ATLANTIC CHARTER

ATLANTIC CHARTER

By Cecil King

With text illustrations by the author

Essay Index Reprint Series

BOOKS FOR LIBRARIES PRESS
FREEPORT, NEW YORK

First Published 1943

Reprinted 1972

Library of Congress Cataloging in Publication Data

King, Cecil, 1881-1942.
   Atlantic charter.

   (Essay index reprint series)
   Reprint of the 1943 ed.
   1. United States--History, Naval. 2. United States.
Navy--History. I. Title.
E182.K5 1972   973   72-4504
ISBN 0-8369-2955-1

TO

PRESIDENT

FRANKLIN DELANO ROOSEVELT

Commander-in-Chief of the United States
Naval and Military Forces

whose work as Assistant Secretary of the
United States Navy during the First
World War has not been forgotten in
Great Britain

this book is respectfully dedicated.

CONTENTS

CONTENTS

LIST OF PLATES

PREFACE

ONE of the most significant events of modern times has been the signing of the Atlantic Charter. Its conclusion and the power to give effect to its provisions would not have been possible without the joint sea-air forces of the two nations who live on either side of the Atlantic.

How many Britons learned at school a little Greek, Roman and English history? How many learned anything about the Americas? In these pages an attempt has been made to set out the salient facts in the history of the U.S. Navy, which is now of such a status as greatly to influence the future of the world.

There was a time, not so many years ago, when in Great Britain a boast was heard in some political circles that she would live in " splendid isolation " ; times have changed. The immunity from European interference which the United States were able to enjoy, for a hundred years, was mainly due, as Colonel Knox generously admitted on a recent occasion, to the British Fleet. It may be that for the future the safety of both nations and the peace of the world will depend upon the joint efforts of both Navies, which have often co-operated in the past, both in peace and war.

Twenty-five years ago the United States became for the first time officially the Allies of Great Britain ; now they have become so once more. *Eendracht maakt macht*, [1] and when the English-speaking people are in danger, the ranks are closed.

I am particularly indebted to the Admiralty Librarian, Mr. L. G. Carr Laughton, for many valuable suggestions and for giving me the benefit of his knowledge and experience ; I am equally indebted to Mr. Francis McMurtrie, who has also read a part of my manuscript. To Lieutenant Peter G. Van der Poel, U.S.N.R., of the American Embassy, London, I am especially grateful for reading my proofs and for his assistance and sympathetic interest throughout.

Others to whom I am indebted in various ways include the Press Division of the British Admiralty ; the American Division of the Ministry of Information ; Captain Dudley Knox, U.S.N., Chief of the Historical Section, Navy Department, Washington ; Professor Sir Geoffrey Callender, Director of the National Maritime Museum ; Captain H. Taprell Dorling, D.S.O., R.N. (" Taffrail ") ; Lieutenant-Commander Allan Baddeley, R.N. ; Mr. H. H. Brindley, M.A., F.S.A., of Cambridge University; and The Old Print Shop, New York. To all of them I offer my sincere thanks.

[1] Unity is strength.

July, 1942.   CECIL KING.

CHAPTER I

THE AMERICAN CONTINENTS

A PHRASE has been heard during the present war which was previously unfamiliar to most ears. " Atlantic Life-Line " is the phrase, and this usually connotes the stream of war-like supplies coming. from the United States to Great Britain and the guarding of those supplies from enemy attacks ; the phrase has still greater meaning since the passing of the Lease-Lend Act early in 1941.

It is perhaps not generally realized that, in a sense, the Atlantic has provided a life-line during a period of peace from very early times, even before the re-discovery of America by Columbus. As some nations ceased to be entirely self-supporting, and some luxuries came to be regarded as necessities of life, those commodities which could not be produced in any one country had to be imported from abroad. One of the earliest of these commodities to come from the West had to make its way across part of the Atlantic. This was the Icelandic cod, for which a fishery was developed by a man named Bacon in 1400. Iceland from early times had been a dependency of the Danish crown, until it obtained dominion status in 1918, and Greenland was colonized at an early date by Icelanders.

Columbus's discovery of the West Indies took place at the end of the fifteenth century ; though a Genoese, he was acting on behalf of Spain, and was quickly followed by Spanish explorers and adventurers. These " Conquistadores " rapidly overran Central America and the West coasts of the Northern and Southern Continents, Portugal, which was still independent of Spain, taking Brazil. Magellan, a Portuguese acting on behalf of Spain, sailed round the world for the first time, through the Straits which bear his name, and took the Philippine Islands and other possessions in the Eastern Seas ; this

" Santa Maria."

voyage took place nearly thirty years after Columbus's first crossing of the Atlantic in the *Santa Maria*.

Trade did not follow the Spanish flag, in the ordinary sense, and little trade existed between Spain and America. Since America had been divided between Spain and Portugal by the Papal Bull and Treaty of Tordesillas, Spain regarded any attempts from outside to engage in commercial activities in that sphere as an encroachment upon her rights ; but gold and silver had been found in Peru, Mexico and elsewhere, and this was constantly being shipped back to Spain in the " Plate Ships."

The plate ships then assured Spain's life-line across the Atlantic for three centuries, and America became to Spain a kind of " Tom Tiddler's Ground " ; with the result that ordinary legitimate methods of trading were largely ignored, and Spain neglected her overseas trade, relying rather on the gold of the Indies for her national wealth. She established viceroyalties in Peru and Mexico, and continued to administer her American Empire until the beginning of the nineteenth century. The islands on the Eastern side of the Atlantic, Cape Verde, Azores, etc., were Spanish or Portuguese, and served mostly as rendezvous or victualling points for the plate ships, which were the frequent prey of men like Francis Drake and other English adventurers.

Meantime two other countries were beginning to be interested in the North American Continent—England and France. In 1497 John Cabot, another Genoese, went out from Bristol, on behalf of King Henry VII, and discovered Newfoundland and Labrador ; Jacques Cartier, of S. Malo, landed near Quebec in 1533-4 and pushed inland into Canada. Cabot was followed, eighty-six years later, by Sir Humphrey Gilbert, who founded an English colony in Newfoundland ; and the rich cod-fisheries of the locality, in which both British and French had, and still have, an important interest, fed the life-line in that commodity which had previously extended only from Iceland. Izaak Walton,[1] quoting Sir Richard Baker, says that about a hundred or so years before his own, Walton's, time :

> Hops and turkies, carps and beer
> Came to England all in a year.

From this we may conclude that the turkey, which is an American bird, was among the commodities brought to Europe by the earlier Spanish explorers.

Jacques Cartier was succeeded by Champlain, who went out to Canada in 1608. In 1609 he founded Quebec; he also developed the French Canadian fur-trade, discovering Lake Champlain and becoming later Governor of Canada. The English fur-trade farther North was put on a firm footing in 1670, under the *ægis* of Prince Rupert, by the Charter establishing the Hudson's Bay Company. The Southern part of Canada remained French until it was ceded to Great Britain as a result of the Seven Years' War, and the Russians, who had settled in Alaska in 1784, sold that territory to the United States in 1867. At the beginning of the eighteenth century the North of Canada was largely unexplored ; it was dotted with fur-posts, equipped as forts, for protection against the

---

[1] *The Compleat Angler.*

native tribes, and these forts and the territory surrounding them belonged to the Hudson's Bay Company. The Southern portion of Canada was French, and this country included the maritime provinces on the Atlantic coast, which were known at that period as Acadia.

In the " Wonderful Year," mentioned in David Garrick's song " Heart of Oak," or in other words in 1759, a naval and military expedition, under Admiral Sir Charles Saunders and General Wolfe, went up the St. Lawrence River, and Wolfe captured the Heights of Abraham, dying in the attempt, as did Montcalm, his French opponent. Quebec was seized, Montreal fell soon afterwards, and thus the British became the possessors of Canada, which was duly ceded at the Peace of 1763. When the country became a dominion in 1867, the Hudson's Bay Territory was taken over, compensation being paid, and was incorporated with Quebec, Ontario and other provinces to form the Dominion of Canada.

English colonization was now developing farther south. In 1584 Sir Walter Raleigh was beginning to colonise Virginia and in 1587 he obtained a Charter for that colony. In 1606 Captain John Smith sailed there and founded Jamestown ; he also sailed up the coast as far as Cape Cod, naming the intervening coast-line " New England." An important trade in tobacco began to spring up between America and England, which, according to some authorities, was originated by Raleigh ; potatoes also began to find their way across the Atlantic.

The " Pilgrim Fathers " landed from the *Mayflower*, near Cape Cod, in 1620, and founded a Puritan settlement in what is now known as Massachusetts. Such native names are very common in North America ; the native Indian population was alternately friendly and hostile to the Colonists, and finally these difficulties were overcome by establishing Indian " Reservations " in various parts of the country, in which the natives could live their own lives undisturbed ; this development occurred in comparatively recent times.

Another European country began to interest itself in North America during the seventeenth century ; this was Holland. The Dutch West India Company established a colony on Manhattan Island, which was purchased from the Indians, and here the Dutch founded an important settlement, which they called New Amsterdam. In 1664, just prior to the Second Dutch War, it was seized by the British and, in honour of the Duke of York, Charles II's brother, it was renamed New York. In 1673 it was retaken by the Dutch, taken again by the British in 1674 and eventually became the Federal capital, until replaced by Washington, D.C. Some of the most distinguished families in America are of this ancient Dutch stock.

British Colonists gradually spread over the Eastern side of North America, from Canada down to Florida, which was Spanish, and nearly as far West as the Mississippi River. Florida became British in 1763, following the Seven Years' War, but went back to Spain in 1783, as a result of the War of Independence. The colonies were divided from the Spanish colonies in the south-west and the unknown lands to the west by a vast territory, a quarter the width of the present United States, which extended from Canada down to the Gulf of Mexico ; the whole of this territory was then known as Louisiana, and was mainly French until the days of Bonaparte. A fear that the French might move eastwards, pushing the Colonists into the sea, was one of the causes of the Seven Years' War in 1756.

The North American colonies were quite independent, one of the other, and differed in religion or in national origin. The New England

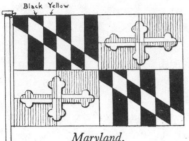

Maryland.

colonies to the north were Puritan ; farther south they were Dutch Lutherans or Quakers, while the Southern colonies were mostly Church of England or Catholic and royalist. Some of them were Crown Colonies, some were practically chartered democracies, and some were under lords proprietors ; the State flag of Maryland still bears the arms of the Earls Baltimore. In 1643 and again in 1754 an attempt was made at federation, but these efforts came to nothing.

Signs of a break-away were already visible after the Seven Years' War, and this was mainly due to a feeling of resentment at what the colonies regarded as excessive taxation resulting from that war. The Stamp Act of 1765 was the first serious bone of contention and, after its repeal by the Houses of Parliament, and the removal of other taxes, a tax was still left on tea. In 1773 a number of men, disguised as Indians, boarded some of the ships in Boston harbour and threw their cargoes of tea overboard. The retaliatory measure for this " Boston Tea Party " was the Boston Port Act, which was in effect a blockade. Matters were now in a bad way ; the Colonists united under the military direction of George Washington, and in 1775 the War of Independence broke out.

Such commodities as rice and timber, and later cotton, wheat and the products of the whale fishery had long found their way across to Europe, and other commodities, tea included, came in the opposite direction. By the time of the War of Independence the principal trade routes were those from the Southern colonies to Great Britain and from the Northern colonies to Southern Europe and the West Indies ; Southern Europe also had an important trade with Georgia and South Carolina. These parts of North America were " sea-minded," and more than a third of the American merchant ships in 1775 were American-built.

PLATE I

THE PILGRIM SHIP *MAYFLOWER*
NEARING AMERICA, 1620

(By courtesy of the U.S. National Archives, Washington, D.C.)

In 1620 The " Pilgrim Fathers " left Plymouth to sail across the
Atlantic. They landed at Plymouth Rock, near Cape Cod, and
founded a colony not far from the present city of Boston, Massachusetts.

South West View of Fort George with the City of New York.

This fort protected the entrance to New York in the Eighteenth Century when New York was a very small place. Originally called New Amsterdam, New York became British in the Seventeenth Century and was for a time the Federal Capital, being succeeded by Washington, D.C.

We are not concerned here with the subsequent political history of the British Colonies, after they developed into the United States of North America, as a result of the War of Independence ; but it may be said that the admission, into the States, of citizens belonging to many nationalities, during the last hundred years, is largely due to Anglo-Saxon generosity.

The United States, like Great Britain, have always been ready to open their doors to political refugees and other luckless men.   Furthermore, a need was felt, in the middle of the nineteenth century, for labour for the development of the country.   The free immigration, which commenced in 1847, only became restricted following the last war, in about 1920.

It was only the colonies abutting on the coast that were sea-minded. A sense of the vital importance of the sea did not penetrate at first inland ; it has taken time for that sense to spread universally.   During the hundred and sixty years during which the United States have been independent of Great Britain, they have, however, built up an important Navy, until at the outbreak of the present war it was second only in size and strength to the Royal Navy.   Some account of the naval history of the United States appears in the succeeding chapters.

*   *   *   *   *

South of the United States, yet still regarded as a part of North America, is the Republic of Mexico, of which the provinces of Chiapas, Yucatan and Tabasco are in Central America.   Formerly Mexico extended up the west coast of North America and included Texas and the whole of the California region ; Texas was annexed to the United States in 1845, California being ceded in 1848.   Mexico was discovered by Hernando Cortes, who conquered the Aztecs and made this vast country into a Spanish possession in 1521 ; it was one of the first portions of her American empire to break away from Spain, and the revolt occurred less than thirty years after the British Colonies of North America obtained their independence.

Mexico's War of Independence broke out in 1810 and lasted for twelve years.   In 1821 a man named Iturbide declared himself Emperor. The Mexican Empire, however, lasted only three years ; for in 1824 Iturbide was shot, and the country adopted a republican government. Another empire was formed in 1864, when the Austrian prince Maximilian became Emperor ; he also was shot, and in 1867 Mexico again became a republic and so remains.

East of Mexico and Central America are two large stretches of sea ; these are known as the Gulf of Mexico and the Caribbean Sea, and they and the surrounding area are freely dotted with islands.   The principal islands on this, the western, side of the Atlantic are known as the West Indies.   The history of these islands has been varied and romantic ; they have been a haunt of buccaneers, pirates and adventurers, and many of them have known more than one master ; Columbus made his first land-fall here, at Watling Island, in the Bahama Group. The

Buccaneers.

leasing to the United States of naval and air bases in the islands of the Western Atlantic, from Newfoundland down to Trinidad, is one of the most significant facts in the history of Anglo-American naval co-operation.

The Spaniards occupied Cuba, Puerto Rico, Santo Domingo and other possessions, including Jamaica, which was first discovered by Columbus and taken by the British in 1654, the British taking also Bermuda, the Bahamas and eventually most of the chain of islands forming the Leeward and Windward Group. The French held, and still hold, Martinique, Guadeloupe and islands contiguous and, since the Spanish War of 1898, the United States own Puerto Rico ; Cuba has become an independent republic.

Santo Domingo has passed through various vicissitudes. Originally known as Hispaniola, it was a haunt of buccaneers in the seventeenth century ; its Western end became the site of a French colony, and Bonaparte tried in 1802 to re-enslave the negro population, which had been liberated eight years previously. A revolt followed, and eventually this part of the island became the negro republic known as Haiti. The greater portion of the island remained Spanish until 1821, when it rose against Spanish rule, becoming the Republic of Santo Domingo in 1844.

From the West Indies to Great Britain a life-line has existed ever since it was discovered that Jamaica produced fine cane sugar. Since then other commodities have found their way across the Atlantic, including cocoa, rum, coffee and West Indian fruits.

Central America is on the isthmus which connects Mexico with South America, and includes the six Republics of Guatemala, Honduras, Salvador, Nicaragua, Costa Rica and Panama. It also includes the Crown Colony of British Honduras and that portion of Panama which is known as the Canal Zone and which is controlled by the United States. All of this area was previously Spanish. Honduras was settled by Spain at the beginning of the sixteenth century ; Nicaragua was discovered by Columbus in 1502, was overrun by Davila, and became Spanish at about the same time, being a part of the Captaincy-General of Guatemala, which the Spaniards first occupied in about 1522. Salvador was a part of this territory, and was taken on behalf of Spain in 1526 by Pedro Alvarado. Costa Rica was not occupied by Spain until 1530, and Panama was, until forty years ago, a part of Colombia, which is in South America.

In 1821 Central America embarked on a War of Independence, and in that year the old Captaincy-General of Guatemala declared itself independent, and became a part of Augustin Iturbide's Mexican Empire, as did Costa Rica and Nicaragua. Two years later they broke away and were joined by Salvador and Honduras, in forming the United States of Central America, or the Central American Union. This lasted until 1842 ; Rafael Cabrera was the Guatemalan leader and Francisco Marazan was leader of Honduras ; the latter was defeated in battle by Cabrera in the same year and executed. The Union was then dissolved. In 1850 Salvador, Nicaragua and Honduras attempted to form a Union, but they were defeated by Cabrera and the attempt came to nothing. Subsequent attempts of this nature have been equally unsuccessful, and the States of Central America remain independent republics.

During the seventeenth century the British also had interests in Honduras, notably near Belize and on the Mosquito Coast. Here they cut "logwood," with the aid of the local buccaneer population, and exported it to Great Britain. In 1850 they converted their rights, by arrangement with the United States, and gave up the Mosquito Coast ; the Crown Colony of British Honduras was then formed in the neighbourhood of Belize, which is now the capital of the colony. Central America produces, among other commodities, coffee, rubber and cocoa, and is more particularly famous for its mahogany, much of which comes from British Honduras.

South America consists of ten independent republics, of which Brazil is by far the largest, and the colonies of British, Dutch and French Guiana. The republics are those of Brazil, Colombia, Venezuela, Ecuador, Peru, Bolivia, Paraguay, Uruguay, Chile and the Argentine. These ten countries became independent between roughly 1810 and 1830, and were referred to in a speech by George Canning who, as Foreign Secretary, had supported the movement for their independence ; he said in 1826 : " I have called the New World into existence, to redress the balance of the Old," some of the countries of the Old World being then in a very disturbed state.

The British have occupied Guiana at various dates, from the end of the eighteenth century until 1814, when the Crown Colony of British Guiana was formed, the Dutch and the French having settlements in those parts dating from the seventeenth century. The island of Curaçao, which was discovered in 1527, became Dutch in 1634, and after two British occupations at the end of the eighteenth and beginning of the nineteenth centuries, reverted to Holland in 1814. Trinidad, the most southerly of the West Indian islands, is really a part of South America ; it became British in 1797.

Brazil was discovered by the Portuguese explorer Cabral in about

1500, and it fell to Portugal in the sixteenth century, as part of her share of the newly-discovered world ; Portuguese is still spoken there. In 1807, after the signing of the Treaty of Tilsit, Napoleon endeavoured to force Portugal to join his " Continental System," and sent his general Junot to occupy Lisbon. Junot then overran the country, this being one of the causes of the Peninsular War. The Regent João, with the Royal Family, sailed to Brazil and directed the affairs of Portugal and Brazil from there ; but in 1822 his son Pedro made Brazil a separate empire and became its Emperor. In 1889 the Brazilian Empire fell, and was succeeded by a republic.

About thirty years ago fears were expressed, in some quarters, lest the Germans, who at that time formed a large proportion of the population of the Provinces of São Paulo and Santa Catharina, might stir up a revolt, with the object of making Brazil, or a portion of it, German. Such action *contra* to the Monroe Doctrine had been attempted before, notably in the case of France and Mexico ; fortunately for Brazil, this danger, if it existed, came to nothing.

Apart from Brazil, South America was Spanish since the beginning of the sixteenth century, all except Patagonia, at the southern end. This territory was left unoccupied till a later date, when it was divided between Chile and the Argentine. Spanish rule lasted till 1810, when Colombia, Chile and the Argentine began to revolt. Venezuela had made such an attempt in 1749, and again in 1797, but on each occasion the uprising had been suppressed.

Colombia was formerly known as Nueva Granada, which was conquered by Quesada in 1537. Bogotá, now the capital, revolted in 1810, but the insurrection was at first unsuccessful. Simon Bolivar, the great " Liberator," was a Colombian ; he had visited the United States in the previous year, and had become impressed with the success with which they were conducting their independent existence. He energetically supported the Colombian movement for breaking away from the mother-country, and issued a Declaration of Independence in 1811. A long struggle followed between Spain and the Colonists. In 1819 the Congress of Angostura made Bolivar commander-in-chief, and he won the Battles of Tunja and Boyaca ; Bolivar's victory at Carabobo concluded the war in 1821, and he was chosen as President of Colombia.

Venezuela's coast-line had been first seen by Columbus on his third voyage, and Venezuela was then occupied by Spain, Ecuador being conquered in 1534 by Diego d'Almagro and Sebastián de Benalcazar. In about 1820 Ecuador and Venezuela became independent of Spain ; after the Battle of Boyaca, Ecuador, Venezuela and Colombia (Nueva Granada) were united as the Republic of Colombia, but in 1829 Venezuela broke away, and in the year following Nueva Granada also,

PLATE III   NEW YORK, 1855   General view taken from the Brooklyn Shore

Large engraving, by Mottram after Hill

In the Nineteenth Century New York had considerably increased in size, and was an important centre of mercantile shipping activity. In this picture the Hudson River is seen in the background with the New Jersey shore beyond. Manhattan Island, on which New York City stands, is bounded on the north by the Harlem River and on the east by the East River. Old New York was confined to the lower end of the island, seen to the left. The spire of Trinity Church (left foreground) is to-day dwarfed by the great skyscrapers in and around Wall Street.

23

PLATE IV

THE *DELLWOOD* CABLESHIP IN ALASKAN WATERS

An American cableship of to-day. The cable is seen being paid out aft. Since the first Atlantic cable was laid, ships have completely changed in design, and specially-designed cableships are constructed, the projection over the bow being a very noticeable feature.

forming a separate republic entitled the United States of Colombia ; this was after the death of Bolivar in 1830. The Westernmost of these States, that lying to the North of the Gulf of Panama, broke away in 1903 and became the separate republic of Panama.

Another country which revolted early in the proceedings was the Argentine. This country broke away from Spain in 1810-16 and became the Provincias Unidas del Rio de la Plata. In 1526 Sebastián Cabot went there, and he was followed by Pedro de Mendoza, who founded Buenos Aires in 1535. Despite the river's name " la Plata," no silver was found there, and Mendoza, disappointed, returned to Europe, leaving Juan de Ayolas in charge of the enterprise. De Ayolas went up the Paraná River, in an attempt to reach the gold of Peru, and then perished, after founding the fort of Asuncion on the River Paraguay.

In the years which followed, the Spanish settlers brought over horses, cattle, sheep and goats, few of which previously existed in the Argentine ; they bred and multiplied to such an extent that the life-line from east to west was transformed into one running in the opposite direction. To-day the Argentine and the districts around the Rio de la Plata are among the richest sources of beef, mutton, hides and wool. This trade began to develop in the nineteenth century, aided by the coming of steam. At first the animals used to come across the Atlantic on the hoof, but with improvements in refrigerating machinery, they come in the form of chilled or frozen meat. The South American life-lines are among the most valuable which cross the Atlantic, and convey not only the Argentine and Uruguayan beef, but many other useful commodities also, including the rubber, cocoa and coffee of Brazil.

In 1806 the Monroe Doctrine was not yet in existence ; the Rio de la Plata had been made into a viceroyalty in 1776. A period of unrest followed and, Spain being then at war with Great Britain, Admiral Sir Home Popham brought a fleet to Buenos Aires ; the British marched into the city and the Viceroy fled. The Argentinians then drove out these British invaders, and another attempt in the following year was also unsuccessful. In 1810 they rose against Spanish rule, and a period of dissension followed until 1826, when Juan Manoel Rosas became Dictator. His rule was marked with arrogance and cruelty ; trade suffered ; Britain and France were defied and blockaded the country, sending a joint naval expedition against Rosas and defeating him at the Battle of Obligado in 1845. ·

The Argentine had made itself independent of Spain by a decree of the Congress of Tucumán in 1816, but it had not yet a settled form of Government. The Governor of the Eastern province of Entre Rios then revolted and took a large army across the estuary of the Rio de la Plata, and completely destroyed the power of Rosas at the Battle of Caseros in 1852. The Santa Fé Convention framed a republican constitution, in the following year, somewhat on the lines of that of the United States.

A third country to lead the South American revolutionary movement in 1810 was Chile. In the fifteenth century this territory was invaded by Indians from Peru. Almagro, who was Pizarro's rival in Peru, followed and after his death, Chile was granted to Pedro de Valdivia, who founded Santiago de Chile in 1541. Chile led a somewhat isolated existence, and the inhabitants went through various periods of unrest for more than two centuries. In 1810 they revolted, but the revolt was put down, and a period of repression followed. Then in 1817 de San Martin collected an army, part of which was under General O'Higgins, and defeated the Spaniards at Chacabuco ; the victory of Maipú in the following year gained for Chile its independence.

A man who may be classed as a deciding force on the side of the " Liberators " was Cochrane ; he was a British naval captain, who had performed many deeds of valour during the Napoleonic War, and was unjustly accused by a political junta of being implicated in a financial swindle, losing his commission. Cochrane, who was afterwards Earl of Dundonald, accepted the command of the new Chilean Navy, arriving in Valparaiso in November, 1818 ; he had previously been offered a naval command by Spain. Among the valorous deeds performed by him was the attack on and capture of Valdivia with the flagship *O'Higgins* and two small ships. He subsequently served with the Navy of Brazil and then took command, in 1827, of the Greek Navy ; he was afterwards reinstated in the Royal Navy, dying as an Admiral in 1860.

General O'Higgins was Dictator of Chile until his abdication in 1823. He was succeeded by Freire, and in 1831 a proper republican Government was established. His name, like that of Cochrane, has often been given to vessels of the Chilean Navy.

Almirante Cochrane, 1874.

Uruguay, at the north side of the Rio de la Plata, was Spanish since 1512, when Diaz de Solís landed seventy miles east of what is now Monte Video, the capital. The Indians invaded the country and defeated the Spaniards ; then Jesuit missions established themselves there. It was long a territory disputed between Spain and Portugal, and in 1776 the Spaniards established themselves in Monte Video and demolished the Portuguese settlement of Colonia shortly afterwards. At this time the country was known as the " Banda Oriental " del Uruguay ; and in 1811 it threw off the Spanish yoke, being conquered soon afterwards by the Brazilian dependency of the

Portuguese crown. In 1828 it ceased to belong to the Brazilian crown, and became a republic in 1830.

The activities of Juan de Ayolas have already been mentioned in connection with the Argentine. After he had founded Asuncion, on the River Paraguay, the Spaniards used this as a base for exploration ; Sebastián Cabot had also built a fort in 1527, called Santo Espiritú. The name Paraguay was given to the whole territory around the Paraná and Paraguay Rivers, including parts of Brazil and of the Argentine. In the seventeenth century Paraguay and the Rio de la Plata, or Argentine, had separate governments, but subordinate to the Viceroy of Peru till 1776 ; then Paraguay came under Argentinian direction.

As in the case of Uruguay, the Jesuit missions had considerable influence. In 1750 Spain ceded to Portugal a part of Paraguay in exchange for Colonia, or Colonia del Sacramento, in Uruguay ; the Jesuits resisted this transference of territory, and were evicted in 1769. Paraguay eventually obtained its independence in 1811.

The last two countries of South America to obtain their independence were Peru and Bolivia. Peru was formerly ruled by the Incas and was conquered by Francisco Pizarro in about 1531 ; Pizarro entered Cuzco in November, 1533. One of his lieutenants, named Diego d'Almagro, undertook an expedition to Chile, and Pizarro founded the Peruvian city of Lima in 1535. Quarrels then arose between the two men, each of whom had his supporters. D'Almagro fought against Pizarro, was defeated and executed, Pizarro himself being murdered in 1541.

Peru remained in an unsettled state until 1569, when Don Francisco de Toledo became Viceroy, and Lima became the centre of military strength. In 1820 a fleet, officered by British, took an Argentinian and Chilean army from Valparaiso to the coast of Peru, San Martin being the general, and in 1821 Peru gained its independence ; the republic was proclaimed in Lima in the same year. The Viceroy and the Spanish troops retired into the interior, and in 1823 Bolivar came across from Colombia and arranged to attack them. In the following year he gained the Battle of Ayacucho, and became for a time Dictator of Peru, leaving the country again in 1827.

Bolivia's history has been to some extent linked with that of Peru. After the defeat of the Incas in the sixteenth century, the natives became practically serfs, and the territory was a dependency of the Viceroy of Peru ; the Indians attempted then to revolt, but were defeated. Bolivia was formerly known as " Alto Peru," and in 1776 it ceased to belong to Peru and came under the Viceroy at Buenos Aires. The independence movement commenced in 1809, and it had varied fortunes until Bolivar and General Sucre won the victory of Ayacucho, when Bolivia gained its independence. Bolivar entered La Paz in the following year, and the republican constitution was drawn up in August, 1825, Bolivia becoming a separate nation, named in honour of Bolivar.

Since these countries have gained their independence, their tranquillity has at times been disturbed by internal dissension, or by differences between one country and another, notably the " Pacific War " of 1879, in which Chile, Peru and Bolivia were involved. A more recent quarrel has been that between Paraguay and Bolivia, concerning the ownership of the territory known as the " Gran Chaco " ; war in this case broke out in 1932 and lasted until 1935. Danger from European countries was averted by President Monroe's famous declaration, known as the " Monroe Doctrine."

In 1823 James Monroe, who was at that time President of the United States, made a declaration of foreign policy on behalf of his country, which has formed the cardinal maxim of United States foreign policy ever since. He announced that the American continents were henceforth not to be considered as subjects for colonization by any European powers, and that the United States would regard any attempt on their part to extend their system to any portion of the Western Hemisphere as dangerous to the peace and safety of the United States.

This declaration, as Colonel Knox has recently pointed out in a speech, was made at a time when some danger of the kind was anticipated from the " Holy Alliance " of Prussia, Austria and Russia, which had been formed in 1815. It was not retrospective, so that no existing arrangements were affected, and various shades of meaning have been read into it from time to time ; President Theodore Roosevelt held that it applied only to occupation of territory.

One has no means of knowing if President Monroe, in his natural anxiety for the safety of his own country and of the rest of the Americas, ever foresaw the time when America would, so to speak, find herself jostling both Europe and Asia ; it is a possibility. The rapid increase in the speed and reliability of communications since his day has undoubtedly made for the furthering of international friendships ; but modern invention has also imported dangers, so that the Americas are no longer alone, far out in the Atlantic ; to the airplane a thousand miles or so is as nothing. Most of the States in the American continents are now banded together among the numerous nations united in the struggle against Axis aggression.

Since the Americas have obtained their independence, communications with Europe have developed at a great pace. At the end of the eighteenth century there was no regular means of bridging the Atlantic, except by the Postal Packets ; these vessels were usually brigs which, under the direction of the Admiralty, maintained a postal service from Falmouth to the West Indies. Increasing trade between the United

States and Europe called the "packet-ships" into existence in 1816, soon after the termination of the War of 1812. This was due to American enterprise, the pioneer line in 1816 being the Black Ball Line, which sailed from New York to Liverpool. Liners of to-day usually have their funnels, and sometimes also their hulls, painted in distinctive colours ; these packets had a large black ball painted on one of their topsails.

These earlier packets sailed on the first of every month, carrying passengers as well as goods, and made the outward passage from New York in the average time of twenty-three days, taking forty days on the westerly voyage. They were followed by the Red Star, Swallow Tail, Dramatic and other lines. A service to London was run in about 1823 and to Havre at the same time. For the carrying of freight, these packets were largely superseded by the clipper ships, which began in 1840 and lasted on the transatlantic run for about fifteen years.[1]

Steamers now began to appear ; the *Curaçao*, *Savannah*, *Sirius* and *Great Western* made the transatlantic voyage, and in 1840 the Cunard Line inaugurated the first transatlantic passenger-mail service with the paddle-steamer *Britannia*, running from Liverpool to Boston, Massachusetts. The development of the "Atlantic Ferry" since that date, and the lines, British, American, French and others, which have come into being during the last hundred years, have made it possible to reduce the time of transit to such an extent that it is phenomenal to-day if it occupies more than a week, and is generally considerably less—a mere matter of days.

British and American ships co-operated directly in the next stage in transatlantic communication. In 1832 an American artist named Samuel Morse invented the electro-magnetic telegraph, and by 1844 he was able to send messages by its means between Washington and Baltimore ; his name is best known to us to-day through the telegraphic code of which he was the inventor.

In 1857 an attempt was made to lay a telegraph cable across the Atlantic, from the United States to Great Britain, the sea-portion of it lying between Newfoundland and Valentia, in Ireland. The United States ships *Niagara* and *Susquehanna* and H.M.S. *Agamemnon*, aided by the small paddle-steamers H.M.S. *Leopard* and *Cyclops*, undertook the task. The American ships were to lay from Valentia to mid-Atlantic, and the British ships from there to Newfoundland. An attempt was made on the 7th of August, but after three hundred and fifty miles of cable had been paid out, the cable parted. A second attempt was made, but was defeated, owing to a violent storm.

A third attempt was made in July of the following year ; in this case the splice was to be made in mid-Atlantic, and the ships were then to

[1] *Harper's Magazine*, January, 1884.

steam in opposite directions. The same vessels were employed in laying the cable, and this time their efforts were crowned with success. On the 5th of August messages of good will were exchanged between Queen Victoria and the President of the United States by the transatlantic cable.

Communication failed however after a time, possibly owing to some fault in the insulation, and it was decided to try again ; this time the  *Great Eastern* made the attempt. She left Valentia in July, 1865, but the cable parted. In July, 1866, she tried again and this time the attempt succeeded. Cables to France, Denmark, Brazil, etc., followed, until the Atlantic was traversed by a perfect network of cables. The efforts

" *Great Eastern.*"

of Morse, Wheatstone and others had bridged the Atlantic.

Senator Marconi's invention of wireless telegraphy in 1895-1900 has brought the American and the European continents still closer together. To-day a British or an American audience can hear speeches by President Franklin D. Roosevelt or Mr. Winston S. Churchill with the greatest of ease in their own homes.

Sea-communications have been improved still more by the opening of the Panama Canal, which makes a way through from the Atlantic to the Pacific. A canal across the isthmus of Panama had been designed in 1879 by Ferdinand de Lesseps, who had completed the Suez Canal ten years earlier. The construction failed, owing to a variety of circumstances, and the company formed for the purpose collapsed in 1888. Owing to American enterprise, the project was taken up again in 1894, and a new canal was made and completed in 1914.

Five years later the Atlantic was crossed for the first time by air. The voyage, which extended from Newfoundland to the Irish coast, was made in the summer of 1919, immediately after the Great War. Subsequent airplane voyages have so developed transatlantic air-transit that the American continents are now within half a day's journey from Europe.

CHAPTER II

WAR OF INDEPENDENCE

THE War of American Independence broke out in 1775, and during this war a number of important fleet actions took place—such as the Battles of Martinique, Chesapeake Bay and the " Saints " ; but these actions were fought by the ships of Great Britain against those of France, Spain or Holland, after France's entry into the war in 1778. In 1775 the Colonists had no Federal Navy, and the efforts of their embryo sea-forces were mainly confined to commerce-destruction and privateering activities, more than fifteen hundred letters of marque being issued by the Continental Congress during the war.

When the " Continental Navy " was formed late in 1775, the nucleus of it and of its *personnel* was the merchant navy ; merchant ships in those days were armed, and could easily be converted into men-of-war ; eleven of the thirteen States had also small navies of their own. With this material George Washington decided to form what is called " Washington's Fleet," in order to capture British store-ships and transports, and so obtain the much needed munitions of war ; he arranged to send a vessel of the Rhode Island State Navy to Bermuda, in an attempt to obtain gunpowder, and a number of British vessels were captured by a small squadron commanded by Commodore John Manly, of the schooner *Lee*. In October, 1775, it was decided to purchase a number of merchant ships and fit them out as men-of-war ; this was the beginning of the Continental Navy.

As the revolt spread, the Colonists adopted their own flags ; some of these displayed trees of liberty or rattlesnakes, and some of them were striped. When Washington left Philadelphia in 1775, he was escorted by a troop of horse ; the silk standard of this troop displayed, in the upper corner, a small " Union " consisting of thirteen stripes of light blue and silver. The first appearance of the stars was probably in the flag worn in the schooner *Lee*, when she formed part of Commodore Esek Hopkins's squadron in November, 1775.[1] This was a white flag, having a Union consisting of thirteen white stars *semés* in a blue field ; an anchor surmounted by a ribbon, bearing the word " Hope," occupied the fly. A somewhat similar flag was afterwards used by the troops of Rhode Island, at the Battles of Trenton, Yorktown and Brandywine.

In December, 1775, the " Grand Union Flag " was hoisted in the

---

[1] The family shield of George Washington was *argent*, charged with two bars *gules*, and bore, in chief, three *mullets* of the second.

Alfred, flagship of Hopkins's squadron, off Philadelphia ; John Paul Jones was First Lieutenant of the *Alfred* and he is said to have hoisted this flag himself. Its origin has been disputed, but it is thought by some to have been derived from the British red ensign, striped with white ; it also bore a strong resemblance to the " Gridiron," the ensign of the Honorable East India Company. The Grand Union Flag is sometimes referred to as the " Cambridge Flag," since in January, 1776, it was hoisted also over Washington's headquarters at Cambridge, Massachusetts. The Declaration of Independence was made on the 4th of July 1776, but the British Union device remained in these American colours, which continued to be displayed at sea until June, 1777.

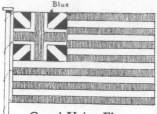

Grand Union Flag.

The man who captured the popular imagination, more than any naval officer who served in the War of American Independence, was John Paul Jones, who was the son of a Scot named John Paul, and born in Kirkcudbrightshire. His earlier maritime career appears to have been somewhat varied, but in 1775 he adopted the surname of Jones, and became one of the earliest lieutenants of the new Continental Navy.

In December, 1775, he was appointed First Lieutenant of the small frigate *Alfred*, of thirty guns, flagship of Commodore Esek Hopkins, who was " Commander-in-Chief of the Fleet," a title which was unique in Hopkins's case. In February, 1776, Hopkins sailed in the *Alfred* from the Delaware River, directing his course to New Providence in the Bahamas, and arrived there with six ships on the 3rd of March. He at once sent a strong landing party ashore, consisting of bluejackets and marines, under Captain Nicholas of the *Alfred* ; his intention was to secure a large quantity of powder, which was reputed to be stored in the island of New Providence.

Captain Nicholas's force landed successfully and proceeded up to Fort Montague, which opened fire, and then held a parley ; as a result the British spiked their guns and retired to another fort in the town of Nassau. Subsequently Hopkins was able to make such arrangements, with the Governor of the Bahamas, as enabled him to bring his squadron peacefully into harbour, where he spent a fortnight in loading the powder into his ships. Some of this powder had been sent away previously, but he secured a considerable quantity.

Having carried out his orders, Hopkins sailed back, capturing several vessels on the way but, encountering the *Glasgow*, a British frigate of twenty guns, in the neighbourhood of Long Island, he fought an action with her. The *Glasgow*, however, retired before superior numbers, and was pursued, but Hopkins's squadron had suffered in the action,

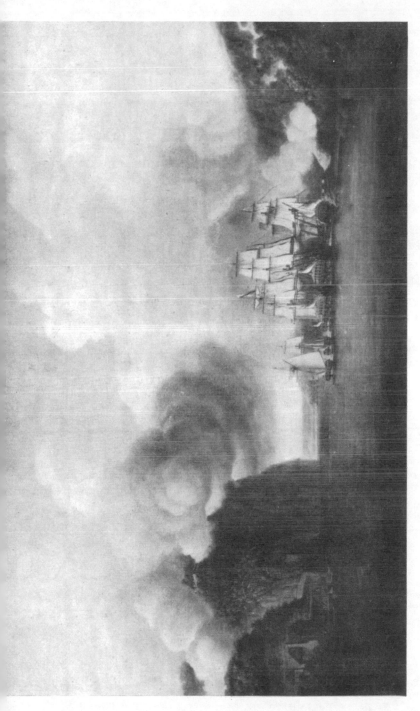

PLATE V   FORCING THE HUDSON RIVER   Oil painting, by Thomas Mitchell

Hyde Parker, in the *Phœnix*, forcing the passage of the Hudson River, 1776. Lord Howe sent Parker, with four ships from New York, and he went up as far as Tarrytown. The ships are seen in the picture, under a fierce bombardment from the shore batteries.

REFERENCES.

Nº 1 Inflexible Ship. 2. Carleton Schooner. 3. Maria Schooner. 4. Congress Galley run a Shore, with other Vessels Blowing up. 5. Washington Galley striking. 6. Gun Boat coming up.

PLATE VI

FIRST BATTLE OF LAKE CHAMPLAIN, 1776

Benedict Arnold had retired from Quebec on to the lake, pursued by
Commodore Pringle. An action was fought in which Arnold was
defeated. Pringle's flagship *Inflexible* is seen in the foreground, also
some schooners and galleys.

and he decided to give up the chase and arrived in New London on the 8th of April.

This successful enterprise gave considerable encouragement to the Colonists, who had suffered from the commencement from a serious shortage of munitions, and greatly enhanced the prestige of the Continental Navy. The Navy had now been increased, some ships being specially built. One vessel of this Navy was the *Lexington*, Captain John Barry, which captured a sloop near Chesapeake Bay ; another vessel, the schooner *Wasp*, also aided some Pennsylvania State Navy ships, when in the Delaware River, in attacking two frigates, the *Liverpool* and *Roebuck*.

Need of munitions was still felt, and it was decided to export American commodities to the French West Indies in exchange for them. The *Lexington* was employed on this service, together with five other vessels, among them the *Reprisal*, Captain Lambert Wickes. In July, 1776, the *Reprisal* convoyed a number of merchant ships to Martinique and, after an inconclusive action with the British sloop *Shark*, brought her charges in in safety. Captain Biddle, in another Continental Navy ship, the *Andrew Doria*, captured some troop-transports, and the *Cabot* and *Columbus* took some prizes also.

John Paul Jones was now captain of the sloop *Providence*. He sailed from the Delaware River in August, 1776, and took sixteen vessels ; his duties were to harass British commerce and to convoy American troops along the coast. In September he encountered the British frigate *Solebay*, of twenty-eight guns, near Bermuda ; he mistook her for a merchant ship. The *Providence* was armed only with twelve four-pounders, so had no chance against a vessel like the *Solebay* and, after a chase lasting four hours, the *Solebay* got into an advantageous position on the *Providence's* lee quarter. Gradually Paul Jones edged away to leeward, till he brought the *Solebay* on to his weather quarter, when he suddenly shifted his helm, went off dead before the wind, and made good his escape. A few days later he escaped successfully from another frigate, the *Milford*, a vessel somewhat similar to the *Solebay*.

He was now given command of the *Alfred*, in which he sailed in November from Newport, with the *Providence* in company, taking three prizes off Louisbourg ; the *Providence* then returned home, and the *Alfred* continued her cruise, meeting with more success. After resuming command of the *Providence*, John Paul Jones was then appointed to the *Ranger*, a frigate of twenty-six guns, and in her he was ordered to proceed to France, his appointment being conveyed in a Resolution of Congress on the 14th of June, 1777.

Meantime there was naval activity also on Lake Champlain. In June, 1776, Benedict Arnold advanced on Quebec but, being defeated, he retired to Lake Champlain later in the month, finding there a few small vessels, in which he embarked his men. The British, who were in pursuit, found that there were no roads running down the lake, and were obliged to build some small ships at the north end, in order to continue their advance. Some time was occupied in this, but in October Commodore Pringle, the British naval commander, had got together a fleet, consisting of twenty-five small vessels, his flagship being the *Inflexible*. Arnold's force consisted of only fifteen vessels, and an action was fought on the 11th of October near Valcour Island.

The British attacked from leeward, and the *Congress* and *Washington* suffered badly in this action, the *Philadelphia* being sunk.[1] Arnold's

force retired and, during the pursuit next day, the *Congress* and *Washington* were taken ; the rest of the vessels were run ashore not far from Crown Point, or escaped. Although defeated, Arnold's force succeeded in delaying the British, and thus stopped an invasion from Canada, until too late in the season for such an invasion to be effective.

A Lake Galley.

Until the year 1778, when the powerful French fleet had thrown its weight into the scale, the British Navy was able to concentrate on the small Continental Navy and the privateers, and so to limit their activities ; none the less some very daring forays were made on the European side of the Atlantic.

Captain Conyngham made several raids in British waters, in the *Surprise* and the *Revenge*, and Captain Lambert Wickes did likewise in January, 1777. Wickes had previously taken Benjamin Franklin to France, in the *Reprisal*, on a diplomatic mission, which resulted in France coming into the war on the side of the American Colonies. The *Reprisal* sailed again from St. Nazaire in January ; she was a ship of the Continental Navy and mounted eighteen guns ; she made a successful raid on British shipping in the English Channel, during which she captured five vessels. The British Ambassador in Paris made a vigorous protest to the French Government for its action in allowing a belligerent ship to shelter in a neutral port, but his representations were ignored.

The brig *Lexington*, Captain Johnson, arrived in April, 1777, and Wickes, who had fitted out the cutter *Dolphin*, then sailed with his three ships on a raid round the coast of Ireland. He was chased in the Bay of Biscay by a British ship of the line, but got away and, passing north round the west of Ireland, he came south again, down the Irish Channel, capturing nearly twenty prizes ; he then made for Land's End, and passed between that point and the Scilly Islands. Near Ushant he fell in with the British seventy-four gun ship *Burford*. Wickes now dispersed his force and went eastwards, with the *Burford* in pursuit. For some hours

[1] *A History of the U.S. Navy.* Captain Dudley W. Knox, U.S.N.

the British ship gradually gained on him, then opened fire with her bow guns ; but Wickes threw overboard his main armament, thus lightening his ship, and drew ahead ; eventually the *Burford* abandoned the pursuit. Wickes succeeded in escaping into St. Malo, and the *Lexington* was taken by the British cutter *Alert* not long afterwards.

This raid caused some perturbation in Great Britain, whose Ambassador again protested.   Wickes, however, was able to refit his ship at St. Malo, and eventually got away in September, 1777, making for America ; on the way over, the *Reprisal* foundered in heavy weather, and Wickes himself was lost.

On the 14th of June, 1777, a Resolution of Congress was passed to the following effect :

" *Resolved*, That the flag of the thirteen United States be thirteen stripes alternate red and white ; that the union be thirteen stars, white in a blue field, representing a new constellation."

The thirteen stars may at first have been arranged in a circle, but were usually disposed *semés* in five or three rows.   John Paul Jones was appointed to the *Ranger* on the same day as that on which the resolution was passed, and it is said that some ladies of Philadelphia presented him with a flag made according to this design.   These were the first Stars and Stripes.

A new frigate called the *Raleigh*, of thirty-two guns, sailed in August, 1777, to France, in company with the *Alfred*.   In September they captured the snow *Nancy*, overtaking the returning West Indian convoy, from which she was a straggler, the next day.   They fought a brief action with the British sloop *Druid*, but were unable to capture any more ships from this convoy.

General Howe had now moved his troops in the direction of Chesapeake Bay and had occupied Philadelphia ; it was essential for him to open up his communications down the Delaware River to the sea.   The British had three sixty-four gun ships, and a number of other vessels, at the mouth of the river ; opposed to them, in the upper reaches, were the frigate *Delaware*, of twenty guns, and six other vessels of the Continental Navy, plus the Pennsylvania State Navy, under Commodore Hazelwood, in the *Montgomery*.

By the 22nd of October the British had broken their way up through the obstructions near Billings Island, as far as Fort Mercer, where they lost a sixty-four gun ship, the *Augusta*, also the *Merlin*, of eighteen guns. Shortly after this, Fort Mercer had to be evacuated, also Fort Mifflin, on an island opposite, and the British secured the Delaware River.   The American ships had to be destroyed, in order to keep them out of the enemy's hands, all except a few Pennsylvania State vessels, which escaped.

In February, 1778, a small squadron, under Commodore Nicholas Biddle, sailed from Charleston. Biddle's flagship was the frigate *Randolph* of thirty-two guns, and he had with him four smallish vessels of the South Carolina State Navy. When near Barbados, in March, he fell in with and attacked the British sixty-four gun ship *Yarmouth*. After a short action, the *Yarmouth* lost her topmasts and bowsprit and seemed likely to strike her colours. Unfortunately, while approaching her, the flagship *Randolph* blew up ; the remainder of the squadron succeeded in getting away safely.

By the Spring of 1778 John Paul Jones was in France where, in February, he received the first salute to the American flag in European waters, this being given off Quiberon by Admiral Lamotte Picquet. The first American naval officer's uniform, established in 1776, seems to have had red facings, and the marines to have worn, since 1777, green coats faced with white. Paul Jones appears to have been unique in giving his officers gold button-holes and epaulettes, and in dressing his marines in red, somewhat after the British fashion.[1]

Paul Jones's ship, the *Ranger*, went from Nantes to Brest, where she refitted, and then proceeded on a cruise in April. Her captain was well acquainted with the waters around his native county down to the Isle of Man, and he intended to raid the Irish coast, Cumberland, Wigton and Kirkcudbrightshire. His first objective was the shipping at Whitehaven, but here he was driven off the coast by adverse weather conditions. On the 21st of April, however, he learned that the sloop *Drake* was in Belfast Lough, and he resolved to attack her. His original intention was to go in under cover of darkness, drop his anchor on top of the *Drake*'s anchor, swing across her bows, and then take her by boarding. It was a cold night, the *Drake*'s men were not expecting an enemy raider and were keeping a bad look-out and everything seemed right for such an enterprise. The *Ranger* let go her anchor, but had too much way on and went along past the *Drake*, bringing up on her quarter ; here Paul Jones cut his cable, so as to make it appear that it had parted accidentally and the *Ranger* drifted out to seaward. He proposed to make another attempt, but the weather worsened, and he was obliged to take shelter on the Scottish coast.

Next day the weather improved, and he intended to have another try at Whitehaven. The *Ranger* came up off the town at about midnight and put off two boats, containing thirty-one officers and men. Before these had reached the pier, day was beginning to dawn ; the strong ebb tide had held them back. The harbour was dry at low water and all the ships in it were aground. One boat was sent to burn the shipping on the north side ; Paul Jones himself landed on what was called the

[1] *Naval Customs, Traditions and Usages*. Captain Leland Lovette, U.S.N.

John Paul Jones

Commodore au Service des Etats-Unis de l'Amérique,

tel qu'il était dans le combat du 22.7.bre 1779. contre le Cap.ne Pearson. son Vaisseau le bon homme Richard montait 40. canons. la frégate Anglaise le Serapis 32. avait l'avantage du calibre et de la légèreté; le Commodore saisit l'instant ou le Beaupré de l'ennemi passa près de son Artimon, il attache ces 2. mâts, et combattant bord à bord s'empara du Serapis. l'action dura 2 h. et 34. le bon homme Richard coula 36. h. après.

PLATE VII

CAPTAIN JOHN PAUL JONES

Line engraving by Carl Guttenberg from the portrait by C. J. Notté.

The celebrated naval leader in the War of Independence. His best-known action was that in which, when in command of the *Bonhomme Richard*, he defeated the British ship *Serapis*.

39

COMBAT MEMORABLE *entre le 23 7bre 1779, entre le Capitaine Pearson commandant le SERAPIS, et Paul Jones commandant le BON-HOMME-RICHARD sur les Anglais*

PLATE VIII

SERAPIS AND *BONHOMME RICHARD*

The 27th of July, 1779

From a black-and-white line-engraving published in Paris by Esnaut and Rapilly shortly after the event. Engravings are sometimes reversed. In this case the ships are shown port side to port side ; in reality they were starboard to starboard.

New Quay. Here there were two old batteries, which were taken unopposed ; they had some ancient guns in them, and these were spiked.

After this had been done, the *Ranger's* captain returned to where he had left the two boats, and was infuriated on discovering that his orders to burn the ships had been disobeyed, the lieutenant in charge of the other boat expressing the view that " nothing could be gained by burning poor people's property "—an old-fashioned attitude of mind which would be even more unpopular to-day. Paul Jones managed to kindle with his own hands a fire in one ship only, and then got back to his boat and out to the *Ranger*.

There was no time to lose ; it was now getting light, and the towns-people were aroused and gathering in considerable numbers. This was due to the treachery of a Whitehaven man named David Freeman, one of the crew of the *Ranger*,[1] who had deserted from the ship's landing party during this raid. The *Ranger* escaped unscathed, and Whitehaven was saved, partly through treachery, and partly through the sentiment of a lieutenant.

Kirkcudbright Bay was the *Ranger's* next objective. Here there is a small island, on which was the house of the Earl of Selkirk. Paul Jones held an opinion which seems to have been held also by Rudolf Hess, during the present war, namely that a nobleman in Great Britain had immense political influence ; he intended to capture the Earl and hold him as a hostage, and doubtless he would have done this, but the Earl happened to be from home.

He then ordered the men down to their boat ; but they protested, saying that the British did not spare private property, and they thought they should be given leave to loot the house. This was accorded them, under certain conditions, and the men got away with a silver tea-set, which was afterwards returned to the owners ; Paul Jones was strongly opposed to this action on the part of his men, and was only obliged to give way, owing to a certain want of discipline among them. He has been criticized for his part in this episode, but quite unjustly.

On the 24th of April the *Ranger* was again off Belfast Lough, where the *Drake*, which had now been warned of the *Ranger's* presence, still lay at anchor. In weighing her anchor, she had found another anchor and a considerable quantity of newly-cut cable entangled

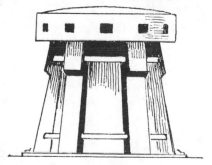

A Capstan.

with it. Seeing the *Ranger* off the entrance to Belfast Lough, she sent a boat off to her, to ask for news ; the boat, not unnaturally, was detained.

[1] *Studies in Naval History.* Sir John Knox Laughton, M.A.

The *Drake* then came out herself, beating against an easterly breeze, and the *Ranger* ran down towards her and then lay-to and hailed ; before the reply came, she passed across the *Drake's* bows and raked her.

This gave an initial advantage to the *Ranger*, which was well handled throughout the ensuing action and well fought ; also she had a heavier armament than her opponent, and a captain who was a most doughty antagonist. The two ships exchanged broadsides for over an hour ; at the end of that time the *Drake* was reduced to a wreck and struck her flag to the enemy. Her captain, her first lieutenant and three others were killed and twenty more were wounded ; the *Ranger's* losses were only three killed and five wounded.

This action was the first really important success scored by the Continental Navy and met with proportionate acclamation ; after the action, Paul Jones refitted the two ships, as well as he could in the circumstances, and brought them round the north of Ireland ; thence, down the west coast to Brest, where he arrived back on the 8th of May.

Commodore Barry, in the frigate *Raleigh*, left Boston for a cruise during the autumn of 1778. Soon after leaving port, he fell in with the British fifty-gun ship *Experiment*, accompanied by the *Unicorn*, which chased Barry's ship. An action followed, in which the *Raleigh* lost a topmast and mizen topgallant mast ; she was subsequently run ashore. Barry and his men succeeded in getting to land by night, and he arranged to set fire to his ship ; for some reason this was not done, and the *Raleigh* was afterwards refloated by the British and taken into their service.

A successful squadron cruise was made by Commodore J. B. Hopkins, in the *Warren*, accompanied by two other ships, early in 1779, when he captured several prizes ; similar success attended the cruises of Commodore Samuel Nicholson, in the frigate *Deane* and of Commodore Whipple, in the *Providence*. The frigates *Deane* and *Boston* were able during July and August to capture a sloop, the *Thorn*, of sixteen guns, and Captain William Pickles took the sloop *West Florida* in Lake Pontchartrain, near New Orleans.

During his stay at Brest on this occasion Paul Jones met with vexations and delays, due to jealousy and other causes ; a curious lack of sympathy was also shown him by M. de Sartine, the French Naval Minister. At length he was given, in the Spring of 1779, leave to commission, under the American flag, an old East Indiaman, lying at Lorient. This ship had forty guns and was called the *Duc de Duras* ; her timbers were in a very bad state, many of her guns were honeycombed, and altogether she was rather a makeshift. Her forty guns included twelve-pounders, nine-pounders and six-pounders, and she had also six eighteen-pounders down in the gun room.

" Poor Richard's Almanac " is perhaps best known in Great Britain to-day through the proverbs and sayings, extracted from it, which appear in books of quotations. It is possibly not so well known that it was written in the earlier half of the eighteenth century by Benjamin Franklin, and translated into French as *La Science du Bonhomme Richard*. Out of compliment to Franklin, Paul Jones obtained permission to change the name of his new command to *Bonhomme Richard* ; Richard Dale was her First Lieutenant.

The *Bonhomme Richard* may be regarded as the flagship of a small squadron, consisting also of the *Alliance*, an American thirty-six gun-frigate, commanded by a Frenchman named Pierre Landais, the *Pallas*, a French ship commanded by Captain Cottineau and armed with thirty-two guns, the *Cerf* of eighteen guns and the *Vengeance* of twelve guns. All five ships sailed under the American flag on the 14th of August, 1779. The crew of the *Bonhomme Richard* numbered about three hundred and eighty men. There were a few American citizens among them, but about a hundred and fifty were French volunteers, lured no doubt by promises of loot or prize money, the rest being made up of citizens of many countries ; to maintain discipline in such a mixed assembly must have been extremely difficult. Furthermore, though the French Revolution did not break out for another ten years, *égalité* sentiments evidently were present to some extent, and Paul Jones was obliged to conduct the affairs of his squadron rather on the lines of a committee, of which the captains of the other ships were members.

It is not surprising then to know that, within ten days of the squadron leaving Brest, the *Cerf* parted company in a fog and did not rejoin, preferring to pursue an independent course ; the third lieutenant of the *Bonhomme Richard* deserted with twenty men, taking two of the ship's boats, and Landais came aboard and was most insolent and insubordinate concerning the whole affair. At this point the squadron was off Cape Clear, in the south of Ireland, and in this neighbourhood it made several captures. It then went north, up the west coast of Ireland, to a point near the coast of Donegal ; here Lambert Wickes, on his raid two years previously, had turned east and come south down the Irish Channel ; but Paul Jones continued his course northwards, so as to come round the North of Scotland and down the North Sea coast.

Near Cape Wrath he captured two very valuable prizes ; Landais, of the *Alliance*, without any orders to that effect, sent these into Bergen and, a few days later, himself parted company with the squadron, which was now reduced to three ships and, continuing its course round Scotland, arrived off the Firth of Forth on the 14th of September. Here Paul Jones thought that he could capture a twenty-gun ship, which was anchored in Leith Roads, and also that he could attack Leith and Edinburgh, exacting a heavy ransom from them both. Furthermore, he calculated that this attack would coincide with an attack on the South Coast of England, which was projected by the joint Franco-Spanish fleet, under d'Orvilliers.

Intelligence in those days was a leisurely affair, and Paul Jones could not possibly know that, though the British had been compelled to retire up Channel, this formidable armada had collapsed through carelessness, incompetence and the ravages of disease, and was now back in Brest. None the less the idea was sound, and it would undoubtedly have been attempted, but for the extraordinary conditions on which the squadron-command rested.

The Commodore of the squadron had no real authority to make any decision, and Captain Cottineau and the commanding officer of the *Vengeance* opposed the scheme. The argument went on far into the night, and these two officers only gave way when it was brought home to them that two hundred thousand pounds was the prize to be aimed at. The breeze had previously been easterly ; next morning it had gone round to the westward, and the opportunity of making a surprise attack was lost.

It was decided, however, to make the attempt, and on the 16th and 17th of September the ships beat slowly up the Forth, causing great alarm. They had got nearly as far as Leith, when the wind suddenly freshened to a full gale, and they were driven back and far out to sea. Paul Jones then proposed to make an attack on the Tyne, but again Cottineau did not agree, and this project also came to nothing.

On the 23rd of September the *Alliance* rejoined the squadron, which sighted a large fleet of merchantmen a few hours later, coming south around Flamborough Head. This was the British " Baltic Trade," escorted by two warships, the *Serapis* of forty-four guns, Captain Richard Pearson, and the *Countess of Scarborough*, Captain Piercy, of twenty guns. These two ships at once took up a position between their convoy and the American squadron. Paul Jones made the signal for line of battle, to which Landais paid no attention, but stood over towards the convoy, perhaps hoping to make a few captures on his own account ; his subsequent behaviour was very extraordinary, and it is not surprising that he was afterwards retired from the Service as insane.

The *Pallas* made for the *Countess of Scarborough*, which was obliged, after an hour's fighting, to surrender. The *Pallas* was so much occupied in securing her prize that she was unable to take part in the fight which now took place between the *Bonhomme Richard* and the *Serapis*.

It was a fine autumn evening, and the moon was just rising when the action commenced. It took place in full view of the shore, and crowds of sightseers assembled on the cliffs to see what might befall. The wind was southwesterly and the two ships were now standing in for the land, on the port tack ; by half-past seven the *Bonhomme Richard* was a little to windward and on the port quarter of the *Serapis*. Both ships opened the action with almost simultaneous broadsides.

The *Serapis* was a forty-four gun ship, the armament of the *Bonhomme Richard* has been already mentioned ; of her forty guns, the eighteen-pounders appeared to be the most formidable, but they were old, and two of them burst before they had fired three rounds, blowing up part of the deck overhead and causing many casualties. The panic which followed was quelled by Paul Jones, whose example and personality it was upon which the conduct of the whole action depended.

His opponent was a much handier vessel ; at the commencement of the affair she was to leeward, but she soon went ahead and passed across the bows of the American ship, and back again, raking her on both occasions. After an hour's engagement, the captain of the *Bonhomme Richard* decided that the only thing to do was to grapple his adversary.

He was now to windward and, putting his helm up, he ran across the bows of the *Serapis*, whose jibboom was caught in the starboard mizen rigging of the enemy's ship ; her captain lashed it to his mizen mast with his own hands ; the *Serapis's* starboard anchor also hooked itself into the quarter of the *Bonhomme Richard*, and the two ships swung together, starboard to

A Figurehead.

starboard, and heading either way. Captain Pearson let go his port anchor, hoping that the two ships would drift apart, but without effect.

The *Serapis's* eighteen-pounder guns now kept up a devastating fire and silenced her adversary's main deck guns ; the men were driven up on deck and into the tops, whence they replied with a furious musketry fire, which drove the men of the *Serapis* below ; no attempt was yet made by either side to board. Meantime the *Alliance* was skirmishing around both adversaries, firing indiscriminately at friend and foe, which was somewhat dispiriting to Pearson, but by which Landais probably did far more damage to the *Bonhomme Richard* than to the *Serapis*.

It seemed as if the devastating fire of the *Serapis* against the rotten timbers of the *Bonhomme Richard* must decide the issue, when an unforeseen circumstance occurred, and turned the tide in favour of the American ship. One of her seamen was out on the main yard of his ship, with a bucket of hand grenades, and one of these he succeeded in throwing down the main hatch of the *Serapis* on to her lower deck. A number of cartridges had been placed there and the grenade fell among them ; the explosion was terrific. Many of the guns were disabled and there were numerous casualties among the guns' crews ; there was a question whether, or not, the *Serapis* should surrender.

Meantime the carpenter of the *Bonhomme Richard* came running up to her captain and said that the ship was sinking. The gunner ran to haul down the ensign, which he found had been shot away, and began to call for quarter ; but Paul Jones stopped his noise, by crashing in his skull with a pistol-butt. Pearson tried to board and so did Paul Jones, but both attempts were unsuccessful. The master-at-arms, who had heard the shouts of the gunner and the carpenter, now released the prisoners, and over a hundred of these rushed up from the hold and on to the deck. They might well have tried to take possession of the ship which had been so long their prison, but Paul Jones, with superb coolness, set them to work at the pumps ; only one of them escaped, through a port, to the *Serapis*, where he revealed the true state of affairs.

By this time both ships were beaten, and the only question which remained undecided was which of them should surrender the first. The number of killed and wounded on both sides is uncertain ; some say two hundred for the *Serapis* and one hundred and twenty for the *Bonhomme Richard* ; some put the figure as high as three hundred for each ship. It may be said, however, that considering the small numbers engaged on each side, the victory was dearly bought. The *Serapis* struck her colours at half-past ten the same night, and was boarded by the crew of the *Bonhomme Richard*, whose ship sank during the next forenoon.[1]

The *Serapis* and the *Countess of Scarborough* were taken, but the convoy was saved and the *Bonhomme Richard* sunk. Thus Paul Jones gained a notable victory, mainly through his personal courage, skill and grim determination, in face of lack of discipline, insubordination and the treacherous conduct of Landais, victory which was the more notable since it was gained off the enemy's coasts. Pearson was knighted by the King, on his return, and the London merchants presented him with a sword of honour, out of gratitude to him for having saved the convoy, at the sacrifice of his ship. Paul Jones is said to have remarked, " Should I have the good fortune to fall in with him again, I'll make a lord of him."

After this victory Paul Jones was desirous of going to Dunkirk, but he was ordered to proceed to the Texel, and thither he directed his course with his small squadron. The ships stayed in that port for some little time, but the British Minister at the Hague protested, on the ground that Paul Jones was a rebel. France had entered the war in 1778, and Spain in the following year ; Holland did not come in until December, 1780, and was therefore still a neutral. Later the ships of the squadron hoisted French colours and were afterwards bought in by the French Government.

[1] *Studies in Naval History.* Sir John Knox Laughton, M.A.

Paul Jones subsequently took command of the *Alliance* ; he succceded in getting through the British blockade, and arrived at Lorient ; he then went to Paris, where he was ordered to take a captured British ship, the *Ariel* of twenty guns, across to America ; he arrived at Philadelphia in February, 1781. This seems to have terminated his service with the American Navy ; afterwards he took service with the Russian Government as a Rear-Admiral, but had a quarrel with Potemkin, and eventually retired to Paris, where he died in 1792.

In January, 1780, Commodore Whipple's squadron, consisting of four ships, was sent to assist in the defence of Charleston, in South Carolina ; Charleston was anticipating an attack by General Clinton, operating from the direction of New York. The *Providence* and the *Ranger* succeeded in capturing seven enemy vessels, and the squadron supported the troops who were defending the city ; when Charleston eventually surrendered, the squadron was cut off and had also to be surrendered. On the 1st of June Commodore James Nicholson, in the *Trumbull*, a frigate newly built for the Continental Navy, fought an action with a privateer near the coast of Bermuda ; in this affair he lost his main and mizen masts, and his adversary got away.

Thirteen frigates had been specially built for the Continental Navy, and all had been lost by the beginning of 1781, with the exception of the *Trumbull* ; the Continental Navy had only four frigates remaining on active service and one sloop. France's entry into the war had now caused the major naval interest to be centred on the activities of her own fleet, American ships playing a somewhat subsidiary part. During the last three years of the war the following operations took place in which the latter were concerned.

In May, Commodore Barry fought an action, off Nova Scotia, with the British ship *Atlanta* and the brig *Trepassy*. Barry's flagship was the frigate *Alliance* ; he was wounded and, after a severe engagement, succeeded in capturing both his antagonists. During the month of August Commodore James Nicholson, in the *Trumbull*, left the Delaware River, in charge of a convoy ; she became separated from her charges in heavy weather, which caused her to lose her fore topmast and main topgallant mast. Damaged as she was, she then fell in with two British ships, the *Iris*, a thirty-two gun frigate, and the *General Monk*, of eighteen guns. The *Trumbull* suffered severely in the action which followed and had eventually to surrender, being towed into the port of New York by the *Iris*.

Barry left New London, in the *Alliance*, in order to make a cruise near the Newfoundland Banks in August, 1782 ; he made several captures, and then went on to Havana, in order to load specie and to escort back to America a newly purchased French ship, the *Duc de Lauzun*. His ships left Havana in March, 1783, and, while on their return journey, were chased by the British frigates *Alarm* and *Sybil* and the sloop *Tobago*. After a short action, Barry succeeded in saving his two ships, together with his valuable cargo.

As in the days of the Spanish Armada, when the English merchant navy made up a large part of the English fleet, so in the War of American Independence, the merchant ships bore the strain of the earlier part of the war ; furthermore, roads were bad, and the communications of both sides had to be maintained by sea. By the peace which was concluded with Great Britain in 1783, the American Colonies obtained their independence, and became the United States of America. Hostilities having ceased, trade began to revive and reached considerable proportions, but the need for protecting commerce was not at first apparent, and the fleet was dispersed. The last ship of the Continental Navy, the frigate *Alliance*, was sold out of the Service in 1785.

COMMODORE STEPHEN DECATUR

From a painting by Gilbert Stuart

(Independence Hall, National Museum, Philadelphia, Pa.)

One of the most distinguished of America's naval heroes.   Decatur first came to the fore during the war with Tripoli, where he set fire to the *Philadelphia*, captured by the Tripolitans.   In the War of 1812 he was Commodore and commanded the *United States* against the *Macedonian* ; his broad pendant was flying in the *President* when she was taken by the British in 1815.

NAUTICAL EXPLOIT.

PLATE X

NAUTICAL EXPLOIT

Engraved by Aubertin, after Binsse

The action off Tripoli in February, 1804, when Stephen Decatur went in and set fire to the captured *Philadelphia* in Tripoli Harbour. On the left is seen the ketch *Intrepid* escaping.

Engraving of Commodore Preble's Squadron whilst engaging the gun boats and Forts of Tripoli on August 3rd, 1804. His six gunboats attacked the town in two divisions, one under Decatur, the other under Richard Somers.

PLATE XII

MEDAL OF COMMODORE EDWARD PREBLE

Medal bearing on the obverse side an effigy of Commodore Preble, with a Latin inscription drawing attention to his energy and his activities on behalf of American commerce off Tripoli in 1804.   Reverse side : his squadron in action.

CHAPTER III

FRANCE AND TRIPOLI

AS a result of the admission to the Union of Vermont and Kentucky in 1791–2, the Stars and Stripes underwent a modification. The stripes, as well as the stars, were increased to fifteen in 1795. This form of the national flag and naval ensign remained in use until 1818, when the stripes were reduced to thirteen, their original number.

After the War of Independence the United States naturally required a period of peace for attention to their internal affairs. The friendly feelings towards France, which had their origin in gratitude for assistance given in that war, were perhaps augmented by republican sentiments, after the French Revolution of 1789 ; but the wise statesmanship of George Washington was able to keep the United States out of any embroilment in the affairs of Europe, despite French attempts to drag them in on their side during the War of the French Revolution.

In April, 1793, President Washington issued a Proclamation in which the United States declared that they would remain friendly and impartial to the belligerent Powers. At about the same time Citizen Genet arrived in America, as Minister of France to the United States ; he at once began issuing commissions to privateers, a matter which seriously embarrassed the United States Government. His general behaviour and that of the French consuls was so outrageous that his recall was demanded, and he was replaced by Citizen Fauchet and

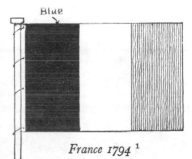

France 1794 [1]

subsequently by Citizen Adet. For a long time negotiations went on in Paris, with a view to adjusting the differences between the two Powers, and these were of an unsatisfactory nature ; finally, in 1798, undeclared hostilities commenced between France and America. At the conclusion of George Washington's second term of office, John Adams senior was elected President, and in July, 1798, Washington became Commander-in-Chief of the armies of the United States.

Meantime the United States had no Navy and, realizing that a naval force was essential to their safety, they at once began to construct a certain number of powerful frigates. These were designed by Joshua

[1] The present proportions of the bands in the French flag are :—width—blue 30 ; white 33 ; red 37.

Humphrey of Philadelphia, and the first three were the *United States*, *Constellation* and *Constitution*, which were forty-four gun ships. These were the first ships of the " New Navy " and were supplemented by vessels more lightly armed. This foresight on the part of the authorities was not at first understood by the generality of American subjects, who still believed that American interests had no need of naval protection.

On the 6th of July the *Croyable*, a French privateer-schooner, was captured by the *Delaware*, of twenty guns, and she was taken into the American naval service under the name *Retaliation*. A captain in command of a squadron was still known as a " Commodore," and Commodore John Barry had a small squadron, consisting of the *United States* and *Delaware* ; with these ships he sailed to the West Indies, picking up two French prizes. In July, 1798, the *Constitution*, last of the three large frigates to be completed, was ready for service, and she went to sea under the command of Captain Samuel Nicholson.

In September the *Montezuma*, a merchant ship in the naval service, went to the West Indies, in company with the brig *Norfolk* and the *Retaliation*, Lieutenant William Bainbridge. They recaptured an American ship from the French, and on the 20th of November, when near Guadeloupe, two sails appeared to leeward. The *Montezuma* and *Norfolk* at once went off to investigate. The *Retaliation* and the prize were left behind, and fell in with two frigates, which they thought at first to be British ; they turned out to be French, the *Insurgeante* of thirty-six guns and the *Volontaire* of forty-four. The *Insurgeante* hoisted French colours and opened fire on the *Retaliation*, which was obliged to surrender to superior force and was taken to Guadeloupe. Bainbridge and his men were repatriated soon afterwards, without an exchange of prisoners ; for the French Governor-General held that, since no war had been declared, there was consequently no war. These hostilities are, in fact, sometimes referred to as the " Quasi-War."

During the winter of 1798–9 Commodore Barry had a considerable squadron, consisting of the *United States*, *Constitution* and eight other ships, and Commodore Truxton, in the *Constellation*, had four other ships in his command. The " New Navy " was growing in size, and American public opinion was now becoming reconciled to the idea of possessing a naval force. American prisoners of war were now, in some cases, impressed into the French naval service, and this produced a feeling of resentment towards France ; retaliatory measures were contemplated, but were not carried out. A renewal of ordinary relations with the West Indies was proposed, however, provided that the activities of the privateers in those localities came to an end.

In January, 1799, Commodore Barry was cruising there, when he was joined by the *Merrimac*, of twenty-four guns ; he at once sent her to the

United States in charge of a large convoy of merchant ships. The captain of the *Merrimac* afterwards wrote to Barry saying that, although the convoy system was regarded with favour, the masters of ships would not keep together and there was much straggling, entailing danger to the convoy, especially at night. History repeats itself, and the " New Navy " was finding out the truth of this part of it for itself.

While cruising among the Leeward Islands in February, Commodore Truxton's squadron made out a large ship near the island of Nevis ; Truxton's broad pendant was in the frigate *Constellation*, which started off in chase ; it was then about noon on the 9th of February. An hour later a squall came on, and carried away the main topmast of the strange vessel, which tried to make for St. Eustatius, hoisting American colours. She then hoisted French colours and fired a gun, allowing Truxton's ship to come up. The French captain was apparently unaware of the fact that there was a war on in those latitudes and was greatly surprised to receive a broadside from a presumably friendly ship. To this he replied with vigour and, during the action which followed, he lost also his mizen topmast ; he was raked several times by the *Constellation* and at half-past four was obliged to surrender.

This vessel was the French frigate *Insurgeante*, rated as a thirty-six gun ship, but carrying forty guns. The first lieutenant of the *Constellation*, John Rodgers, was put in charge of the prize, with a prize crew which included Midshipman David Porter, and he succeeded in navigating her, through heavy weather, to St. Kitts, in the Leeward Islands. The French Governor-General of the West Indies endeavoured to obtain the release of the *Insurgeante*, on the ground that the United States and France were not at war ; his efforts were vain, and he then declared war on the United States.

Affairs in Haiti, or Santo Domingo, were causing a great deal of trouble. Toussaint l'Ouverture, a negro slave who had joined the French Republicans in 1794, bringing most of the negro population with him, was now virtually dictator of the former French colony at the western end of the island ; Toussaint agreed to stop privateering and opened two ports for commerce to American and British ships ; he had a rival in a mulatto called Rigaud, who held the extreme south-western portion of Haiti, where he carried on piratical activities.

Rigaud's men employed similar tactics to those used by the old buccaneers, who used formerly to frequent this area. They embarked in large boats, in which they hid close to the shore, dashing out to attack any vessel which passed ; when becalmed, these ships had little chance of escape. Their crews were often murdered and the ships themselves taken into one of the ports under Rigaud's control ; in 1799 Rigaud declared his loyalty to the French Directory.

On the 1st of January, 1800, the schooner *Experiment*, convoying four merchant vessels, was lying becalmed, with her charges, when she was set upon
by twelve boats full of Rigaud's desperadoes. As soon as they got near the
convoy, they opened fire with swivel-guns and musketry ; the *Experiment*
and the merchantmen replied, doing much damage to the pirates
These retired, putting their dead and wounded ashore and, embarking
a fresh lot, sallied forth again. Attempts to capture the *Experiment*
failed, but the pirates eventually retired with two ships of the convoy
which they had succeeded in detaching.

Measures had been taken during 1799, as we have seen, to protec
American shipping against French depredations in the West Indies, bu
in 1800 steps were also taken to protect it from any French privateer
which might be lurking in Eastern seas. In January the *Congress*
Captain Sever, and the *Essex*, Captain Preble, set out with a convoy o
three ships for the East. Bad weather was encountered ; the convoy and
the two frigates became separated and they lost sight of each other
The mainmast of the *Congress* was carried away, taking the mizen top
mast with it ; the foremast followed, and the *Congress* was left dismasted
she eventually succeeded in getting back under jury rig.

The *Essex* suffered little damage ; she reached the Cape of Good
Hope, and thence sailed to the Straits of Sunda, where she recaptured an
American ship taken by a privateer, and picked up a convoy of fourteen
sail, which she brought back. Just before reaching the Cape, on the
return journey, the convoy ran into a heavy gale ; the ships were dis
persed ; nine of them eventually turned up at the rendezvous at St
Helena, and duly reached New York.

Probably the most important action of this war was that between
Truxton's ship, the *Constellation*, and the French " frigate " *Vengeance*. The
Vengeance was described by Truxton as having at least fifty-four guns and
was sighted off Guadeloupe in the early morning of the 1st of February
Truxton gave chase, hoisting British colours ; the wind became light a
about noon, but at one o'clock it freshened and Truxton was able, by
setting every inch of canvas that his ship would carry, to get nearer
the Frenchman. By eight in the evening he was within hailing distance
and was about to demand the surrender of the *Vengeance*, when the last
named ship suddenly opened fire from the guns on her quarter and stern

Truxton then put the *Constellation* on the weather quarter of the French
man, and action commenced and continued until one o'clock in the
morning, when the *Vengeance* ceased firing and sheered off. At this
moment the *Constellation's* main rigging was found to be shot to pieces
during an attempt to save the mainmast, the mast fell, together with
the mizen topmast. Truxton was now compelled to devote all his
energies to saving his own ship, and the Frenchman got away to Curacao

The *Vengeance*, Captain Pitot, also received much damage to her masts and rigging, losing her mizen topmast, mainmast and fore topmast. It s said that she hauled down her colours twice or three times during the action, but since the *Constellation* continued to fire, she had to do the same. The battle may be regarded there-fore as a drawn game, with the advantage to the *Constellation*, since the Frenchman first withdrew from the fight, and the news of the action was received with great satisfaction in America.

Rigging Block.

Since the autumn of 1799 Commodore Talbot, in the *Con-titution*, had been on the Santo Domingo station, supporting Toussaint l'Ouverture and protecting ·American commerce. One of his squadron, the *General Greene*, was sent in April, 1800, to cruise round the island and to intercept supplies for General Rigaud's forces ; she aided Toussaint, in his attack on Jacmel, in the south. By the capture of this place, Toussaint was able to strike a decisive blow at Rigaud's authority. Rigaud was forced to capitulate in July, 1800, and left the island.

While the *Constitution* was still on the Santo Domingo station in the spring of 1800, a cutting-out expedition was arranged. The intention was to capture a French armed ship, which was lying at Porto Plata ; this port was in the Spanish part of the island, nearer its eastern end, and the Frenchman was lying under the guns of the Spanish fort. The sloop *Sally* was requisitioned for the enterprise. Lieutenant Isaac Hull, the first lieutenant of the *Constitution*, was given command of her, and ninety seamen and marines placed on board. Hull entered the harbour in broad daylight on the 11th of May, with his men concealed below decks, ran alongside the French ship, and boarded her without the loss of a man ; at the same time a landing party went ashore and spiked the guns of the fort.

The French ship had her topmasts down and the sails unbent ; by sunset, however, she was in order and ready waiting for the land breeze to take her out of harbour. She was sent to New York, but afterwards had to be returned to the French, since it was held that in " cutting her out," Spanish neutrality had been violated.

Affairs in the Dutch island of Curaçao called for some co-operation between the United States and Great Britain, which was also engaged at this time in war with France. American property there was unpro-tected, and in July, 1800, a French force from Guadeloupe arrived off the island ; some men were landed and the surrender of the forts was demanded, a demand which was refused by the Dutch Governor. An American subject named Robinson was then sent by the U.S. Consul for help to the island of St. Kitts ; [1] he returned with the *Merrimac* and

---

[1] *Our Naval War with France.* Gardner W. Allen.

Patapsco. In the meantime the British frigate *Nereide* had arrived, and the Governor had placed the island under British protection. The *Nereide* landed a party of marines ; so did the *Patapsco* ; several American citizens had volunteered to serve in the defence of the place and, as the result of their joint efforts, the French were compelled to abandon their project.

In June the *Enterprise*, Lieutenant Shaw, captured the French privateer *L'aigle*, also the *Flambeau* and three other armed vessels. The *Experiment*, Lieutenant Charles Stewart, also made important captures, including the privateer *Deux Amis* and the schooner *Diana*, on board which was found the Haitian General Rigaud.

The frigate *Boston*, Captain Little, was cruising near Guadeloupe in October, 1800, when she saw a French ship and gave chase, hoisting her colours. The Frenchman also hoisted his colours and shortened sail. At a quarter to five in the afternoon action commenced and lasted about half an hour ; both ships had their rigging much damaged and had to discontinue the fight, in order to effect repairs. At nine at night the action recommenced and continued until 10.20, by which time the Frenchman's fore and main topmasts were shot away. He then struck his colours and proved to be the man-of-war *Le Berceau*, Captain Senes, of twenty-four twelve-pounders and eight nine-pounders. The prize was towed most of the way back and arrived in Boston in November. Negotiations for peace were now proceeding with France, and in the following year she was given up.

These were the principal episodes of the " Quasi-War " with France ; the war came to an end with the ratification of the Peace Treaty on the 3rd of February, 1801.

Concurrently with the War with France there was trouble also with the Barbary States ; these consisted of Morocco, Algiers, Tunis, Tripoli and Barca. For long their ports had been haunts of piracy, and any ship proceeding to the Mediterranean, which was too weak to protect herself, was liable to capture at any moment ; she and her cargo were then taken into one of these African ports and her passengers and crew cast into slavery. Sallee, near Rabat in Morocco, was a well-known headquarters for these pirates on the Atlantic coast.

From early times the pirates of the Barbary States had been a menace to European merchant shipping in the Mediterranean. The Dutch in the seventeenth century found it necessary to keep warships there for the protection of their nationals, and the Knights of Malta were continually waging war on these marauders. Algerine pirates even raided the coast of England and Ireland, carrying off their victims into slavery.

Several punitive expeditions were organized against the Barbary States. Great Britain, France and Holland made attacks on Algiers

Tunis and Sallee, at different times, releasing a certain number of captives ; but the trouble went on well into the nineteenth century, when France began to occupy Algeria. At the beginning of that century Great Britain was fully occupied in the wars with France ; the United States had now no claim on the protection of her warships and, having no fleet of their own, were forced to submit to the insolent depredations of these sea-rovers, who made full use of their advantages.

For many years negotiations had been proceeding, between the United States and the Barbary Powers, for the ransom of American captives and for the purchase of peace between the countries concerned ; in 1792 the Senate approved of a payment of a hundred thousand dollars a year, to secure peace with Algiers, Tunis and Tripoli, and forty thousand dollars as ransom for the prisoners.[1] The building of frigates and other ships in the United States, shortly before the war with France, no doubt affected the situation ; some of these ships had been built with an eye to the Mediterranean before that war broke out. Oriental dilatoriness was speeded up with such effect that peace had been concluded with Algiers on the 3rd of September, 1795, and the American flag saluted. The Treaty of Peace with Morocco was confirmed in the same year, and Tripoli and Tunis made peace shortly afterwards—at a price—through the good offices of the Dey of Algiers.

Treaties with the Barbary States, however, were of a kind which carried little weight. In September, 1800, the frigate *George Washington*, Captain Bainbridge, arrived at Algiers with some of the money to be paid in tribute, according to the peace settlement. The Dey of Algiers had incurred the displeasure of his overlord, the Sultan of Turkey, and wished to ingratiate himself, by sending an ambassador with presents to Constantinople. He conceived the idea that an American warship would do admirably for the journey and applied to the United States consul for the use of the *George Washington*.

The request was refused, whereupon the Dey waxed indignant and changed his polite request into a peremptory demand. The *George Washington* had been anchored close in under the guns of the town and Bainbridge was forced to comply, and sailed for Constantinople under the Algerine flag. On arrival there, he was well received ; but the message from the Dey was not, and Bainbridge was sent back to Algiers with demands from the Sultan, which the Dey was not in a position to refuse.

It was apparently the first visit to Constantinople to be made by an American warship and the American flag was at first unrecognized. The Grand Vizier tried to make trouble, presumably in an attempt to extract backsheesh, and Bainbridge applied for advice to Lord Elgin, the British Ambassador. Lord Elgin, having had by this time considerable

[1] *Our Navy and the Barbary Corsairs.* Gardner W. Allen.

experience of Oriental customs, settled the matter privately. Bainbridge then became friendly with the Turkish naval commander-in-chief, and by him he was given a *firman*, granting him protection in all ports of the Turkish Empire ; this document was of considerable value to Bainbridge subsequently.

He arrived back in Algiers in January, 1801, and visited the Dey bringing the Sultan's message. The Dey was in a bad mood, and at once flew into a violent temper, which threatened unpleasantness all round ; Bainbridge at once thought of his *firman*, at the sight of which the Dey collapsed, and the incident was closed. Captain Bainbridge had no alternative but to act throughout as he had done, and his actions were approved, on his return to the United States, by the President.

The Pasha of Tripoli was an usurper ; a man of ambition, he had murdered one of his two brothers, and assumed power ; his other brother, Hamet, was the legitimate successor on the death of their father, and he was an exile in Tunis. In February, 1801, the Pasha, scenting a chance of obtaining more tribute-money, repudiated the peace treaty and proposed either to conclude another treaty, on more advantageous financial lines from his own point of view, or else to declare war. The first suggestion was refused, and Tripoli declared war on the 10th of May, 1801. The Tripolitans were much disappointed to find that American merchant shipping did not fall such an easy prey as had been anticipated, owing to warnings having been sent broadcast by the American consul, but they despatched two large ships to Gibraltar, to operate against the American flag in the Atlantic.

The United States were beginning now to realize that the continuous giving of " Danegeld " was not a paying proposition, and that they would have to abandon the Mediterranean altogether, or else maintain a naval force there, possibly " in rotation " with the other Powers.

In June, 1801, Commodore Dale was sent out to the Mediterranean in the *President* of forty-four guns, having with him the *Philadelphia*, *Essex* and *Enterprise*, and he found the two Tripolitan ships in Gibraltar, where he put in in July ; he at once detached the *Philadelphia* to watch their movements. With the *President* and *Enterprise* he cruised down the Barbary coast, visiting Algiers, Tunis and even Tripoli, but off none of these ports did he meet with any hostile demonstration.

A Polacre.

In August the *Enterprise* fell in with a polacre from Tripoli of about her own size ; she had fourteen guns against the twelve of the *Enterprise*. This Tripolitan ship was commanded by Reis Mahomet Sous, and the *Enterprise* by Lieutenant Sterrett. Sterrett raked the polacre several imes and finally compelled her surrender ; his first lieutenant was the elebrated David Porter, who was sent on board and had guns, equipment, verything of any real utility cast into the sea, except the bare necessities or navigating the vessel back to Tripoli. On his return there the unfortunate Reis Mahomet Sous was humiliated and punished ; as a esult of this affair, Tripolitan corsairs were rather chary for the future bout venturing out of harbour.

Tripoli was now being blockaded ; food was scarce and the Pasha was beginning to chafe under the effects of the blockade. It was quite a new dea to the Barbary States, and it was evidently having a salutary effect. he Pasha of Tripoli and the Bey of Tunis protested vehemently against vhat was to them a new and barbarous form of warfare, and they endeavoured to enlist the support of the Dey of Algiers.

The two Tripolitan ships had been abandoned by the bulk of their rews and left at Gibraltar, thus releasing the *Philadelphia* for other duties. he and the *Essex* cruised down the Barbary coast in September, escorting onvoys. The *Enterprise* went home, followed soon after by the *President*. he *Essex* was directed to keep an eye on the two Tripolitans and the *Philadelphia* had gone to Syracuse for the winter, with instructions to go o Tripoli occasionally, in order to see that the blockade was effective. he frigate *Boston* arrived from America and aided the *Philadelphia* in naintaining the Tripoli blockade. The *George Washington* was also in he Mediterranean.

A bombardment of Tripoli was then contemplated, together with a nd attack. It was believed that the Tripolitans were dispirited and ould welcome this method of restoring Hamet Pasha. Hamet was nduced to go to Malta, and there await a squadron which should convey im in triumph to Tripoli.

In February, 1802, the *Enterprise* went out again to the Mediterranean, llowed by the *Constellation, Chesapeake, Adams, New York* and *John Adams*, ll under the command of Commodore Richard Morris, whose broad endant was in the thirty-six-gun frigate *Chesapeake*. This time the naval rce was of some strength, comprising about ten vessels, including those ft in the Mediterranean during the preceding year.

The *Constellation*, while lying off Tripoli in July, saw some Tripolitan unboats coming along from the westward close in shore. She made all ail and stood in, in an endeavour to cut them off ; by the time she was ithin range, the water was shoaling rapidly and the gunboats had got nder the shelter of the forts, which at once opened fire, as did the gunoats. The *Constellation* made a vigorous reply, lasting about half an our, and was then obliged to abandon any attempt to cut them off. was apparent that the ease with which small vessels could creep in and ut of port and along the coast rendered the blockade ineffective unless

the U.S. naval forces in that locality disposed of some light-draugh
vessels.

The Emperor of Morocco was now becoming difficult. He wanted t
send corn to blockaded Tripoli, and asked for passports for the ship
intended for this service ; he also laid claim to the possession of th
Meshuda, one of the two Tripolitan ships at Gibraltar. These reques
were refused, whereupon the Emperor declared war on the United State
The *Chesapeake* put in an appearance off Tangier and this seemed t
quiet the Emperor's intransigence ; subsequently the passports wer
granted, the *Meshuda* was given up to him and " peace " was restored.

In May, 1803, Commodore Morris's squadron put into Malta. Her
some time was spent in taking in stores and in effecting repairs to th
New York, which had now joined the squadron and had met with a
accident just previously ; she was now the commodore's flagship, th
Chesapeake, with the *Constellation*, having returned to the United State
On the 3rd of May the *John Adams* went for a cruise off Tripoli, an
captured the Tripolitan ship *Meshuda*, now under the Moroccan fla
bringing her into Malta.

Shortly after Morris sailed for Tripoli with the *New York*, *Adams*, *Jo
Adams* and *Enterprise*. On approaching the port eleven lateen-rigg
coasting vessels were seen, with several gunboats, and these coasti
craft the *New York* succeeded in cutting off from Tripoli ; whereup
they got into a neighbouring port. The gunboats succeeded in getti
in under the guns of Tripoli itself. The coasting vessels were hauled
on the beach, and temporary defences were hastily built near them a
manned by a large force.

Lieutenant Porter then volunteered to take a boat in and make
night reconnaissance, and the following day he took charge of a bo
attack in which all the boats of the squadron took part ; Lieutena
James Lawrence was one of those who distinguished themselves in t
attack. As the boats approached the shore, they became the targ
for an intense musketry fire from the Tripolitans, concealed behind th
improvised defences. Porter's men succeeded, however, in setting f
to the vessels, which were drawn up on the beach.

He then re-embarked his men, opening his boats out to right and l
so as to leave a space free for the squadron to use its guns. This it
with great effect, but the Tripolitans rushed out, regardless of loss of li
they succeeded in putting out the fire and saved their ships.

An attack was then made on the gunboats off Tripoli ; they w
moored at the entrance to the harbour. The *John Adams* was sent
and opened fire, but the enemy withdrew, the wind being too light
the *New York* and *Adams* to come up in support of the *John Adams*. N
day some negotiations were started with the Pasha, but his demands w

so exorbitant that they were broken off, and the *New York* and *Enterprise* sailed for Malta, leaving the *Adams* and *John Adams* to continue the blockade of Tripoli ; they were joined soon afterwards by the *Enterprise*, commanded by Lieutenant Isaac Hull.

Captain Rodgers was in command of this force, and on the 21st of June he sent the *Enterprise* to the eastward and the *Adams* to the westward, remaining himself off the port, in the *John Adams* ; he had reason to think that preparations were being made for a large ship to leave or to enter the port. At six the next morning a large polacre was seen making for Tripoli, and the little *Enterprise* intercepted her and drove her to anchor in a small bay, about fifteen miles to the eastward of the town.

Rodgers approached the *Enterprise*, and saw nine gunboats coming to the aid of the polacre ; he opened fire, which was returned, and after forty-five minutes the polacre's fire was silenced, when her crew precipitately abandoned ship. The *John Adams* then hoisted out her boats, in order to take possession, when the enemy ship hauled down her colours and at once blew up with a tremendous explosion. Rodgers then chased the gunboats, but ineffectively, owing to the small draught of water.

Commodore Morris discontinued the blockade of Tripoli at the end of June, thinking that, with this success and the capture of the *Meshuda*, the Tripolitans had no ships at sea. He subsequently returned to the United States in the *Adams*, leaving the squadron under the temporary command of Captain Rodgers, pending the arrival of Commodore Edward Preble from the United States, with a new squadron.

Preble's flagship was the *Constitution* ; he had also in his squadron the *Philadelphia, Siren, Argus, Nautilus* and *Vixen* ; the four last-named were vessels of comparatively light draught. The *Enterprise* had been left in the Mediterranean, and she now came under Preble's command, Stephen Decatur being appointed to command her, and Hull being appointed to the *Argus*. Charles Stewart commanded the *Siren* and Bainbridge the *Philadelphia*.

In August Bainbridge arrived at Gibraltar, where he had news of two Tripolitan ships off Cape de Gata, and on the 26th of August he found at that place a ship and a brig. He ordered the ship's papers to be sent on board, and discovered that she was called the *Mirboka* and belonged to the Emperor of Morocco ; the brig was a captured American merchant vessel, called the *Celia*, and on board her were imprisoned her master and seven of the crew. Bainbridge at once took the *Mirboka* into Gibraltar and the *Celia* was given back to her master.

It was becoming obvious that something must be done to impress the Moors. Commodore Preble made a naval demonstration before Tangier in October, and the Emperor happened to be there with his army. He at once professed the most friendly sentiments and the squadron saluted him with twenty-one guns ; later the Treaty of Peace of 1786 was ratified, and the *Mirboka* and *Meshuda* were returned to him.

Just previously Bainbridge in the *Philadelphia*, having the *Vixen* in company, was ordered to proceed to Tripoli, and to blockade it. Bainbridge sent the *Vixen* to Cape Bon, to look for two Tripolitan ships which had been reported in that locality, and continued the blockade alone. On the 31st of October he saw a Tripolitan ship making for the port and, in trying to intercept her, ran his ship on to an uncharted rock. Attempts to get her off failed, and Bainbridge had the mortification of having to haul down his ensign and of finding himself a prisoner of war, together with his ship's company ; before giving up his ship, he threw the guns overboard and everything else of value.

Some days later the weather changed and the Tripolitans were able

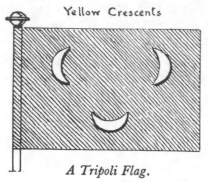

A Tripoli Flag.

to refloat the *Philadelphia* ; they also recovered her guns and brought her triumphantly into port. The ship's company remained prisoners for over eighteen months and, though roughly used, the deaths among them during that time did not exceed six men. This loss was a serious blow to the U.S. Navy, and no doubt had a tendency to lengthen the war.

Syracuse now became a naval base for the squadron ; it had advantages over Malta and Gibraltar, where desertions to the Royal Navy were not unknown ; captains of British ships refused to give up the deserters. In December Preble left Syracuse in the *Constitution*, with the *Enterprise*, for a cruise off Tripoli. The *Enterprise* succeeded in capturing a Turkish ketch called the *Mastico*. Her master had been very active in plundering the *Philadelphia*, and he and the passengers and crew were sent on board the flagship, while the prize was taken to Syracuse by the *Enterprise*. She subsequently passed into the U.S. naval service under the name *Intrepid*.

It was proposed at first to make an attempt to cut out the *Philadelphia*, but consideration of this plan showed it to be almost impossible ; it was therefore decided to destroy her. This attempt was entrusted to Lieutenant Stephen Decatur, and volunteers from the ship's company of the *Enterprise* ; the *Intrepid*, which was lateen-rigged, was to be used for the purpose. She left Syracuse on the 3rd of February, 1804, with the *Siren*, Lieutenant Charles Stewart, in company.

Four days later the two ships arrived off Tripoli, but for some days the weather was bad and they were carried away to the eastward. On the 16th of February they were again off Tripoli and, the weather having improved, it was decided to make the attempt the same night. The *Siren* stayed a little distance away from the port, so as to have the appearance of being in no way connected with the *Intrepid*, whose men included Lieutenant James Lawrence and Midshipman Macdonough. The *Intrepid* drifted into the harbour, and at half-past nine she was close to the *Philadelphia*, whose guns were loaded ; she was now in a perilous position ; but her pilot, who was a Sicilian, engaged the Tripolitan crew of the *Philadelphia* in conversation, without arousing suspicion, and asked permission to lie alongside the frigate for the night. A rope was passed and gradually the two vessels came together.

Immediately the men concealed aboard the *Intrepid* sprang on board the *Philadelphia*, and in a very short time the frigate was in their possession. The Tripolitans escaped overboard, only one man being made prisoner. The various combustibles were then transferred to her, and in a few minutes the ship was on fire, Decatur being the last to leave her, as the *Intrepid* cast off.

In order to take the *Intrepid* out to sea, her sweeps had to be brought into play, owing to the lightness of the wind ; the process was slow, and she was exposed to a hot fire from the shore, but without receiving serious damage. The guns of the burning ship went off and did some damage ashore, and after a time her cables were burned through and she drifted ashore herself and blew up. On rejoining the *Siren*, the *Intrepid* set sail in her company for Syracuse, where Decatur and his doughty men, none of whom was killed in this gallant affair, had a great reception. Nelson, hearing of this exploit when he was blockading Toulon, called it " the most bold and daring act of the age."

During the same month the *Vixen* was sent on a mission to Algiers and the *Nautilus* to Tripoli, where she captured the brig *Fortunata Barbara*, which she brought into Malta. The *Siren* captured a polacre and during March, an armed brig, the *Transfer* ; this ship was sent to Syracuse and served in the U.S. Navy under the name *Scourge*. The force maintaining the Tripoli blockade was now under Lieutenant Charles Stewart, and consisted of the *Siren*, *Vixen*, *Argus* and *Enterprise* ; these were joined at a later date by the *Scourge*.

Commodore Preble had been in correspondence with Bainbridge, now a prisoner of war, and Bainbridge was constantly urging that an attack should be made on Tripoli. In May Preble went to Naples, where he obtained from the King of the Two Sicilies—on something not unlike a " lease-and-lend " basis—six gunboats and two bomb-vessels. With these and the rest of his squadron he joined the blockading force before Tripoli on the 25th of July.

Bad weather then set in, but it improved by the 3rd of August, when the six gunboats were split into two divisions, one being under Decatur and the other under Lieutenant Richard Somers. The bomb-vessels and gun-boats were ordered in to attack the town, which responded with a hot fire. In the course of this operation the gunboats came up against a force of enemy gunboats, and Decatur succeeded in taking two of these, one of them after a fierce hand-to-hand fight. At about four o'clock the action terminated, the only American killed being Lieutenant James Decatur, Stephen Decatur's brother.

On the 7th of August another attack was made ; in this one of the gun-boats in Decatur's division was hit in the magazine and blew up. At about this time the *John Adams* arrived from the United States with news that the Mediterranean squadron was to be strengthened by the addition of the frigates *President, Constellation, Congress* and *Essex* ; the squadron was to be put under the command of Commodore Samuel Barron.

Between the 24th of August and the 3rd of September Preble made three night attacks, but these did not accomplish much, though some of the Tripolitan flotilla were sunk or driven ashore. On the night of the 4th of September, an attempt was made to send in a fireship to be blown up amongst the enemy's ships. The *Intrepid* was selected and was filled with explosives. From the volunteers for the enterprise, ten men were chosen and were placed under the command of Lieutenant Richard Somers, aided by Lieutenant Wadsworth ; at the last moment Lieutenant Joseph Israel, of the *Constitution*, pleaded to be allowed to go, and this request was granted.

The *Intrepid* approached the harbour at about nine-thirty and the shore batteries opened fire on her ; a few minutes later and just as she was entering the port, there was a terrific explosion, followed by commotion ashore, which was succeeded by a dead silence. The boats which the *Intrepid* had taken with her, for the escape of her crew, did not reappear, and it was concluded that Somers and his brave companions had perished ; in fact the thirteen bodies were afterwards found by the Tripolitans. The cause of the premature explosion was never known.

As the winter season was approaching, active operations before Tripoli were suspended, and on the 10th of September the *President* and *Constellation* arrived, with Commodore Barron ; Commodore Preble returned home soon afterwards, receiving the thanks of the United States authorities. The blockade of Tripoli continued and several vessels were taken, but on the 22nd of May, 1805, Commodore Barron was obliged to give up his command to Captain Rodgers, for reasons of ill-health.

Hamet Pasha had settled at Derna in the autumn of 1802 ; he made war on his brother, the Pasha of Tripoli, and being unsuccessful, he retired in 1804 to Egypt. Barron sent Captain Isaac Hull, with the *Argus*, to Alexandria, with orders to search for Hamet Pasha. He was greatly assisted in his dealings with officials in Egypt by letters from Sir

Alexander Ball, one of Nelson's captains, who was now Governor of Malta, and officers were sent up the Nile to look for Hamet.

Hamet was found and an international force was assembled, which proceeded to march westwards, across the Libyan Desert, towards Derna. Hamet was decidedly " infirm of purpose," but after meeting almost incredible obstacles, the column reached Derna in May, 1805, where with the aid of the *Argus*, *Hornet* and *Nautilus*, the place was taken. Peace negotiations, however, were already proceeding and, at the beginning of June, 1805, Hamet, a weak and irresolute character, was abandoned and peace was signed with Tripoli.

The Barbary States problem was not yet settled. Troubles arose again first with Tunis and then with Algiers. The difficulty with Tunis was quickly settled ; not so that with Algiers. In 1807 two American merchant ships were captured and taken into that port and for some years similar depredations continued. The situation was complicated in 1812 by the fact that war had broken out between the United States and Great Britain, which fully occupied the ships of the first-named ; as soon as these hostilities came to an end, war was formally declared on Algiers.

CHAPTER IV

WAR OF 1812

THE causes of the War of 1812 have been fully described in Admiral Mahan's great work on that subject ; [1] they might be summed up by saying that the war was due to Britain's interference with trade and to her impressment of British seamen found in American ships.

By the Decrees of Berlin and Milan in 1806, Napoleon established his " Continental System," whereby the Continent of Europe was forbidden to trade with Great Britain ; that country then retaliated with the " Orders in Council," blockading the Continental ports. The United States had at that time a considerable trade with Europe, and were consequently among the countries affected by this decision, as Great Britain was affected by the Continental System.

According to the provisions of the British Navigation Acts, all overseas trade from or to Great Britain and its colonies must be carried in British and British-manned ships, or in ships of the country of origin. This worked satisfactorily, as regards the carrying trade of America, so long as the North American colonies remained British ; as soon as they gained their independence, the whole matter was altered ; but traders in the West Indies continued to send their goods out in American ships, to a great extent, the new conditions being winked at, and Nelson got into great trouble with his Admiral and the West Indian trade interests because he protested against this breach of the law. Indeed the interests in question, aided by some ingenious legal gentlemen, brought charges against Nelson, which led to his being kept ashore, and not given command of a ship for about two years.

These were some of the difficulties which were left unsettled after the Peace of 1783, and in 1794 John Jay went to Great Britain and signed the " Jay Treaty " with Lord Grenville, by which, among other provisions inland trade could be freely conducted between the United States and Canada, and American seamen should not be liable to impressment in the British Navy.

In 1812 The Napoleonic War was in full swing, and British merchant seamen were freely impressed for service in the Royal Navy ; it was known that they often deserted, and obtained employment for good pay in American merchant ships. Britain therefore exercised her time honoured " right of search," and frequently held up American ships

---

[1] *Sea Power in its Relations to the War of* 1812. Captain A. T. Mahan, D.C.L., LL.D., U.S.N.

PLATE XIII

CAPTURE OF THE *JAVA*

Painting by Nicholas Pocock

In October, 1812, the British frigate *Java*, Captain Lambert, was on the Brazilian coast, when she fell in with the *Constitution*, Captain Bainbridge. Lambert was killed and his ship almost dismasted. She was captured and set on fire.

PLATE XIV

COMMODORE WILLIAM BAINBRIDGE
In the full-dress uniform of a naval captain

Bainbridge distinguished himself in the "Quasi-War" with France and afterwards in that with Tripoli. In the War of 1812 he commanded the frigate *Constitution* when she captured the British ship *Java*.

PLATE XV

THE *CONSTITUTION* AND *GUERRIÈRE*, 1812

Engraved by T. Tiebout

Captain Isaac Hull of the U.S. Frigate *Constitution* fought an action with the British frigate *Guerrière*. The *Constitution* had forty-four guns against the *Guerrière's* thirty-eight. The latter ship, commanded by Captain Dacres, lost her fore and main masts during the fight and was finally compelled to surrender.

FIRST IN VICTORY   FIRST IN BATTLE

Captain I. Hull

Eluded the British Fleet July 1812 — Captured the Guerriere Aug. 1812.

PLATE XVI

COMMODORE ISAAC HULL

Aquatint by W. Strickland

Isaac Hull, Commodore, commanded the *Constitution* in her action with the British ship *Guerrière* in August, 1812.

removing from them any British seaman who might be found on board. Too close a discrimination was not always shown, regarding the nationality of the seaman in question. Bismarck is said to have observed, on one occasion, that in his opinion the most significant thing, in its influence on world affairs during the last hundred years or so, was the fact that North America speaks English ; and this fact did not make the difficulty any easier.

Captain Marryat, who was a contemporary writer, records or imagines a scene, in one of his books,[1] where a British naval officer is having a friendly chat with the master of an American privateer, captured at the commencement of the War of 1812.

" ' Some of them, I suspect, are English,' said the naval officer, referring to the crew of the privateer.

" ' It is not for me to peach,' said the wary American. ' It is difficult always to know if a man who has been in both countries is a native of Boston in Lincolnshire, or Boston in Massachusetts ; and perhaps they don't always know themselves. We never ask questions when a seaman ships for us.' "

The speaker went on to say that the British Press Gang really acted in American interests, because the British could not endure impressment, and for every two men whom they got by force, the Americans got one as a volunteer. This knotty question eventually led to war, and Mahan gives, as its causes, " the impressment of seamen from American merchant ships, upon the high seas, to serve in the British Navy, and the interference with the carrying trade of the United States by the naval power of Great Britain."

It was impossible for the United States Navy, owing to its small size, to cross the ocean in any force, consequently the sea operations were mainly confined to the American coasts and here, and on the great lakes, the principal actions were fought, mostly frigate actions. The superior fleet of Great Britain enabled her ships to dominate the Atlantic, and so to exercise pressure on the American coast-line by means of blockade, notwithstanding the fact that she was already engaged in fighting Napoleon in Europe. Admiral Mahan draws attention to the fact that American roads were still in very bad condition, and that nearly all communications had to be assured by water. Thus a blockade of the American coasts practically put a stop to trade, while the war continued.

On the 18th of June, 1812, President Madison's Government declared war on Great Britain, and a small force was formed of five ships under Commodore John Rodgers. This consisted of the frigates *President* and *United States*, of forty-four guns, and the *Congress* of thirty-eight ; also the sloop *Hornet* of eighteen guns and the brig *Argus* of sixteen. Stephen

[1] *Frank Mildmay.* Vol. iii.

Decatur had a part of this force under him, consisting of the *Congress*, *United States* and *Argus*.

By the 21st of June, Rodgers had left New York with his five ships, his

Ship's Boat.

broad pendant being in the frigate *President*. It was known that a large convoy was proceeding from Jamaica to England, and this he determined to intercept, if possible ; an American brig had seen the convoy, and reported it as steering east about three hundred miles away. All sail was set, and soon afterwards a large vessel was seen coming towards the American ships. This vessel was the British ship *Belvidera*, of thirty-two guns, which at once put about and tried to escape. The chase continued all day, the *Belvidera* jettisoning anchors, boats and other matters, in her efforts to get away : finally she succeeded, making for Halifax, in Nova Scotia.

Rodgers then directed his course in pursuit of the convoy ; he went most of the way across the Atlantic, but with no success, and returned, reaching Boston on the 31st of August. The *Belvidera* had presumably announced at Halifax that a strong American squadron was at sea, and this suggested that a state of war existed, though news had not yet arrived there to that effect.

This news was confirmed a few days afterwards, and Admiral Sawyer sent from Halifax a force commanded by Captain Philip Vere Broke, of the *Shannon*, thirty-eight guns ; Broke had also the *Belvidera* and *Æolus* of thirty-two guns ; the *Guerrière* of thirty-eight guns joined him a few days later. He did not find Rodgers's force, and towards the end of July he joined a convoy, which was homeward bound for Jamaica, under the escort of the frigate *Thalia*.

On the 6th of August, Broke ordered the *Guerrière*, which was badly in need of an overhaul, back to Halifax ; Broke's squadron then went to a position off New York. Meantime the *Constitution*, of forty-four guns, was in Chesapeake Bay and Captain Isaac Hull, fearing to be blockaded there, put to sea. He sighted Broke's squadron, which gave chase and, the weather being calm, the *Constitution* had great difficulty in getting away ; after a long and laborious pursuit, in which the ships' boats had to be employed, she at last eluded her British pursuers, and made for Boston.

From here she sailed on the 2nd of August, and went up to a point off Halifax ; thence to the Gulf of the St. Lawrence, where she made several captures. She then sailed south towards Bermuda, and on the 19th of August, she fell in with a strange sail. This proved to be the *Guerrière*, which was leisurely returning to Halifax. The wind was north-westerly and the *Constitution* was to windward of the *Guerrière*, which was on a south-westerly course.

Shortly before four o'clock the *Guerrière* backed her main topsail, thus lessening her way. The *Constitution* directed her course towards the *Guerrière's* starboard quarter and, as the American ship approached her adversary, the latter swung across in such a way as to present her starboard broadside, which opened on the *Constitution*. Captain Dacres, of the *Guerrière*, then altered course again and presented his port broadside ; this had the effect of bringing the two ships nearer together : the *Constitution* avoided being raked, as she approached head on, by yawing from side to side.

This went on for about three quarters of an hour, until the two ships were close together, with the *Constitution* a little astern, and both vessels running before the wind. Captain Hull now ordered the main top-gallant sail to be set, and the *Constitution* drew ahead and came up on the *Guerrière's* port side. It was now six o'clock, and a furious exchange of broadsides commenced at close quarters. Twenty minutes later the *Guerrière's* mizen mast had gone, falling over on the starboard side ; her main yard was also damaged. The effect of the mizen mast and its gear falling overside was to lessen the speed of the ship, and to slew her head round to starboard. Hull ported his helm, so as to follow the movement round, and at the same time to get into a favourable position for raking, on the *Guerrière's* starboard bow, since his superior sail power now carried him forward.

The braces of the *Constitution* had now been shot away, and she was difficult to manage, with her sails shaking in the wind. She raked the *Guerrière* on two occasions, and was then able to turn across to port, on her starboard side, and a little ahead of her. The *Guerrière's* bowsprit became entangled in her port mizen rigging and the two ships came together side by side. The moment had now arrived to make an attempt to board, and Captain Hull and Captain Dacres presumably both had this in mind ; men were gathering in both ships, ready to make the attempt ; a hot musketry fire was also being exchanged, by which the *Constitution's* senior officer of marines was killed and her first lieutenant and sailing master were wounded ; casualties were also inflicted on the ship's company of the *Guerrière*.

At half-past six the fore- and mainmasts of the *Guerrière* were shot away, and the ship was left helpless ; an attempt was then made to get the sprit sail on her, and so get her under some sort of control in the heavy sea, but this was ineffective ; she was a beaten ship.

Captain Hull then took the *Constitution* a little way off, so that he could repair damages, and half an hour later he returned and received the *Guerrière's* formal surrender. The *Constitution* had a thirty per cent. superiority over her adversary in weight of metal, but was magnificently fought, and her gunnery was of a superior order.

Night was now coming on, and the hours of darkness were employed in transferring the prisoners of war across to the *Constitution*, a task which presented some difficulty, owing to the heavy sea which was running. Next day it was obvious that the *Guerrière* could not be brought back to port as a prize, so badly was she shattered by her adversary's gunfire, and so she was set on fire during the afternoon, and soon afterwards she blew up. This victory caused some jubilation in the United States, which had previously been a prey to some despondency.

Fighting was now going on on the Canadian border, and here are two large lakes, Lake Erie and Lake Ontario, which supply the St. Lawrence River ; Captain Isaac Chauncey was placed in naval command there on the 3rd of September. At the southern side of Lake Ontario is the town of Oswego, and farther East a place called Sackett's Harbour. Lieutenant Wolsey was in command on Lake Ontario, with one brig named the *Oneida*, but when Captain Chauncey arrived he found no organization on the American side of Lake Erie, and at once set about to create one.

Jesse Elliott was the lieutenant chosen for command on Lake Erie, and he arranged for two ships to be built and others fitted out. Efforts

A Brig.

were then concentrated on Lake Ontario, where Sackett's Harbour was fitted out as a naval base ; some skirmishing with British vessels occurred on the lake, and in November the *Madison* was launched, a ship of twenty-four thirty-two-pounder carronades. At the end of 1812 the American naval force was in Sackett's Harbour, where two ships were building, and at the eastern end of Lake Erie, where two brigs and other vessels had been laid down.

Before the winter set in, that is on the 8th of October, the British armed ships *Detroit* and *Caledonia* had arrived off Fort Erie, near the Falls of Niagara ; the following day Elliott took a number of seamen, who had just arrived overland from New York, alongside these two ships, and captured them in a surprise attack. The *Caledonia* he was able to beach in an advantageous position, but the *Detroit* had to be set on fire and abandoned.

A great deal of privateering was a feature of this war, and here Joshua Barney was very active ; he had been a Commodore in the War of Independence, and early in this war he had a schooner, called the *Rossie* of Baltimore, with which he again embarked on an adventurous career. He sailed on the 15th of July from the mouth of the Chesapeake to the neighbourhood of Halifax, where Sir John Borlase Warren held the British naval command, and up to the beginning of August he had made eleven captures. On the 30th of August, he went up to Rhode Island, and thence to the Caribbean Sea ; he returned to Baltimore late in October, having captured or destroyed property estimated at a million and a half dollars.

The ship *America* was also a privateer. She was a merchantman of four hundred and seventy tons. Since it was useless or extremely difficult to carry on her ordinary business, she had her spars greatly increased in size and was equipped with a strong armament ; thus she could fight or run, having considerably more speed than she had in her ordinary rig. During the whole war the *America* took forty-one prizes, operating usually between the English Channel and the Canary Islands, and her prizes, which she succeeded in bringing to port, were estimated in value at eleven hundred thousand dollars.

Three squadrons were formed in September, 1812: one under Captain William Bainbridge, who now commanded the *Constitution,* one under Stephen Decatur in the *United States,* and one under Rodgers, in the *President* ; Rodgers had also the *Congress,* Decatur had the brig *Argus* and Bainbridge had the *Hornet,* commanded by Captain James Lawrence, and the *Essex* of thirty-two guns, commanded by Captain David Porter.

Rodgers and Decatur left port together on the 8th of October, but three days later Decatur parted company. Rodgers then captured the British packet *Swallow* and another ship, but the British regulations concerning ships proceeding in convoy were so rigidly enforced that he had little success in interfering with the enemy's trade, and saw comparatively few British vessels.

On the 13th of October, Captain Jacob Jones, commanding the sloop *Wasp,* left the Delaware River, for a cruise to the eastward. Three days afterwards he lost his jibboom in a strong gale. On the night of the 17th he saw several large sail passing, and found them to be part of a convoy proceeding from Honduras to England, escorted by the British brig *Frolic,* Captain Whinyates, which had just lost her main yard. Whinyates sent the convoy on and dropped astern, endeavouring by various means to delay the enemy.

When the action between the two ships of war commenced, they were nearly side by side and closing, and ten minutes later the *Wasp* lost her main topmast, her mizen topgallant mast and spanker gaff, also much of her running rigging. The *Frolic* was firing too high ; the *Wasp's* fire, on the other hand, was well directed and did conspicuous harm to her opponent, who lost fifteen killed as against the American's five. The *Frolic's* bowsprit came across the deck of the *Wasp,* which grappled her and submitted her to a raking fire. She then boarded the *Frolic,* which surrendered.

The *Frolic* hauled down her colours, and soon afterwards a British seventy-four-gun ship, named the *Poictiers,* came up, and the American vessel was unable to escape. The *Poictiers* overhauled them both, and took them into Bermuda, where the *Wasp*, under the name *Loup Cervier*, was taken into the British service.

Decatur, on getting out to sea, had detached the *Argus*, for a cruise to the coast of South America, and himself, in the *United States*, stood south-east for some days. On the 25th of October, he sighted the British frigate *Macedonian*, Captain John Carden, which altered course for the *United States*. The two vessels approached each other on opposite courses, the *Macedonian* being a little to windward, and the wind being S.S.E., and almost on the beam. The *United States* had twenty-four-pounder guns against her opponent's eighteen-pounders ; therefore it was to her advantage to keep at long range from her adversary, where her guns would be more effective.

After a time she wore, thus bringing her into the same course as the *Macedonian*, and ahead of her, but she soon came about again onto the opposite course, and passed at a distance of half a mile, discharging her broadside, which was within range. The *Macedonian* now wore in her turn, and approached the *United States*, coming up on her port quarter. Broadsides were exchanged for about fifteen minutes, and the *Macedonian* endeavoured to close, having by this time lost her main topmast, main yard and mizen topmast ; the *United States* had only lost her mizen top-gallant mast. Casualties were heavy aboard the *Macedonian*, which continued fighting for another half-hour, but at the end of that time the fore and main topmasts fell and she was practically helpless. The *United States* passed on and crossed her bows, and then returned, to find that the British frigate's mizen mast had gone by the board and that she had surrendered.

The British were a little puzzled at the American frigate crossing their bows without delivering a raking broadside, and it has been supposed that this was due to the fact that no cartridges were available at this precise moment ; Mahan hints that to rake an already beaten enemy, unless his surrender were refused, was not a sporting thing to do and, bearing in mind that the two opponents were Anglo-Saxons, where such niceties of conduct were regarded as being of some importance, one can accept such an explanation as being the most probable.

Bainbridge took his squadron to sea in October, 1812 ; the *Essex* was under repair and did not leave till later, but the *Constitution* and the sloop *Hornet* left Boston on the 26th of October, and went to the Brazilian coast, arriving at Bahia on the 13th of December. In the port of Bahia was the *Bonne Citoyenne*, a British sloop of war, and the *Hornet* was detached to watch her. Bainbridge then took his ship to sea, and about five miles out he saw the British frigate *Java* approaching the coast in company with an American prize. Captain Lambert, of the *Java*, thereupon ordered the prize to go into the port of Bahia, and himself prepared to meet the *Constitution*.

The Portuguese authorities had shown some anxiety as to violation of territorial waters ; therefore, in order to avoid any question of this nature, which might arise, Bainbridge stood out some distance from the coast in a south-easterly direction ; the *Java* followed at a good speed. At one-thirty the *Constitution* went about and made for the *Java*, which bore up so as to present her broadside, whereupon the *Constitution* wore back to her south-easterly course, the wind being north-east.

Soon after two o'clock the *Java* was within half a mile of her adversary, and hoisted her colours, to which the *Constitution* replied with two broadsides, and the two ships came alongside each other, the *Java* being to port. The manœuvres which followed are too complicated to describe here ; the ships circled round each other, presenting either broadside and alternately raking and being raked. At half-past two the *Constitution* had her wheel shot away, and had to steer by means of relieving-tackles. Half an hour later the *Java's* bowsprit-head and jibboom went ; her fore and main masts were damaged and all her gear cut to pieces.

Thereupon Captain Lambert decided to board ; but on putting the *Java's* helm over, the foremast went over the side, and what was left of her bowsprit caught in the *Constitution's* rigging. The latter ship then got clear, and came across the bows of the *Java*, which now lost her main topmast ; her mizen mast followed soon after, and she was left helpless.

Though a beaten ship, she continued to fight till four o'clock, or soon after. Captain Lambert was mortally wounded, and the *Java's* casualties numbered one hundred and twenty-four, against her adversary's thirty-four. The *Constitution* retired, to repair her own damages, and she returned before six o'clock, to receive the *Java's* surrender.

This ship was so badly knocked about that she had to be set on fire ; the *Constitution* landed her prisoners at Bahia and returned to the United States, arriving at Boston towards the end of February. Bainbridge left the *Hornet* at Bahia, warning her against the expected approach of a British ship ; soon after his departure this ship arrived, being a seventy-four-gun vessel named the *Montagu*, and caused Captain Lawrence some discomfiture ; but he managed to escape from Bahia by night and got away in safety.

The *Hornet* then cruised off the Brazilian coast till the 24th of February, when she was off the Demerara River, where she fell in with the British brig *Peacock*. The engagement between these two ships was brief, the *Peacock* having an inferior armament, and only lasted about a quarter of an hour, when the *Peacock* surrendered, leaking heavily and with six feet of water in her hold. Soon afterwards she sank, taking down nine of her own crew and three of the enemy's. Lawrence had now a large number of prisoners on board the *Hornet* ; food was running short, and he therefore decided to return to the United States, where he arrived in the middle of March, 1813.

In this earlier period of the war, five frigate or small ship actions had been fought, all with results highly favourable to the United States Navy. These actions were those between the *Constitution*, sometimes called " Old Ironsides," and the *Java*, and the same ship and the *Guerrière*, and that between the *United States* and *Macedonian* ; smaller actions were those between the *Wasp* and *Frolic* and the *Hornet* and *Peacock*. Interest begins now to centre on the Canadian border or, as it is sometimes called, the " Lake Frontier."

Admiral Warren had not entirely neglected the defence of the frontier, from the naval point of view, and Captain Sir James Yeo had been selected to command on Lake Ontario ; he reached Kingston, at the north-eastern end of Lake Ontario, in May, 1813 ; the Americans were building ships at Sackett's Harbour, on the opposite side of the lake, and were generally getting into a state of readiness, and Captain Barclay was sent by the British to Lake Erie to assume that command, where he was opposed to Captain Oliver Hazard Perry.

At this time British naval units were partly building and partly afloat, and were divided between Kingston and York, now known as Toronto, at either end of Lake Ontario. The *Prince Regent*, of twenty guns, and the *Duke of Gloucester*, with sixteen, were at York, and two vessels were reported to be on the stocks there.

In April, 1813, an American expedition was organized by Chauncey and crossed to the north side of the lake, arriving off York on the 27th of April. York was taken, together with the *Duke of Gloucester*, but the *Prince Regent* had been sent to Kingston some days before, and so escaped. Some demolition was carried out, and the expedition returned to Sackett's Harbour. On the 27th of May, Chauncey sailed thence to Niagara, and drove out the British forces there and in the immediate neighbourhood. A British vessel, named the *Queen Charlotte*, which had been at Fort Erie, had been sent to Amherstburg, or Fort Malden, at the north-western end of Lake Erie, and with the capture of the connecting link between the two lakes at Niagara, including Fort Erie, the Americans were enabled to release some ships which were immobilized there, and to put them into a proper state of repair.

A British attempt was then made to create a diversion by attacking Sackett's Harbour, where a ship was building for Chauncey's force. Captain Chauncey was away at Niagara, leaving a lieutenant in charge of the base at Sackett's Harbour. The British expedition started from Kingston on the same day as that on which Captain Chauncey had

STREFFEN ZWISCHEN DEM AMERIKANISCHEN SCHIFFE „United States" UND DEM BRITTISCHEN SCHIFFE „Macedonian"

PLATE XVII

UNITED STATES AND *MACEDONIAN*, October 25th, 1812

Engraved by R. Weber

Commodore Stephen Decatur, in the frigate *United States*, sighted the British frigate *Macedonian* and engaged her ; the *Macedonian* was commanded by Captain John Carden.   After fifteen minutes of broadside fire, this vessel lost her main topmast, main yard and, when her mizen mast also fell, she surrendered.

PLATE XVIII

PERRY'S VICTORY, LAKE ERIE, 1813

Engraved by B. Tanner

In September, 1813, Commodore Oliver Perry fought a successful action against Captain Barclay on Lake Erie. Perry had a number of brigs and smaller vessels and the opposing force was very similar. Perry's flagship, the *Lawrence*, was badly damaged during the action, and he had to transfer his flag to the *Niagara*.

sailed for Niagara ; a number of barges from Oswego were captured, but no immediate attempt was made to land.

It had been arranged that if Sackett's Harbour could not be defended, the naval base should be set on fire. The British made a landing on the 29th of May, but the attack was not pressed, and they failed to take the place and were compelled to re-embark. A false report reached the American officer in command, during the affair, to the effect that the place had been already taken and must be set ablaze. The *Duke of Gloucester*, captured previously at York, and another ship were set on fire, but as soon as the mistake was discovered, the flames were got under control ; considerable damage however had been done to the naval base and its contents. The British attempt on Sackett's Harbour had failed and the expedition returned to Kingston.

In a few weeks Captain Yeo found himself with a superior fleet on Lake Ontario to that of his adversary, who now had his new ship in commission ; she was named the *General Pike*, and was equipped with twenty-six twenty-four-pounders. A ship-building race had been going on ; the British made a demonstration before Oswego, but no active operations took place. On the 21st of July, Captain Chauncey sailed, proceeding west, and arrived off Niagara on the 27th of July. On the 7th of August, Yeo's squadron appeared off that place, consisting of the *Royal George* (ex-*Prince Regent*) and the *Wolfe*, together with two brigs and two large schooners. Chauncey had the *General Pike* and the *Madison*, one brig, the *Oneida*, and ten schooners ; he lost two schooners through capsizing in a heavy squall, before the two forces engaged.

The opposing forces manœuvred for three days, and on the 10th of August, the British line of battle, consisting of six ships, was on a parallel course and to windward of the Americans, whose squadron was in two parallel lines, most of the schooners being to windward, that is, on the side nearest to the British. Just at the commencement of the action, the two schooners leading the windward line tacked over, for some reason, and crossed the head of the British line, which pursued them and eventually effected their

A Small Sloop.

capture. This completed the affair, and afterwards Chauncey returned to Sackett's Harbour.

A different state of affairs existed on Lake Erie. Here Captain Oliver Perry was pressing on with ship building in like manner, but with results far more favourable to the American cause. In June, 1813, the famous action had taken place between the *Chesapeake* and the *Shannon*,[1] in which

[1] Chapter V.

the gallant Lawrence lost his life, and one of Perry's new ships was named the *Lawrence*, in his memory. At the Battle of Lake Erie in September, 1813, Perry hoisted a flag which bore the words attributed, during the *Chesapeake* action, to Lawrence : " Don't give up the ship."

Chauncey, who was on Lake Ontario, was senior to Perry and had control of all naval reinforcements sent to the lakes, and Perry was unable to obtain all the men he required for manning his fleet ; he had to do the best he could with the personnel at his disposition. He had now ten ships in his force : the *Lawrence* and *Niagara*, brigs armed with thirty-two-pounders ; another brig, the British *Caledonia*, which had been taken by Elliott off Fort Erie in 1812 ; and some schooners and small vessels, including the *Tigress, Ohio, Somers, Trippe, Ariel, Scorpion* and *Porcupine*. Lieutenant Jesse Elliott acted as Perry' second-in-command.

This force was built and equipped largely at the town of Erie, or Presqu'isle, at the south of the lake, and for a time it was blockaded by Barclay, who came over from Long Point, at the other side of the lake, but eventually he went away, and Perry set himself to get his squadron out from Presqu'isle. The brigs had to be lightened of their guns and their hulls lifted on " camels," so as to get them over the harbour-bar ; the smaller vessels were ordered outside the harbour, so as to protect the operation. The *Niagara* and *Lawrence* were safely taken over the bar, and on the 4th of August the force was outside in the lake.

Barclay was still awaiting the completion of a new ship, the *Detroit*, and he retired to Amherstburg, leaving Perry in control of the lake, where he received the welcome reinforcements. On the 12th of August, Perry sailed westwards, making for Amherstburg, off which he appeared on two occasions, but Barclay still postponed action. The American squadron went to the Bass Islands, about thirty miles south-west of Amherstburg, where it was in a position to watch Barclay's force, and awaited developments.

On the 10th of September the British line, commanded by Barclay, was sighted in the north-west. The *Detroit* was now ready, and this ship and the *Queen Charlotte*, together with the *Hunter*, were in the centre of the line, the American force being similarly disposed, with the heaviest ships in the centre. Perry's ships went into action in this order : the flagship *Lawrence*, the *Caledonia* and *Niagara*, Lieutenant Elliott ; two schooners, the *Ariel* and *Scorpion*, formed the van of the American line, and four brought up the rear. Barclay's force numbered six vessels, including schooners, and Perry's numbered nine.

The wind was south-east and the British line at the commencement of the action was heading south-west and was on the leeward side of its adversary ; Barclay waited for a time for the enemy's squadron, hove-to. At about a quarter to twelve the *Detroit* opened fire, and the

Americans replied ten minutes later. The American line was approaching the British obliquely, until it was within carronade range ; then the *Lawrence*, headed by the *Ariel* and *Scorpion*, altered to a parallel course, having the *Detroit* opposed to her. Much of the *Lawrence's* rigging was shot away by now and she was becoming difficult to handle ; she and the two schooners got somewhat ahead of the rest of her squadron ; the *Caledonia*, which was next astern, gave her some support, but the *Niagara's* carronades did not render adequate assistance.

The *Detroit* was leading the British line and was opposed to the *Lawrence*. Following the *Detroit* was the *Hunter*, and then the *Queen Charlotte*. The *Queen Charlotte* was opposed to the *Niagara* but, finding that he could give no support to the *Detroit* in concentrating on the *Lawrence*, owing to her being out of range of his carronades, her captain increased speed, passed the *Hunter*, and took the second place in the line ; the wind was light, but sufficient to enable the *Queen Charlotte* to come up, past the *Hunter*, to the aid of Barclay's flagship, the *Detroit*. The *Niagara*, Elliott's ship, lagged astern, possibly in order to preserve the order of sailing, she being astern of the *Caledonia*, which was a slow ship. Thus there was a gap in the American line between the *Caledonia* and the *Lawrence*, on which vessel the British ships were now concentrating.

By two o'clock the wind had died away almost to nothing. The *Lawrence* had been in action since noon, and she was reduced to a wreck, only one of her guns being left capable of firing. The *Detroit* was also badly smashed, partly through the raking fire of the two schooner-gunboats *Ariel* and *Scorpion*. Elliott, though he realized that his chief was hard pressed, was unable to come to his assistance, there being now no wind to speak of which would enable him to come up and close the gap.

Barclay had been severely wounded, and the captain of the *Queen Charlotte* killed, more than half the ship's company of the *Lawrence* being either killed or wounded ; the British ship *Lady Prevost* had gone to leeward, with a damaged rudder. At about two-thirty the breeze freshened and Elliott was able to bring up the *Niagara* past the *Caledonia*, and to windward of the *Lawrence*. As she passed this ship, Perry got into a boat and transferred his flag to the *Niagara* ; a few minutes later the *Lawrence* struck her colours.

As soon as Perry came aboard the *Niagara*, Elliott left her, in order to visit the gunboats in rear, and urge them forward. The *Niagara's* helm was then put over to port, so as to bring her across the bows of the *Detroit*. This ship tried to bear away, and bring her port battery into action, her starboard guns being largely disabled ; she fell foul of the *Queen Charlotte*, and the two vessels, locked together, were for a time a target for the American ships, which by this time had the aid of the gunboats in rear of the line, and which had now come up.

Soon the *Queen Charlotte* was obliged to strike her colours ; the *Detroit* was the only ship of any power left, for the *Hunter* was very lightly armed. The *Detroit* was out of control ; with one of his flagship's topmasts down,

Perry's Flag.

braces shot away, guns disabled and raked fore and aft, the gallant Barclay was compelled at last to surrender.

After his victory, Perry sent the *Lawrence* back to Erie for extensive repairs ; the *Queen Charlotte*, *Detroit* and other prizes being also reconditioned, and very soon the American squadron was again fit for action ; but the season was becoming advanced for further activities on the lake ; Perry was removed for duty on the coast, and Elliott was left in command on Lake Erie.

This action is known as the Battle of Lake Erie, and was the most important, from the naval point of view, of those fought on the lakes, together with the Battle of Lake Champlain in 1814. These battles, though fought only with small ships, may be regarded as miniature fleet actions, and thus differed from all the other naval engagements which took place in this war.

On Lake Ontario operations continued. Sir James Yeo was at York on the 26th of September, and, fearing that he might interfere with certain American troop movements, Chauncey, who was at Niagara, sailed to meet him on the 27th. On the following morning the force formed line of battle. The flagship *General Pike*, followed by the *Madison* and *Sylph*, each had one of the schooner-gunboats in tow, Chauncey having one other ship and two smaller craft in his squadron, making a total of nine vessels.

During the forenoon the British were sighted, also in line of battle. The flagship *Wolfe* was leading, followed by the *Royal George* ; two other ships came after and two small craft brought up the rear—six vessels in all. The wind was easterly and Yeo's course was southerly, that of Chauncey being in the opposite direction and to windward. When about three miles distant, the American line altered course together to south-west, so as to close the enemy.

Soon after noon Yeo feared that this movement might cut off the two small craft at the rear of his column ; so he altered course to north, and towards his opponent, and opened fire on the *General Pike*. Chauncey at once imitated the manoeuvre and the two forces proceeded north on parallel courses, exchanging broadsides.

Twenty minutes later the *Wolfe* had lost her main yard, and main and mizen topmasts. She therefore turned to port, so as to keep before the

PLATE XIX

PERRY'S VICTORY ON LAKE ERIE

Engraving by Lawson, after T. Birch

Perry transferring his flag.   Perry's flagship was badly damaged during the action, and he was obliged to hoist his flag in another vessel.

PLATE XX

THE *HINCHINBROOK* AND THE *GRAND TURK*, 1813

Engraving by J. Baily, after W. I. Pocock

An action between the Privateer brig *Grand Turk* and the Postal Packet *Hinchinbrook* during the War of 1812. The Postal Packets were brigs which maintained the mail service between Falmouth and the West Indies.

wind, followed by the rest of her squadron ; the *General Pike* conformed, but this movement put her some little distance astern ; also the principal American ships were hampered by having each a schooner in tow.

Chauncey made a signal for all sail to be set and, as the damaged *Wolfe* went to leeward, the *Royal George*, Captain Mulcaster, came across her stern and manœuvred in such a way as to give her the maximum of protection. The wind had now freshened to a gale, and the Americans found themselves on a lee shore and a hostile coast. The British squadron succeeded in anchoring in safety, but the Americans returned to Niagara. No further naval activities took place on Lake Ontario, which froze over at about the end of November.

CHAPTER V

WAR OF 1812 (continued)

WHILE these activities were proceeding on the Great Lakes, a remarkable action took place—remarkable because it was a duel between opponents as equally matched in material force as circumstances rendered possible. The duel between the *Chesapeake* and the *Shannon* was a short action, but one in which the opponents fought with equal valour and determination. It differs from the other actions in this war in that it was the result of a deliberate challenge issued by one commanding officer renowned for his seamanship and prowess in battle to another equally renowned.

Captain Lawrence was appointed to the *Chesapeake* in May, 1813, and took command at Boston on the 20th of May; his instructions were to proceed to the St. Lawrence and there intercept transports and supply-ships going to Quebec. Boston Harbour was at this time being blockaded by Captain Philip Vere Broke, commanding the thirty-eight-gun frigate *Shannon*.

Broke sent a challenge to Lawrence, expressed in a manner similar to that in which one duellist challenges another, and it is said that the challenge was formally accepted ; as a matter of fact, the challenge was never received, for James Lawrence left Boston while it was on its way ; but Broke's presence off Boston Light was equivalent to a challenge, and Lawrence immediately took it up. Lawrence was at some disadvantage, since his crew, though more numerous than that of the *Shannon*, was only partially trained, whereas that of his adversary was very efficient, particularly in gunnery.

At about noon on the 1st of June, 1813, the *Chesapeake* weighed anchor, and sailed out of harbour, there being a light breeze from the westward. Captain Broke, seeing her coming out, then stood out to sea, and hove-to, heading south-east. The *Chesapeake* followed and, taking in her light canvas at five o'clock, got into fighting trim and came up on the *Shannon's* starboard, or weather, side ; but the American frigate had too much headway and, as she overtook her British opponent, the latter opened fire, gun by gun, as she slowly passed ahead. Broadsides were now exchanged, and the action developed, with the *Chesapeake* drawing slowly ahead on the weather side of the *Shannon*, until she was on the latter's starboard bow. Lawrence and his sailing master were wounded, and damage to the *Chesapeake's* rigging forced her head up into the wind, and she began to gather stern-way and to come back onto the weather bow of the *Shannon*.

The *Shannon* was now on the port quarter of the *Chesapeake*, a position from which she could deliver a half-raking fire. Lawrence and his First Lieutenant fell mortally wounded, together with his officer of marines, his master and his boatswain ; the other lieutenants were still on the gun deck, leaving a midshipman in command on the upper deck.

Before the Second Lieutenant could get up from the gun deck, the two ships touched, the fore rigging of the *Shannon* engaging the mizen chains of the *Chesapeake*. Broke then prepared to board, and his ship's boarders occupied the after part of the *Chesapeake*. After a fierce fight on her decks, she was captured, her colours being hauled down by her British captors ; the entire engagement, from first to last, had occupied only fifteen minutes.

On board the *Shannon* there were eighty-two casualties, among them being Broke and his First Lieutenant, who were wounded : there were one hundred and thirty-nine casualties on board the *Chesapeake*, which was afterwards taken into Halifax. About fifty years ago there died in England an aged and very distinguished naval officer, who was regarded as the " Father of the Navy " ; this was Admiral of the Fleet Sir Provo Wallis, who had served as a lieutenant on board the *Shannon*, during this action. When his senior officers were wounded, he found himself, for a time, in command of the ship. It was to this fact that he owed his eventual advancement to the rank of Admiral of the Fleet ; for it was the rule that no officer could be advanced to that high rank who had not commanded a vessel in action, and this Lieutenant Provo Wallis had done on the occasion in question.

Early Broad Pendant.

Decatur succeeded in getting out from New York with the *United States*, the captured *Macedonian* and the sloop *Hornet*, but found enemy forces opposing him and was obliged to take shelter in New London, where he was blockaded, being afterwards transferred to the *President*. The *Constellation* was being blockaded in Chesapeake Bay and the blockade was now becoming general. No naval actions occurred for a while, with the exception of a brief fight between the British frigate *Junon* and some gunboats in Hampton Roads.

In September, 1813, however, the American brig *Enterprise* left Portsmouth, New Hampshire, on a cruise along the coast, and on the 5th of September, she sighted the British brig *Boxer*. The *Enterprise* was commanded by Lieutenant William Burrows, and was armed with fourteen eighteen-pounder carronades and two long nine-pounders, her adversary's armament being twelve eighteen-pounder carronades and two long six-pounders ; the *Boxer's* commanding officer was Commander Samuel

Blyth ; the *Enterprise* began the action by coming up on the *Boxer's* starboard, or windward, side, and engaging at fairly close range.

She then went ahead, raking her opponent with one of her " long nines," and hauled her wind ; she sailed then backwards and forwards across the bows of the British brig, raking her with her carronades, and causing her to lose her main topmast and fore topgallant yard. It was now the *Enterprise's* battle, and soon afterwards the *Boxer* ceased fire. Burrows and Blyth were both killed in the action, in which the American casualties totalled twelve and the British twenty-one. Both the young captains were buried with ceremony at Portland, Maine.

Meanwhile some activity was developing in European waters. The brig *Argus* went across the Atlantic on a mission to France, making a prize on the way, and on her return from Lorient she cruised in the English and Irish Channels, making nineteen captures. On the 14th of August at daylight the British brig *Pelican*, which had sailed from Cork in search of the *Argus*, sighted this ship in the act of setting fire to another prize. The wind was southerly and the *Pelican* went in pursuit, the *Argus* steering east and to leeward of her opponent.

When off St. David's Head the *Argus* wore, followed by the *Pelican*, and the two ships went off westerly, with the wind on their port sides, and engaged with grape shot and musketry. The *Argus* was commanded by Captain William H. Allen, and this officer received a severe wound in the leg, which subsequently cost him his life.

Gear on which the after sails relied, rigging, etc., had been badly damaged in the *Argus*, and the *Pelican* now altered course with the intention of passing under her stern and submitting her to a raking broadside ; but the *Argus* succeeded in thwarting this manœuvre by backing her main topsail, and came across her enemy's bows, raking her instead. The braces of the American ship had been shot away and she fell off slowly before the wind, permitting Captain Maples, of the *Pelican*, to bring his ship first across her stern and then across her bows, firing a broadside on each occasion. The *Argus* surrendered at about 6.30 a.m., the action having lasted three-quarters of an hour ; she was taken to Plymouth, where Captain Allen was buried with military honours.

Two privateers, the *Scourge*, of New York, and the *Rattlesnake*, of Philadelphia, were also operating in British waters during 1813, and made twenty-two captures. The *Scourge* also took ten more prizes during her return to New York. The schooner *Leo*, of Baltimore, had some success of this nature on the Spanish and Portuguese coasts, taking or destroying seventeen vessels ; the *Lion* also operated in the same neighbourhood and destroyed fifteen. The *True-Blooded Yankee* captured twenty-seven off the coast of Ireland ; she was afterwards captured and taken to Gibraltar.

There were other localities also in which American privateers were active, including the Gold Coast and the neighbourhood of the Canaries and the other Spanish and Portuguese islands.   The warship *Adams* succeeded in escaping from the Potomac River in January, 1814, and operated in these latitudes, but without much success.   The privateer *Yankee*, however, of Bristol, Rhode Island, had done better, and when she returned to the United States early in 1813, from a cruise up the West coast of Africa, she was able to report having captured eight vessels.

In the same locality on the 1st of November, 1813, the *Globe*, a privateer schooner of Baltimore, came into contact with two British mail packets, the *Montague* and *Pelham*.   The *Globe* was commanded by Captain Moon, and had one long gun and eight nine-pounder carronades ;   she also had a fairly large crew, which gave her some advantage, when it came to boarding.   The two packets lay off Funchal, in the island of Madeira, and at night they left neutral waters and proceeded to sea, followed by the *Globe*, which lost sight of them in a squall.

Next morning she picked them up again and resumed the pursuit. The *Montague* opened fire with her stern guns, and the *Globe* closed and endeavoured to board ;   in this she was unsuccessful, for the *Montague* met the attack smartly, and the two ships separated, two of the lieutenants of the *Globe* and several seamen being left on board the *Montague*.

Seeing her opportunity, the *Pelham* crossed the *Globe's* bows, raking her, causing much damage to the schooner's rigging and rendering her almost unmanageable.   Ten minutes later the *Montague* was entirely disabled, for in the interval she and the *Globe* had been engaged in a vigorous exchange of broadsides.   The *Pelham* then resumed the action, and as a result the *Globe* was reduced to an almost sinking condition and was obliged to sheer off.   She afterwards went to the Canary Islands, the British packets proceeding to Teneriffe.

Near Madeira at about the same time the privateer schooner *Governor Tompkins* took three British merchant vessels, belonging to a convoy on its way to Buenos Aires from England, they having become detached in a gale, and the *America*, of Salem, took another, a brig.   The blockade was necessarily relaxed, owing to bad weather, during the winter months, and the frigate *Constitution*, Captain Charles Stewart, got out from Boston in the early months of 1814 and cruised among the West Indian islands, but made only four prizes.   The two vessels *Rattlesnake* and *Enterprise* also got out and, after a cruise in the Caribbean Sea, during which they took two British vessels, were afterwards driven into Wilmington, in North Carolina.

On the 5th of August, 1813, the schooner *Decatur*, of Charleston, fell in with the British schooner *Dominica*, a man-of-war armed with two long six-pounders and thirteen carronades.   The *Dominica* was accompanied by a mail packet, which she was convoying. As in the case of the *Globe*, the *Decatur* had on board a superiority of numbers.

At 2.30 the schooners were within close distance of each other, and the *Decatur* tried to board, the *Dominica's* broadsides causing much damage to her sails and rigging in the attempt. The attempt was made on two occasions; finally the *Dominica's* mainsail was pierced by the *Decatur's* jibboom, as she struck her adversary on the quarter. The privateer's crew swarmed on board, and a sharp fight took place on the decks of the British schooner, her captain, Lieutenant Barreté, being killed. The *Dominica* was afterwards taken by the *Decatur* into Charleston, the packet making good her escape.

In April, 1814, the privateer *Saucy Jack*, of Charleston, found herself between Cuba and Santo Domingo when she fell in with the British ship *Pelham*, not to be confused with the *Pelham* previously mentioned; the *Pelham* was of between five and six hundred tons and was armed with ten guns. The action was fierce and lasted for two hours, both ships fighting well. The *Pelham's* captain was dangerously wounded, his ship suffering fifteen casualties in all, as against the *Saucy Jack's* eleven. The *Pelham* was subsequently taken into Charleston.

The *Saucy Jack* was speedily made ready again to go to sea, and she went to the West Indies. When off the west end of Santo Domingo she sighted two vessels, and went in pursuit, opening fire. The stranger shortened sail and replied. At seven in the morning, the *Saucy Jack* began to engage one of the ships and ran alongside, intending to board, only to find her adversary to be full of soldiers; she proved, in fact, to be the transport *Golden Fleece*, taking two hundred and fifty troops to Jamaica. The privateer at once broke off the action, and endeavoured to escape and, after an hour's chase, succeeded in doing so. The bomb-vessel *Volcano*, with which she was first in action, was acting as convoy to the transport; she lost an officer and two men killed and two wounded, the *Saucy Jack* losing eight killed and fifteen wounded.

Another privateer, the *Kemp* of Baltimore, fell in with a convoy of eight ships, one of them Spanish, and a frigate on the 1st of December, 1814; she was pursued by the British frigate, but eluded her during the night. She then went back in search of the convoy, which she found at daybreak. The seven British merchant vessels formed a line of battle, and tried to engage the *Kemp*, but in half an hour they were overpowered; some of them escaped, but four, which were loaded with sugar and coffee, a cargo particularly valuable to a blockaded country, were taken into port.

At the end of 1814 the privateer brig *Chasseur*, of Baltimore, cruised in British waters, capturing eighteen vessels. In those days news took long to travel and, though peace had been signed in December, information on the subject had not been circulated universally; the *Chasseur*, after her exploits on the coasts of Great Britain and Ireland, went for a long cruise in the West Indies, and was quite ignorant of the true state of affairs.

On the 25th of February, 1815, Captain Boyle, of the *Chasseur*, when near Havana, saw a schooner in the north-east. The wind was roughly from the same quarter, and the schooner altered course to the northward, the *Chasseur* conforming, and coming up on her leeward side. The schooner was endeavouring to escape and was carrying all the sail of which she was capable; owing to this fact, her fore topmast went overboard, when she was about three miles away. She cleared away the wreckage, hoisted British colours and fired her stern gun.

A Schooner.

The chase continued during the forenoon, and Captain Boyle crowded on all sail, in an effort to overtake the stranger, coming within range of her at about half-past one. Suddenly the enemy opened her broadside, and showed herself to be a man-of-war, the *St. Lawrence*. The privateer had more way on than the British ship, and went a little ahead on her port side; the *St. Lawrence* tried to pass under her adversary's stern, with the intention of raking her. The *Chasseur* avoided this, by turning to port, and came abreast of the *St. Lawrence* on her starboard side, broadsides being exchanged for about ten minutes.

The *Chasseur* then ran alongside her enemy and boarded; the *St. Lawrence* struck her colours soon after, her losses being six killed and seventeen wounded, out of a ship's company of seventy-five; the privateer lost five killed and eight wounded, out of eighty-nine. The *Chasseur* had no intention of fighting a man-of-war, that being no part of a privateer's duties, but was deceived by her peaceful appearance into thinking that she was a merchant vessel. Captain Boyle showed great consideration for her captured officers and men, which was duly appreciated.

Over five hundred privateers were employed by the Americans during this war, but though their work in capturing or destroying prizes was eminently successful, it was even exceeded by that of the vessels of the U.S. Navy, in proportion to the small numbers of that force employed as commerce-raiders. There were twenty-two of these ships, so engaged at various times, and they took one hundred and sixty-five prizes, including ships of war captured; the privateers accounted for over thirteen hundred, so that the prizes taken by warships, as against those taken by privateers, numbered nearly three to one.[1]

One of these warships carried her commerce-raiding activities into

[1] *Sea Power in its Relations to the War of* 1812. Captain A. T. Mahan, D.C.L., LL.D., U.S.N.

remote quarters ; this was the *Essex*, Captain David Porter. When Bainbridge took his squadron out in October, 1812, the *Essex* followed him to sea, and cruised off the coast of Brazil, hoping to find and rejoin the squadron ; here she remained until January, 1813. Porter then went to St. Catherine's Island, and from there he decided to go south, round Cape Horn, and into the Pacific Ocean, where, being short of provisions, he expected to make some captures among the whaling fleet of the enemy, which was usually well supplied.

Chile had already begun to revolt against Spain, and friendliness was shown to Porter, while he was on the Chilean coast ; on the other hand, the authority of the Viceroy of Peru still held, and he intended, Spain being then an ally of Great Britain, to fit out privateers against the Americans ; some of the British whaling fleet also carried letters of marque. One of the Peruvian privateers was encountered by Porter, who threw her guns and ammunition overboard and sent her back to port with a warning, and one of the prizes taken by this vessel was retaken by him, as she was entering the port of Callao. Consequently Porter's stay in Peruvian waters was not prolonged, since he was not popular in those latitudes.

The Galapagos Islands was the next port of call ; here the *Essex* arrived in April, 1813, and remained about six months, capturing twelve British whalers, one of which was converted into a warship, with twenty light guns, and renamed the *Essex Junior*. This vessel went to Valparaiso, in charge of the other prizes, and returned with news that a squadron of three frigates, under Captain James Hillyar, was now on its way to the Pacific Ocean, one of these ships being superior in force to the *Essex*.

Captain Porter decided that the *Essex* must have a complete overhaul, before risking an engagement ; so he went across to the Marquesas Islands for the purpose, this being a fairly remote spot. Here he stayed, in company with the *Essex Junior*, for nearly two months, and then sailed for Chile, arriving at Valparaiso on the 3rd of February, 1814. The British squadron, with the exception of the *Raccoon*, detached for other duties, came into Valparaiso on the 8th of February.

Captain Hillyar then took his two ships out of neutral waters, and cruised about outside. They consisted of the *Phœbe*, which was armed with thirty long eighteen-pounders and sixteen thirty-two-pounder carronades, and a smaller vessel called the *Cherub* ; the last-named ship had two long six-pounders and eighteen thirty-two-pounder carronades, also six carronades of eighteen pounds. The *Essex* had forty thirty-two-pounder carronades and six long twelve-pounders ; the *Essex Junior's* armament was negligible.

Consequently the force of the British was superior to that of Captain Porter, who sought an opportunity to escape ; but on the 28th of March, as

PLATE XXI

SHANNON AND *CHESAPEAKE*, June 1st, 1813

J. Jeakes after G. Webster

On June 1st, 1813, a remarkable frigate action occurred off Boston, in which the British ship *Shannon*, Captain Philip Vere Broke, defeated the *Chesapeake*, Captain James Lawrence, Lawrence being killed.

Macdonough's Victory on Lake Champlain.
AND DEFEAT OF THE BRITISH ARMY AT PLATTSBURG BY GEN. MACOMB, SEPT 11TH 1814.

PLATE XXII

MACDONOUGH'S VICTORY ON LAKE CHAMPLAIN,
September 11, 1814

Painted by H. Reinagle, engraved by B. Tanner

The picture shows the galleys and other small craft which formed a large pro-portion of the opposing forces.   The town of Plattsburg is seen in the distance.

he result of a south wind, one of the cables of the *Essex* parted, and he drifted out to sea. Sail was made, but a squall carried away her nain topmast, and she had to return towards the coast of Chile, and anchor close inshore about three miles to the northward of Valparaiso and well within territorial waters.

The *Essex* was " wind-rode," that is to say, she lay heading south, and at about four in the afternoon the two British ships, disregarding neutral vaters, came in close under her stern, to attack. Porter tried to get a pring on his cable, so as to bring his ship across and get her broadside o bear, but this spring was shot away. The *Phœbe* and *Cherub* wore, and stood out to sea again, the former having suffered some damage to ails and rigging in this preliminary encounter. It is interesting to note hat one of the midshipmen of the *Essex* was David G. Farragut, aged hirteen ; the action between the *Phœbe* and the *Essex* was probably the ' baptism of fire " of a boy, who afterwards became one of the most amous admirals serving in the Union forces during the Civil War.

At half-past five a fresh attack was made ; the *Phœbe* endeavoured to anchor on the seaward side of the *Essex*, leaving the *Cherub* freedom of action, so that she could choose any point from which she could do most lamage to the American ship. As the *Phœbe* approached the *Essex*, his ship was also seen to be under way, Porter having cut his cable, noping that the wind would bring his ship down onto the enemy, and enable

him to board. In this way the two vessels drifted to leeward, and a furious oombardment developed, the *Phœbe* keeping a distance at which her own guns were effective and those of the *Essex* out of range.

The *Essex* was now in a crippled condition, and Porter decided to destroy her and save the remainder of his crew, half of whom were casualties. He tried o run his ship ashore, but failed in the attempt ; he then gave permission, to anyone who wished to do so, to swim

Compass Card.

ashore, and finally surrendered a little before half-past six. By arrangement between the two captains, the *Essex Junior* was disarmed, in order o act as a neutral transport, and she conveyed the surrendered ship's company of the *Essex* to the United States as paroled prisoners of war.

Another commerce-raider was the *Wasp*, commanded by Commander 'ohnstone Blakeley. She left Portsmouth, New Hampshire, in May, 1814, n order to cruise off the south of Ireland. She had taken seven British ressels, when on the 28th of June she fell, in with the brig *Reindeer* ; this was a ship of war commanded by Captain Manners, and armed with sixteen twenty-four-pound carronades, as against twenty thirty-two-pound carronades of the *Wasp* ; both adversaries had also two long guns.

Commander Blakeley was to leeward and some distance ahead of his enemy, who opened fire on his starboard quarter. Finding that he could not reply effectively, Blakeley turned to windward, in order to bring his starboard battery to bear ; and the two ships were soon at close range alongside each other, when a fierce interchange of broadsides developed, which reduced the *Reindeer* to a wreck. Captain Manners who was already wounded, then attempted to board and, while doing so, was shot through the head. The *Reindeer* then surrendered, with a loss of sixty-five, killed and wounded, as against the *Wasp's* twenty-six.

Blakeley then went to Lorient, for a refit. He left at the end of August and had destroyed three more British vessels by the 1st of September. On that day several ships were sighted, and the *Wasp* went to investigate the nature of that farthest to windward, which happened to be a man-of-war, the brig *Avon*. Blakeley engaged this ship on the leeward side, in order to prevent her from running to leeward, to join her presumed consorts, and at the same time to make it necessary for them, in coming to her assistance, to beat against the wind.

Action between these two vessels began about half-past nine in the forenoon, and at noon there was a pause ; for the *Wasp* believed that the *Avon* had been silenced. Receiving no reply to her hail, except a burst of fire, the *Wasp* renewed the engagement and shortly afterwards the *Avon* surrendered. Just as the *Wasp* was about to take possession, another brig was seen approaching and, soon afterwards, two others. The *Wasp* then made sail, in the hope of enticing the first of these brigs to follow her, but the brig remained where she was, in order to render assistance to the *Avon*, which was now in a sinking condition ; the *Wasp* then went away.

Later she took two more vessels, and on the 21st of September, when near Madeira, she captured a brig called the *Atalanta* ; this was a valuable prize, and was sent into Savannah. After this, nothing more was heard of the *Wasp*, and it was presumed that she was lost at sea.

Her sister ship, the *Peacock*, left New York in March, 1814, and went to St. Mary's, in Georgia ; thence she sailed to the Bahama Islands, meeting with no success, and then went northwards, where she met three merchant ships, under the convoy of a British brig-of-war. This was the *Epervier*, armed with eighteen thirty - two - pound carronades. The *Epervier* ordered the convoy to scatter, and went to engage the *Peacock*, damaging her fore yard with a broadside ; this prevented her from setting her fore sail or fore topsail, and the necessity for relying only on her head sails somewhat impaired her manœuvrability. The fight continued for three-quarters of an hour, after which the *Epervier* hauled down her colours.

A further cruise, on which she took twelve prizes, was made by the *Peacock* subsequently ; but by October, 1814, commerce had become more wary, and stricter regulations were enforced by the British Admiralty with regard to convoys, so that few ships were encountered or even sighted.

At the beginning of 1814 an attempt was made by the British to regain control of the lakes. In April Captain Yeo launched two new ships on Lake Ontario, the *Prince Regent* and the *Queen Charlotte*, and also had under construction a formidable vessel mounting over one hundred guns ; it was proposed to make an assault on Sackett's Harbour, and Oswego was attacked by British ships on the night of the 5th of May and occupied the next day ; after which the British squadron retired, taking with it two small schooners and a quantity of stores.

Yeo then went to Sackett's Harbour, where a new ship, the *Superior*, had been launched, mounting sixty-six guns ; another vessel was on the stocks. He endeavoured to blockade Sackett's Harbour, in which he was thwarted by an ingenious move on the part of the Americans, and returned to Kingston, on the other side of the lake.

On Lake Erie there was some activity during July. American troops crossed over to the north side of the lake, and landed near Fort Erie, which surrendered. The British forces were defeated at the Chippewa River, and the American commander advanced as far as Queenstown, on Lake Ontario ; from here he sent an appeal to Captain Chauncey, at Sackett's Harbour, asking him at once to bring his ships to the west end of the lake, in support of the troops. This was disregarded, and some confusion resulted ; eventually Chauncey, after some delay, left harbour, but by that time the opportunity had been lost.

At the end of July the British were defeated at Lundy's Lane, and this action was followed by attempts by them to recapture Fort Erie, which they besieged. A sortie by the beleaguered Americans, however, compelled them to evacuate their positions. On the 15th of October the British big ship was completed, and the British now felt themselves to be secure on Lake Ontario. On the other lake the Americans had to retire ; they blew up Fort Erie, before abandoning it, and then crossed over again to the south side. The *Caledonia* and other vessels had been lost by accident or capture, but the *Lawrence* and the *Niagara* were safe ; these ships were withdrawn to Erie, and laid up for the winter.

After the capture of Washington by the British troops in June, 1814, the major naval interest centred on Lake Champlain. This lake is a long and narrow piece of water, running north and south, which lies to the east of Lake Ontario. It is south of Montreal, and its southern extremity is near the upper waters of the Hudson River.

When the war broke out the United States had the control of Lake Champlain ; and under the American flag were three sloops called the *President, Eagle* and *Growler* ; the British had one sloop only, but both sides had also a few rowing-galleys and small gunboats. In June, 1813 there were some minor naval operations on the lake and, as a result of these, the *Eagle* and *Growler* were taken and brought into the British service under the names *Chub* and *Finch*. The control of the lake then passed to the British.

In May, 1814, a British naval officer, Captain Everard, went to Lake Champlain, with a number of seamen, with the object of manning these two sloops, which then proceeded to raid the American stations on the lake. Another naval officer, Captain Pring, aided in the construction of a large brig named the *Linnet*, and two gunboats. The Americans were also building, and in April, 1814, they launched a ship named the *Saratoga* Captain Thomas Macdonough was in charge of these activities, and was subsequently in command of the American naval forces.

Near the north end of the lake and on its west side is a town named Plattsburg. This lies on the bay of that name, where the Saranac River flows into the lake ; the bay is protected from the north and east by a promontory known as Cumberland Head. Plattsburg had been held by the American military forces, and the American squadron, consisting of four ships with some gunboats or galleys, lay at anchor in Plattsburg Bay.

British troops entered Plattsburg on the 6th of September, and the Americans retreated south, across the river, where they took up an entrenched position. It was proposed to make a simultaneous naval and military attack, and Sir George Prevost, the British military commander showed great anxiety that these attacks should exactly coincide, and urged the speedier preparation of the naval force, which was under Captain Downie, with the result that Downie had to go into action before his new ship, the *Confiance*, was entirely completed.

Macdonough had his broad pendant in the *Saratoga* and his force was anchored in a line running north and south ; this line consisted of the brig *Eagle* of twenty guns, the ship *Saratoga* of twenty-six, the schooner *Ticonderoga* of seven and the sloop *Preble*, also of seven guns. The galleys and gunboats were in a parallel line to the westward, the Plattsburg side. The British line consisted of the sloop *Finch*, the ship *Confiance*, the *Linnet* and the *Chub*, which was also a sloop. The *Eagle* was a new vessel and she and the *Saratoga* were slightly superior in force to Captain Downie's ship, the *Confiance*, and the *Linnet*, Captain Pring.

The 11th of September was the date chosen for the attack, and on that day the wind was light and from the north-east, and thus favoured Downie who came down from the north ; in rounding Cumberland Head to attack the American line, Downie found, to his stupefaction, that no

COMMODORE THOMAS MACDONOUGH

Engraving by T. Gimbrede

The victor of Lake Champlain. Here, in 1814, he defeated a British squadron, which attacked him, when at anchor off the town of Plattsburg. Macdonough had previously served at Tripoli, under Decatur.

PLATE XXIV

CAPTURE OF THE *PRESIDENT* BY THE *ENDYMION*

Engraved by J. Jeakes, after T. Buttersworth, the particulars and
the position of the ships by Lieut. Ormond of the *Endymion*

The *President*, Commodore Stephen Decatur, escaped from the blockade
of New York on January 14th, 1815, and steered northward. She ran
into the blockading ships, one of which, H.M.S. *Endymion*, held her in
chase. She was finally captured by the frigates H.M.S. *Tenedos* and *Pomone*.

attack had developed on the part of the military, who remained quite inactive throughout.

Once round Cumberland Head, the *Confiance* and *Linnet* made for the *Eagle*, at the head of the American line ; the first broadside of the *Confiance* did great execution on board the *Saratoga*, but the wind failed, and Downie had to anchor some distance from the enemy. A quarter of an hour after the action commenced, he was killed.

The *Linnet* engaged the *Eagle* ; the *Chub*, which was detailed to act in support of the *Linnet*, was much damaged aloft, and she drifted through the American line, where she struck her colours. The *Finch* went too far to leeward and, the wind failing, she eventually drifted ashore on an island to the south of the bay. The *Ticonderoga* had been attacked by the British gunboats, but this attack was inefficiently carried out and she maintained her position, whilst the *Preble* was forced away from her anchorage, at the rear of the line, and went ashore south of Plattsburg.

Fighting now resolved itself into an action between the American *Saratoga* and *Eagle* and the British *Confiance* and *Linnet*. The *Eagle*, finding that her starboard guns were mostly out of action by this time, cut her cable and drifted down the line, in such a way that she was able to bring her port broadside to bear, and the *Saratoga*, by an ingenious manoeuvre, carried out a similar evolution. The *Confiance* was now in a sinking condition, and hauled down her colours at about eleven o'clock in the forenoon. Captain Pring's *Linnet* was the last to strike ; Macdonough's victory was decisive.

Peace was signed in December, but the news took long to travel, and three actions took place subsequently. The first of these was the fight between the frigates *President* and *Endymion*. The *President*, under Stephen Decatur, succeeded in escaping from New York on the night of the 14th of January, 1815, and came up against the blockading squadron under Captain John Hayes, of the *Majestic*, his other ships being the forty-gun frigate *Endymion*, and the thirty-eight-gun frigates *Pomone* and *Tenedos*.

There was a strong gale raging, and Hayes had been driven off the coast, but he anticipated that Decatur would try to get out, and his probable course. The *President* steered east and then south-east. At five the next morning three of the British ships were seen ahead ; the wind was north-west and the American frigate then hauled to the wind, and tried to escape alongshore, with the British ships in chase, the *Endymion* leading.

Captain Hope, of the *Endymion*, knew that his ship was faster than the *President*, and he was able to yaw from time to time and deliver a broadside. This went on for some time ; then the American frigate put her helm over and came across the Englishman's bows. The *Endymion* avoided this attempt to rake her, and the two ships ran off on parallel courses, exchanging broadsides. The *President* aimed at the sails and rigging of the *Endymion*, and eventually stripped the sails from her adversary, leaving her astern, helpless.

Again the American frigate steered east, with the rest of the British blockading squadron in chase. The *Pomone* and the *Tenedos* were fast sailers, and were able to overtake Decatur's ship notwithstanding the fact that she was carrying studding sails; at eleven o'clock in the evening they came up with her, and shortly afterwards she struck her colours, having lost twenty killed and fifty-five wounded, as against eleven killed and fourteen wounded in the *Endymion*.

A Frigate.

The frigate *Constitution* was under the command of Captain Charles Stewart. On the 20th of February, 1815, when not far from Madeira, she fell in with the British ships-of-war *Cyane* and *Levant*. The *Cyane* carried thirty thirty-two-pounder carronades, and two of eighteen pounds, plus two long nine-pounder guns; the *Levant* had eighteen thirty-two-pounder carronades and two "long nines." The *Constitution* was thus the heavier ship.

The wind was light and from the east, and the two British ships, which were previously separated, were able to close each other shortly before six o'clock. They then formed into line, with the *Levant* leading. Soon afterwards the *Constitution* came abreast of the *Cyane*, and action commenced; smoke obscured the progress of affairs and, when this cleared, the *Constitution* found herself abreast of the *Levant*, and came back to the *Cyane*. The American frigate raked both ships, and the *Cyane* soon afterwards surrendered; the *Levant* tried to escape, but was overtaken and surrendered also; she was afterwards retaken.

On the 20th of January, 1815, the sloops *Hornet* and *Peacock* and the brig *Tom Bowline* left New York. The *Hornet* then went to the island of Tristan da Cunha, and was about to anchor, when she saw the British sloop *Penguin*, passing to the westward of the island, the wind being south-south-westerly. The *Penguin*, Captain Dickinson, carried sixteen thirty-two-pounder carronades and three long twelve-pounder guns; the *Hornet*, Commander James Biddle, had eighteen thirty-two-pounder carronades and two "long twelves."

The *Penguin* was to windward and closed her enemy, the two ships running parallel and exchanging broadsides. Just before two o'clock in the afternoon she put her helm over, in order to board her antagonist, and her bowsprit came in between the *Hornet's* main and mizen masts; the manœuvre was unsuccessful; no attempt was made to board, and the *Penguin* got clear with the loss of her fore mast and bowsprit. She

inally surrendered, her captain and thirteen others being killed and
twenty-eight wounded, the *Hornet* losing only one killed and ten wounded.

This, happily, was the last occasion upon which the two English-speaking
nations have been opposed to each other in battle.   The United States
were anxious to bring the war to a conclusion, and negotiations to that
effect had been going on for a long time.   Peace was at last signed at
Ghent in December, 1814.

CHAPTER VI

MEXICO AND THE ORIENT

THE Treaty of Peace with Great Britain was ratified by the President in February, 1815, and in the same month war was declared on Algiers. Two squadrons were sent out from the United States, one under Commodore Decatur, the other under Commodore Bainbridge. Decatur had his broad pendant in the *Guerrière*, and had in his squadron the *Constellation, Macedonian, Epervier* and *Ontario*, together with three brigs and two schooners. Bainbridge's flagship was the new seventy-four-gun ship *Independence* and he had a squadron of almost equal strength. Decatur left New York on the 20th of May, 1815 ; Bainbridge, who was the senior, was to assume command of the force when the two squadrons combined in the Mediterranean ; but his departure from Boston was much later, and he did not arrive in time to take an effective part in the proceedings.

On arriving at the Straits of Gibraltar, Decatur learned that an Algerian squadron under Reis Hammida was off Cape de Gata, and he went there in search. Near that place he found a large Algerian ship and, after a brief action, she surrendered ; she was found to be the flagship of Reis Hammida, who was killed during the action. A brig was also found and taken.

The squadron then made for Algiers, where the Commodore dictated a Treaty of Peace which was characterized by a proper firmness ; this treaty was signed at the end of June. From here the squadron went to Tunis, and from there to Tripoli, where some Sicilian and Danish captives were liberated. Bainbridge's squadron had now arrived and showed itself also off Tunis and Tripoli ; these demonstrations greatly impressed the Tunisians and Tripolitans.

For so long had Algiers and the other Barbary States been indulging in piratical activities, or receiving " Danegeld " from other countries, for the purchase of immunity, that any departure from this principle filled them with astonishment, and was truly shocking to their susceptibilities ; it is not too much to say that non-recognition of it caused alarm and despondency, to such an extent as might even result in the assassination of the Dey himself. Decatur's treaty was much too like a real treaty for their taste, and they became restive under what they regarded as its humiliating terms, of which they took little practical notice.

Shortly after this, a terrific bombardment of Algiers, by the British and Dutch under Admiral Lord Exmouth, resulted in the Dey signing a treaty in 1816, by which he undertook to abolish Christian slavery.

THE U.S. SQUADRON, under Command of Com. DECATUR.
At anchor at the City of ALGIERS. June 30th 1815.

New Haven. Published by N. Wells & G. Munger Pise 1816.

PLATE XXV U.S. SQUADRON, UNDER THE COMMAND OF
COMMODORE DECATUR, AT ANCHOR OFF ALGIERS, June 30, 1815

Engraved by G. Munger and S. S. Jocelin.

Soon after the declaration of War with Algiers, Commodore Decatur took a squadron there and, after capturing a number of Algerine vessels, he anchored his ships off the town and, as a result, negotiations were opened which resulted in a Peace Treaty being signed.

THE YANKEE TAR.

PLATE XXVI

THE YANKEE TAR

An American bluejacket's rig in the earlier part of the Nineteenth Century. The flag suggests a date between 1818 and 1837, but, as the stars in it are six-pointed, it is probably not a very reliable guide.

The appearance of an American squadron off the place shortly afterwards hastened the conclusion of another treaty between the United States and Algiers ; this treaty was formally signed in December, 1816. Difficulties with the Barbary States were now at an end, but for some time it was thought prudent to maintain a naval force in the Mediterranean.

On the 4th of July, 1818, another change was made in the Stars and Stripes. The Stars were increased to twenty, owing to the following States having been admitted to the Union : Tennessee, Ohio, Louisiana, Indiana and Mississippi. If the stripes had also been increased to twenty, the design would have been too complicated ; they were therefore reduced to the original thirteen, and so remain. It was now arranged that a new star should be added to the flag for every new State admitted to the Union, on the 4th of July following its admission, and this practice has continued until modern times.

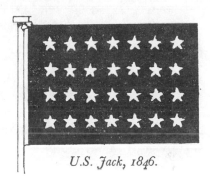

U.S. Jack, 1846.

The title " Old Glory," as often applied to the flag, is said to date from August, 1831, when a flag was presented by a committee of ladies to William Driver, of Salem, master of the brig *Charles Doggett*. When the Federals occupied Nashville, during the Civil War, they hoisted the Stars and Stripes over the place ; these were hauled down a few minutes later, and the original " Old Glory " substituted.

Piracy now made its reappearance. As often happened, when peace was restored after a long period of war, energetic men, of an adventurous temperament, who had been engaged in fighing their country's foes in the capacity of privateers, found no further scope for their activities. Consequently they turned their attention to capturing ships of any nationality, and became frankly " hostes humani generis." Piracy broke out in the neighbourhood of the West Indies and caused great damage to American merchant shipping.

In about 1810 South America had already begun to revolt against Spanish rule, and independent governments were beginning to be set up ; but at first something like a state of anarchy prevailed. There were military dictatorships in Buenos Aires and on the north coast of South America, and these used to issue licences to ships for the purpose of preying upon Spanish commerce, without making too close enquiry. In reality, many of these ships were pirates.

Commodore Oliver Perry was sent to deal with this state of affairs in 1819. He sailed to the Orinoco River with the *John Adams, Constellation* and *Nonesuch*. At the river-mouth he shifted his broad pendant into the *Nonesuch*, and proceeded alone three hundred miles up river ; after a terrible voyage, in which his men were beset with thirst, heat, fever and insects, he arrived on the 26th of July at Angostura, now known as Ciudad Bolivar. Here he asked for a list of the vessels which had been licensed and also for compensation for a captured American ship. Bolivar himself was absent and his deputy procrastinated for a time, but at length Perry obtained a satisfactory reply. Meantime yellow fever had broken out on board the *Nonesuch*, and on the 15th of August, Perry sailed back, making for Port of Spain, in Trinidad.

His arrival at Port of Spain was expected, and a number of British officers, who had fought against Perry at Lake Erie, had prepared a great reception for him. Unfortunately, just as the *Nonesuch* entered the port, the gallant Commodore succumbed, a victim of yellow fever.

In 1821 attempts to deal with the pirates were renewed. Captain Robert Henley went out with the *Hornet, Enterprise* and six other ships, and succeeded in capturing several pirate vessels. In the following year Commodore James Biddle went out in the *Macedonian* ; one of his ships, the *Shark*, under Captain Matthew Perry, captured five vessels, the *Grampus* took another, and also took the *Palmira*, a ship under Spanish colours, which had plundered the American schooner *Coquette*. Numerous other captures were made, and finally Captain David Porter, who took command of these operations in 1823, broke up the pirates' nests and drove this scourge from the seas.

An era of expansion had set in in North America, even before South America had entirely thrown off the Spanish yoke. At the Peace of 1783 the western border of the United States had been roughly the line of the Mississippi River. The vast territory known at that time as Louisiana, west of the Mississippi, had been purchased from the French in 1803, and pioneers and adventurers were pushing farther west. In 1819 Florida was acquired by treaty from Spain as well as the coastline stretching westwards to the Mississippi ; the west was unknown, and the south-west still belonged to Mexico, as part of the old Spanish Empire.

Texas had already been visited by explorers and frontiersmen, who had carried Anglo-Saxon ideas into that " Lone Star State," and it was the first portion of the Mexican possessions to break away. A remarkable man named Sam Houston, a Virginian who had fought in the war of 1812, had become a congressman and also Governor of Tennessee. In 1829 he suddenly abandoned civilization, and was admitted as a chief of the Cherokee Indians. In 1835 Texas was becoming restive and revolted against Mexican rule, choosing Houston as its commander-in-chief ; unsuccessful at the outset and compelled to retreat, Houston turned on the Mexican army, under Santa Anna, and decisively defeated it at the Battle of San Jacinto in April, 1836. Texas then became an independent republic, and chose Houston as its President ; when, in 1845, Texas was annexed to the United States, he became Senator and subsequently Governor of that State.

By the Treaty of Ghent it was agreed that the United States and Great Britain should combine in putting down the slave trade, which still went on between the African coast and the Caribbean Sea. Andrew Hull Foote, afterwards famous in the Civil War, was among those engaged on this duty, which involved the stopping and searching of suspected slavers, in conditions of extreme tropical discomfort. This duty kept American and British warships well employed until after the middle of the nineteenth century.

Meantime the frontiersmen had pushed their way not only into Texas, but into California as well. One of these men was Captain J. C. Frémont, who had made considerable exploration also into the Oregon territory. This territory lay next the Canadian border and included the present States of Washington, Oregon, Idaho and parts of Montana and Wyoming. Some dispute as to its possession had taken place between the United States and Great Britain, and this had been settled in favour of the United States by treaty in 1846, thus giving them a foothold on the Pacific Ocean. California stretched south of Oregon down to what is now the Mexican border, and included the present States of California, Nevada, Utah, Arizona and parts of Colorado and New Mexico.

In 1842 a curious incident occurred in California. Some sections of opinion in the United States feared that Great Britain might attempt to seize that territory, and a strong squadron was sent round Cape Horn to the Californian coast, with a view to preventing this attempt. Lieutenant Catesby Jones was in command, and the squadron included the sloop *Cyane*, which had been captured during the war of 1812.

Life in the U.S. Navy, in the 'forties of the nineteenth century, was not greatly unlike that in other navies. Flogging was not yet abolished,[1] and the gundecks were very like those of Nelson's day. The frigates and other ships were still built of oak, though steam had already been introduced, and the ships were long-lived,[2] so that it is not surprising to find a vessel like the *Cyane*, which served in the War of 1812, serving again thirty years afterwards.

On the way out Catesby Jones learned that Mexico had ceded California to Great Britain, and at once proceeded to Monterey, which he occupied. He then discovered that the rumour was false, and that the North American Continent was still at peace ; he surrendered the town to the Mexican authorities, and all was as it had been.

---

[1] *White Jacket.* Herman Melville.
[2] Nelson's *Victory* was already forty years old at Trafalgar. The U.S.S. *Constellation* and *Constitution* are still preserved in the United States, though built in the eighteenth century.

On the 13th of May, 1846, however, war broke out between Mexico and the United States. Captain J. D. Sloat, who was Commodore commanding the Pacific Squadron, was at Mazatlan in Mexico, in the frigate *Savannah* ; he sailed to Monterey, where he found the *Cyane*, *Levant* and *Warren*, and occupied the place. Commander Montgomery, of the *Portsmouth*, then seized San Francisco Bay.

In the middle of July Captain Frémont arrived at Monterey and was sent in the *Cyane*, with a hundred and fifty men, to occupy San Diego, in the south. Commodore R. F. Stockton, in the *Congress*, took over the naval forces on the west coast at the end of the month, replacing Commodore Sloat, and moved against Los Angeles. He landed about three hundred and fifty men and entered Los Angeles almost unopposed in August ; the Governor, Andres Pico, and General José M. Flores were put on parole. Santa Barbara and San Pedro were also taken and American garrisons left at those places, and Stockton had now won possession of the whole territory between San Diego and the Sacramento Valley.

The Commodore then organized a form of civil government, and an expedition was planned by him against Acapulco ; but a report had been received to the effect that an attack had been made by the Mexicans in the Sacramento Valley, and Stockton went to San Francisco with the *Congress* and *Savannah*, taking most of the Los Angeles garrison and the whole of that at Santa Barbara. The weakening of the garrison at Los Angeles induced the Mexicans to rise, and Pico and Flores broke their parole. The report of the attack in the Sacramento Valley proved to be exaggerated, and the *Savannah* returned, followed by the *Congress* ; Stockton reached San Diego, which was besieged, in October, and raised the siege.

A small body of troops under Brigadier-General S. W. Kearney had now joined the naval forces and they were attacked at San Diego by the Mexicans, who were however driven off. Captain Mervine, of the *Savannah*, had meantime attempted to recapture Los Angeles, but without success. The combined force, under Commodore Stockton, then advanced from San Pedro and, after a difficult march in bad weather, it inflicted two severe defeats on the enemy ; Los Angeles was retaken in January, 1847, and the Commodore remained in possession of the whole of the Californian coast-line.

Operations were also proceeding in the Gulf of Mexico, where Commodore David Conner was in command. Conner was off Vera Cruz in May, 1846, when he learned that General Taylor's expedition at Point Izabel, in Texas, had been cut off by the Mexicans ; he proceeded there, and landed a force under Captain Gregory, of the *Raritan*, to assist the General in crossing the Rio Grande and, as it was then intended to march the troops across to Monterey, a boat expedition was sent up the river, under Captain Aulick, which took Barita, in Mexican territory. Matamoros was evacuated by the Mexicans, and Conner's force then guarded Taylor's lines of communication in the coastal area.

A blockade of Mexican ports in the Gulf was now established, but this was a difficult operation, owing to the deep draught of Conner's squadron, and the distance away of Pensacola, the nearest American naval base. A few minor ports were captured, and Vera Cruz and Tampico were blockaded eventually by vessels of lighter draught, which were added to the squadron. An attempt was made in August to capture Alvarado, a port thirty miles south of Vera Cruz. The river here was too strong to enable the boats to get up against it ; they could not cross the bar, and the attempt failed. A little later the brig *Truxton* was lost on the bar at Tuxpan, to the north of Vera Cruz, under the fire of the shore batteries.

Steam Warship, 1847.

A second attempt was made on Alvarado in October. The steamer *McLane*, a revenue cutter, towed in the schooners *Nonita*, *Petrel* and *Forward*, and the steamer *Vixen* had the schooners *Bonita* and *Reefer* in tow. A strong attack developed, aided by the guns of the steam-frigate *Mississippi*, which bombarded the Mexican batteries at long range. The *McLane* grounded and again the attempt was unsuccessful.

Commodore Conner then sent Captain Matthew C. Perry, of the *Mississippi*, to destroy Mexican shipping in the Tabasco River, in Yucatan. He attacked Fronteria, at the mouth of the river, on the 16th of October, having the *Mississippi*, *Vixen*, *McLane*, and the schooners employed in the previous operations, with the exception of the *Petrel*. The capital of Tabasco, San Juan Bautista de Tabasco, lies up the river from Fronteria, and this river divides the major part of Mexico from the Yucatan Peninsular. Perry, with the *Vixen* and two schooners, crossed the bar at Fronteria, and captured the Mexican shipping, including the steamer *Petrita* ; the land batteries were powerless against his vessels and the town surrendered.

This success at Fronteria was followed by an advance up the river with the *Vixen* and *Petrita* as far as San Juan ; the Mexicans abandoned their guns, and San Juan was taken almost without firing a shot. This city lies more than seventy miles up the river from Fronteria, and its capture resulted in Yucatan being cut off from the remainder of Mexican territory and coming under American control.

Commodore Conner then went to Tampico, where he crossed the bar in small boats and schooners, towed by the *Spitfire* and *Vixen* ; Tampico was surrendered, together with three Mexican gunboats and some merchant shipping. Commander Josiah Tatnall went from there, eighty miles up the river, to Panuco, where he spiked a number of guns and destroyed much material. A garrison was established at Tampico, and Perry then went to Laguna, with the *Mississippi*, *Vixen*, *Bonita* and *Petrel* ; this place was surrendered, without making any resistance.

It was now decided to abandon the plan of making a military advance on Mexico City from the direction of Monterey. Vera Cruz was chosen instead, as the *point de départ*, and plans were made for its capture by the naval and military forces. The taking of Vera Cruz was a difficult business ; yellow fever and other tropical diseases had to be faced, owing to the malarial swamps with which the neighbourhood abounded. General Winfield Scott was in command of the troops, and early in March, 1847, his transports had arrived at Lizardo, ready for a landing at Vera Cruz.

Meanwhile blockade-runners had to be dealt with, and in the previous November a cutting-out expedition against them was made. Lieutenant Parker, in a boat from the brig *Somers*, entered Vera Cruz harbour, with a few men, and burned the *Creole*, under the guns of the forts. Later the *Somers*, while chasing a blockade-runner, capsized through carrying too much press of sail, and lost half her ship's company ; her commanding officer on this occasion was Commander Raphael Semmes, afterwards famous, during the Civil War, as the Captain of the Confederate commerce-raider *Alabama*.

On the 9th of March, 1847, the troops were transferred to boats and these were towed in by the naval craft, Commander Tatnall coming in close inshore with the gunboats and other light-draught naval vessels, in order to support the landing with his guns. The troops were landed and proceeded to invest Vera Cruz. General Scott asked for some heavy naval guns and these were landed by Captain Aulick ; a three days' bombardment of Vera Cruz then commenced on the 22nd of March.

Tatnall went in the *Spitfire*, with the *Vixen*, to clear the beaches, and the *Spitfire* then went in again to draw the enemy's fire ; she drew a heavy fire on herself, to which she replied, shelling the town. The enemy's guns having been located, she retired. Next morning Tatnall, with the *Spitfire*, *Vixen* and four schooner-gunboats, went in to within eight hundred yards of the principal fort, which he bombarded for some time, until recalled by signal ; this fort was the Castle of San Juan de Ulloa, famous for its connection with Sir John Hawkyns and the *Jesus of Lübeck*.

All this time the main bombardment was continuing ; at 2.30 p.m. of the 25th of March firing ceased, and on the 28th of March Vera Cruz capitulated. Commodore Matthew Perry had now succeeded Commodore

Conner in the Gulf of Mexico, and he proceeded to the capture also of other towns on the coast. A third attempt was made on Alvarado by Lieutenant Hunter, in the *Scourge*, but the town was found now to have been evacuated. In April Perry crossed the bar at Tuxpan, with a naval and military landing-party in boats, and captured the local forts, and in June he occupied Fronteria with a large force and went up the Tabasco River ; the capital had been retaken, but he took it again with small loss to his own forces.

On the west coast Commodore Stockton had been temporarily relieved by Commodore Biddle, who had arrived from Japan in the *Columbus*. Commodore Shubrick also arrived, in the *Independence*, and later relieved Biddle. Commodore Biddle sent Shubrick, with the *Independence* and *Cyane*, to blockade Mazatlan and Guaymas, which is in the Gulf of California. Commander Dupont, of the *Cyane*, landed at San Blas and spiked the guns there, afterwards proceeding to Guaymas, where he destroyed some Mexican vessels. He then went to the relief of San José, which was being besieged, and raised the siege. San Blas was finally taken by a landing-party from the *I xington* on the 12th of January, 1848.

Peace between the United Sta s and Mexico was signed a month later and, as a result, California a d New Mexico became a part of the United States.

A story is told of a negro seaman who served in the U.S. Navy during the Mexican War. It appears that, when his service-time had expired, he was duly pensioned ; he still wished to go to sea, and therefore joined the Royal Navy. He found himself in East Indian waters in 1857, when the Indian Mutiny broke out, and was in the naval brigade commanded by Captain Peel, of the *Shannon* ; this brigade performed distinguished services in Oude, and here this seaman won the V.C., thus becoming the recipient also of a pension from the British Government.

The U.S. Navy had to take a hand also in matters connected with the Far East. The American ship, *Friendship* of Salem was attacked by the natives of Sumatra in 1831. The *Friendship*, was lying off a place on the north-west coast called Kuala Batu, and her master was ashore, buying pepper. While this was going on, the natives seized some of the ship's boats, and got on board the ship, which they captured by stratagem, killing the mate. The master succeeded in escaping in another boat, aided by a native chief ; he picked up four men, who were swimming from the captured ship, and got away to a neighbouring settlement called Muké. Here he found three American ships, who volunteered to return with him and recover possession of the *Friendship*. The ships had a few guns between them and, the natives proving defiant, these had to be used against them. Eventually the ship was recovered, but she had been looted and was just an empty shell.

A year later the U.S. frigate *Potomac* arrived off Kuala Batu. She was disguised as a merchantman, but when a ship's boat was sent towards the shore, the natives showed themselves to be hostile ; also they had guns and a system of fortifications. It was therefore decided to send ashore a landing-party by night, and make an attack on the place. By daylight two of the forts had been captured. Three armed schooners were also taken and finally the whole settlement, the citadel being blown up. The *Potomac* then bombarded the place and eventually the natives asked for peace.

In August, 1838, a somewhat similar incident occurred, the ship being in this case the *Eclipse*, which was captured, together with a large sum of money ; her master was killed. The U.S. frigate *Columbia* and the corvette *John Adams* happened to be not far away, under Commodore G. C. Read. The ships arrived off Kuala Batu in December, 1838. The town was known to have been responsible for the murder of the master of the *Eclipse* and for the theft of part of the money, but since neither the criminal nor the money were given up, it was bombarded. The ships then went on to Muké, which was partly incriminated, and that also was bombarded. Treaties were afterwards made with the native chiefs, by which the lives and property of American subjects were secured.

Commodore Kearney went out to China, with the *Constellation* and *Boston*, in March, 1842. At this time the Opium War between British and Chinese was practically ended and was followed, in the same year, by the Treaty of Nanking. As a result the British obtained Hong Kong and the use of five Treaty Ports, including Shanghai. Kearney went to Canton and there demanded indemnity for wrongs which had been suffered by American citizens and, finding the Chinese to be very amenable, he proposed that similar rights to those granted to the British be granted also to the United States. This was agreed to, and was granted also to other nationalities. The International Settlement at Shanghai was established shortly afterwards.

Arctic exploration also began to engage the attention of the United States. Interest had already been focussed on the Antarctic in 1836 ; here Lieutenant Charles Wilkes, afterwards Captain of the *San Jacinto*, made some discoveries. Wilkes had command of the sloops *Vincennes* and *Peacock* and four other ships, and explored among the islands of the Pacific, discovering parts of the Antarctic Continent.

Sir John Franklin had gone to the Polar Seas in a British attempt to discover the North-West Passage, the eastern end of which he succeeded in finding. He left Greenhithe with H.M.S. *Erebus* and *Terror* in May, 1845, and died in the Arctic in 1847. In 1848 relief expeditions, in an endeavour to find him and his men, began to be sent out. One of these

PLATE XXVII

TABASCO RIVER. 1846

From a lithograph by Commander Henry Walke, U.S.N.

During the Mexican War, Captain Matthew Perry took an expedition up the Tabasco River, in Yucatan. With two steamers he advanced up the river and captured the capital of Yucatan.

LANDING OF THE TROOPS AT VERA CRUZ

Coloured lithograph by Wagner and McGuigan, Phila.

The Mexican War of 1847. The U.S. Squadron is seen in the offing. In March, 1847, it was decided to attack and capture Vera Cruz. Troops were landed and the combined naval and military operations resulted in the capture of the place.

was an American expedition under Lieutenant de Haven, in command of
the *Advance* and *Rescue*, and this is known as the First Grinnell Expedition.

The expedition started in 1850 and was away for sixteen months,
during which time it did valuable scientific research work.   The surgeon
and naturalist was Surgeon Elisha Kent Kane who, on his return, at
once toured the country lecturing, in an endeavour to raise funds for a
second attempt.   The Second Grinnell Expedition, financed by Mr.
Henry Grinnell, went out in 1853, under the command of Surgeon Kane
in the brig *Advance*.   He was absent for two winters and reached what
was then the farthest north, 80°, 35′.   The *Advance* had to be abandoned
and the explorers eventually reached Upernivik, in Greenland, in August,
1855, where a relief expedition under Captain H. J. Harstene found
them and brought them home.

A squadron was already maintained on the China Station by the
United States.   In 1845 Commodore Biddle had been sent to Japan,
with the *Columbus* and *Vincennes*, with the object of negotiating a Trade
Treaty ; but he had been unsuccessful.   Japan had been penetrated
during the sixteenth century by Christian missionaries, led in 1549 by
St. Francis Xavier ; but the results of western penetration were held by
the Japanese to be unsatisfactory, since
in the middle of the nineteenth century they were still an artistic nation
and despised western materialism.
They had therefore prohibited any
foreigner from landing in Japan, and
intercourse with the outside world was
non-existent, except for some small
trade facilities granted to the Dutch
at Nagasaki.

U.S. Frigate " Mississippi."

In 1852 it was decided to make another attempt to open up trade
with Japan, and a mission was appointed under Commodore Matthew
C. Perry, the younger brother of Oliver Perry.   His broad pendant was
in the steamer *Mississippi* and he arrived in Hong Kong in April, 1853 ;
here he joined the American China Squadron, and he shifted his broad
pendant to the steamer *Susquehanna*.   The squadron arrived in the Bay
of Yedo, now known as Tokio, in the summer of the same year.

Shore boats, some carrying minor officials, swarmed round the ships,
as soon as they dropped anchor, but any attempt to come on board
was repelled, and it was made clear to the Japanese, through an interpreter,
that none but an official of high rank would be received.   At length a
lieutenant of the flagship was told off to receive an official who appeared
to be of some consequence, and who turned out to be the Vice-Governor
of the district.   He explained that it was lawful only to communicate

with foreigners at Nagasaki, where the Dutch already had some trade facilities.

It was pointed out that this was no ordinary mission ; for the Commodore was the bearer of a letter to the Emperor of Japan from the President of the United States himself, which could only be delivered to a prince of the highest rank and at some place near the capital. The lieutenant also explained that the shore boats must immediately be ordered away, as their presence was most disrespectful to the squadron, otherwise steps would have to be taken, possibly with the aid of the ships' guns.[1]

The boats were sent away, but Oriental temporizing still continued for some time, until the Commodore, who had hitherto maintained a dignified invisibility, sent an ultimatum, saying that he would steam up to Tokio itself, unless a proper reply to his request for a messenger, worthy of the mission, were sent by a named date. This brought the Japanese to their senses, and they replied that a house should be erected ashore for the reception of the letter and of the Commodore's own credentials by a high official of state on the 14th of July.

On the day named the Commodore went ashore in full state, accompanied by guards of honour and by the local Governor and Vice-Governor : bands played and a thirteen-gun salute was fired. A large guard of honour, consisting of bluejackets and marines, was drawn up ashore to salute the Commodore. The documents were delivered in gold caskets and everything conducted with the greatest ceremony. The squadron then sailed away.

In February, 1854, Commodore Perry returned to Yedo Bay, to obtain the reply to the President's letter. He steamed in with the *Susquehanna*, *Mississippi* and *Powhatan*, having the sailing-ships *Lexington*, *Southampton*, *Macedonian* and *Vandalia* in tow, and dropped anchor off Yokohama, a dozen miles from the capital. Similar ceremonies were observed as at his previous visit, and the Commodore took away with him a trade treaty with Japan.

Subsequent dealings with the Japanese were not always quite so agreeable. Despite their apparent willingness to throw open their doors to foreign intercourse, they attempted ten years later to close the Straits of Shimonoseki to the passage of foreign ships. A strong naval force, commanded by Admiral Sir Augustus Kuper, was sent there and, aided by Dutch and French warships, compelled the reopening of the Straits ; in this operation the force had the aid also of a ship of the U.S. Navy.

An example of Anglo-American naval co-operation occurred at Shanghai in April, 1854. The International Settlement at Shanghai had been established following the Treaty of Nanking in 1842. In 1854 the Taiping Rebellion had broken out, and the Chinese Imperial Troops

[1] *History of the United States Navy.* John R. Spears.

were encamped close to the international boundary. The troops caused much trouble, owing to their frequent attempts to cross over into the International Settlement, and steps had to be taken to deal with the nuisance.

At that time there were two British ships at Shanghai, H.M.S. *Encounter*, Captain George O'Callaghan, and *Grecian*, Commander the Hon. George D. Keane ; the U.S. corvette *Plymouth* was also present, under the command of Commander John Kelly. The British picket had to be reinforced against the Chinese, and eventually it was decided to set on fire the camp nearest the boundary. The various consuls then represented the position to Captain O'Callaghan as being serious and he decided on sharp action.

On the 14th of April, Commander Keane and Lieutenant Dew, of the *Encounter*, seized eight junks as hostages, and an ultimatum was sent to the Chinese to move their main camp farther away ; this was disregarded, and some guns from the ships, with landing-parties, were then brought ashore. Two howitzers belonging to an American gentleman, Mr. Edward Cunningham, were offered, and their use accepted.[1] The first shell was fired into the camp about four o'clock in the afternoon and, the American bluejackets co-operating, the camp was stormed shortly afterwards and the incident was at an end, the Chinese losing about thirty or forty killed.

Piracy in China was very prevalent, and called for action in which both British and Americans gave their services. In July, 1855, some ships under convoy of the steamer *Eaglet* were cut off by pirates and taken into a fortified bay. Commander Fellowes, of H.M.S. *Rattler*, was appealed to, and he went to Hong Kong, where he asked for and obtained the help of the U.S. frigate *Powhatan*.[2] On the 3rd of August, the *Rattler* and her boats, with three of the *Powhatan's* boats, entered the bay with the *Eaglet*. A Chinese "lorcha" tried to escape, and was chased by the *Rattler's* pinnace and the *Powhatan's* cutter, which suddenly found themselves close down on a group of Chinese craft. When the rest of the boats came up, these craft, which numbered about thirty-six, made off, being badly damaged by the boats' howitzers.

The boats continued their pursuit of the pirate vessels, one of which was overtaken by the *Powhatan's* launch, containing some British marines, which captured her by boarding, other junks being taken also. One of the captured junks blew up, and Commander Fellowes and Lieutenant Rolando, of the *Powhatan*, were thrown into the water, but were rescued. All the larger junks were secured and, as a result of this affair, five hundred pirates were killed and a thousand made prisoners.

---

[1] *Troubles in China.* The Navy, October, 1937.
[2] *The Royal Navy.* Sir William Laird Clowes.

During the following year Captain Andrew H. Foote of the *Portsmouth* was off Canton, protecting American interests, and at that time fighting

Chinese Junk.

was still going on between the British and the Chinese ; unfortunately the Chinese were making no distinction between nationalities. In November, 1856, when Foote was passing one of the forts in his boat, he was fired on, the American flag being disregarded. Next day the forts were bombarded by the *Portsmouth, San Jacinto* and *Levant*, after which a landing-party attacked the rear of one of the forts and captured it. The guns of the captured fort were trained on its neighbour, which was silenced. Other forts were then taken and the Stars and Stripes were hoisted on four of them. Respect for the American flag was then observed by the Chinese.

An interesting episode occurred in the same year. One of the expeditions in search of Sir John Franklin had been commanded by Admiral Sir Edward Belcher, who went out to the Arctic in 1853. One of the five ships of this expedition was H.M.S. *Resolute* ; this ship was under the command of Captain Henry Kellett, R.N., and a sledge party from her had succeeded in rescuing McClure, the explorer who discovered the western end of the North-West Passage. In 1854 Belcher feared that he might be forced again to winter in the ice, and he embarked the crews of four of his ships on board the fifth, the *North Star*, abandoning the *Resolute, Intrepid, Assistance* and *Pioneer* ; Kellett, McClintock and others vainly protested, and the expedition returned to England.

The derelict *Resolute*, which had drifted a thousand miles, was sighted nearly eighteen months later, in Davis Strait, by American whalers. She was taken to America, reconditioned, and eventually handed back to the British Government, having made the voyage across the Atlantic under the command of Captain Harstene. The ceremony of presentation took place at Cowes in December, 1856, in the presence of Queen Victoria and of the Prince Consort.

In January, 1857, a captain in command of a squadron of the U.S. Navy became known as a "Flag-Officer." The broad pendant had been blue and contained a number of white stars. If a junior captain occupying the same position happened to be present, he employed a red broad pendant of similar design, a white broad pendant being displayed by the junior of three officers in command of squadrons, if all present at the same time.

It will be remembered that in some navies a Rear-Admiral hoisted his flag at the mizen mast and a Vice-Admiral at the fore. In May, 1858,

SERVICE DRESS.

Captain.   Midshipman.   Surgeon.   Purser.

PLATE XXIX

U.S. NAVY OFFICERS' UNIFORMS, 1852

The frock coat is cut high in the neck, and this characteristic continued for
some years (see Plate XXXIX) ; up to the time of the First World War
the "monkey jacket" was also cut high (see Plate XLV). Afterwards
the British fashion was adopted, with lapels, white collar and black tie.

DEPARTURE OF THE U.S.S. COLUMBUS AND VINCENNES

PLATE XXX　　DEPARTURE OF THE U.S.S. *COLUMBUS* AND *VINCENNES*

Painted by S. F. Rosser and J. Eastley.　Engraved by Wagner and McGuigan

The U.S. Ships *Columbus* and *Vincennes* leaving Japan.　In 1845 Commodore Biddle went to Japan in the hope of negotiating a Trade Treaty ; he returned unsuccessful.　Afterwards he crossed the Pacific Ocean and took part in the War with Mexico.

PLATE XXXI COMMODORE PERRY'S EXPEDITION TO JAPAN

From an original water-colour by W. Heine

In 1853 Commodore Matthew Perry went to Japan, in order to negotiate a trade treaty. After some difficulty, a meeting was arranged in a specially erected house on shore. The picture shows U.S. bluejackets and marines forming a guard; the officers are on the verandah behind.

PLATE XXXII

IN JAPANESE WATERS, 1853. By W. Heine

Scene during Commodore Matthew Perry's expedition to Japan in 1853, showing Lieutenant S. Bent in the *Mississippi's* first cutter forcing its way through a fleet of Japanese boats while surveying the bay of Yedo, July 11th, 1853.

these captains were authorized to hoist a square flag the same size as the jack at the mizen, and if of twenty years' seniority, at the fore.

An example of Anglo-American solidarity now occurred, which has since become famous, and which met with particular appreciation on the British side of the Atlantic. Various accounts of it have appeared, and though these differ in detail, they agree in essentials. Trouble in China between the British forces and those of the Chinese Empire was still going on in 1859, the Americans being neutral. In June of that year the British naval forces were under the command of Rear-Admiral Sir James Hope, who made an attack on the forts in the Peiho River. His flag was in H.M.S. *Plover*, but this ship being badly hit, he transferred it to H.M.S. *Cormorant*.

Admiral Hope was wounded early in the attack, and was confined to his cabin on board H.M.S. *Cormorant*. The entrance to the Peiho River is V-shaped, and a strong fort was on the left bank and a line of batteries on the right bank. The *Cormorant* engaged the batteries on the right bank, which was on her port side, having the *Plover* lashed to her starboard side, in such a way that the bow gun could fire across her bows and engage the batteries. A good many casualties had already been suffered by the British.

Suddenly a double-banked cutter displaying the American flag was seen coming up the river. It contained Flag-Officer Josiah Tatnall, who was in command of the American naval forces in the Far East. On the way up, his coxswain was killed by a shot and Lieutenant Trenchard, his flag lieutenant, was wounded. The Flag-Officer came alongside the *Plover* and crossed her blood-stained deck to the *Cormorant*, where he visited the Admiral in his cabin, and expressed his sympathy. Meantime his boat's crew, observing that the crew of the *Plover's* bow gun were quite exhausted, took their places one by one, and continued to serve the gun.

Tatnall came out on deck and, seeing this, said : " Don't you know that we are neutrals ? " Whereupon his men went back to their boat, excusing themselves with a remark about the fellowship of the sea. During these operations the British made a boat attack up the river, which was obstructed with stakes, booms and other obstacles ; this attack was beaten off, with heavy losses, and a steamer called the *Toeywan*, which had been chartered by Tatnall, was lent by him to aid in towing up boats full of British reserves, and towing back boats full of British wounded.

Flag-Officer Josiah Tatnall explained his generous actions by saying simply that : " Blood is thicker than Water."

CHAPTER VII

THE CIVIL WAR

NO actions between powerful fleets had taken place in any of the earlier wars in which the United States Navy was concerned, with the single exception of the War of Independence; no such action occurred again until the Spanish-American War of 1898. Yet the Civil War of 1861–5 was the most important in which the Navy played its part during this period, and it occurred at a time when great changes were taking place in the conceptions of naval armament. It was now that the principle of arming a ship, on each side, with a row of pieces along the gun deck began to give way to the principle of employing one or more powerful guns in revolving turrets. Breech-loading guns had been already invented, but were not yet practicable. Shell-guns had been invented by General Peixhan, some ten years after the Napoleonic War, and muzzle-loading guns, firing shells or solid spherical shot, were still in use, which differed but little from those employed at Trafalgar ; ships were still equipped with sails, though in many cases they had auxiliary steam, which could propel them either with the screw propeller or with paddle-wheels.

The Government forces, known as " Federals," had at their disposal a certain number of steam frigates and sloops, and with these they proceeded to blockade the Southern States, or " Confederates," who had but few of these vessels, and were forced to act on the defensive at sea. In 1842 an armoured ship had been commenced in the United States, but was never completed ; the success attained by this principle in the floating batteries employed in 1855 by the French before Kinburn led to several vessels, Federal as well as Confederate, being armoured. During the 'fifties Captain Cowper Coles, R.N., had been working on these problems also, and in 1862 the razéed *Royal Sovereign* was equipped with four turrets on the centre line, and was thus a forerunner of the *Dreadnought* of 1906 and her successors. In 1862 also the Federals, through the genius of Captain John Ericsson, obtained the use of the *Monitor*, a ship of low freeboard and equipped with a two-gun turret ; this vessel gave its name to ships of a like character, as in the case of the " Dreadnoughts " ; several " Monitors " served on the Federal side. Since that date armour and turret-guns have become a normal feature of warship construction.

Despite their limited resources, the Confederates developed two new weapons—the mine and the submarine. The mine had been employed in the Crimean War and was known as a " torpedo," the mobile torpedo not having yet come into use. The submarine, a submersible boat known as a "David," did great execution in Charleston Harbour, as mentioned below. The Confederates also devised a turtle-decked vessel of low freeboard; this was sometimes referred to as a "ram," a term which seems to have been rather loosely employed, and included a type of armoured gunboat.

The causes of the quarrel are outside the scope of this brief study. Soon after the election of President Lincoln in 1860, South Carolina seceded from the Union, followed, at various intervals, by Mississippi, Florida, Alabama, Georgia, Louisiana and Texas. Representatives of these seven states met on the 4th of February, 1861, at Montgomery, in Alabama, and formed the Confederate States of America. A month later the Confederate States Navy adopted an ensign, which contained seven white stars in a circle on a blue canton, this design being employed also as a jack; the remainder of the ensign consisted of three horizontal bands—red, white and red.

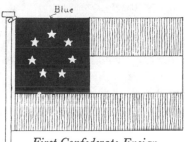

First Confederate Ensign, 1861.

Since 1818 the United States flag had contained thirteen stripes of red and white, to represent the original thirteen states of the Union. Only South Carolina and Georgia, of the seceding states, were among the original thirteen, and the use of three bands, instead of two, was presumably dependent upon the symmetrical appearance of the flag. Prior to the Civil War the United States flag had thirty-three stars and thirteen stripes; this flag continued to be employed in the United States, or "Federal," Navy throughout the war.

In 1861 North Carolina also seceded, together with Virginia, Tennessee and Arkansas; this made eleven states in all. Though there was considerable sympathy with the Southern cause in Kentucky and Missouri, they were divided in opinion and did not formally join the Confederate States; delegates were sent by both to Washington and also to the Confederate Congress. The President chosen by the Confederacy was Jefferson Davis and its capital was established at Richmond, in Virginia.

War broke out in April, 1861, with the capture by South Carolina of Fort Sumter in Charleston Harbour; the Confederates also captured the naval base of Pensacola, in Florida, and that of Norfolk, in Virginia, which the Federals had to abandon, after setting it on fire. These were accompanied by a series of land successes, beginning with the Battle of Bull Run, or Manassas. At sea, however, their operations were mostly directed against Federal merchant shipping, in which such commerce-destroyers as the *Alabama* and *Shenandoah* played a large part. The

Federal naval forces often acted in conjunction with the military, but sometimes served independently, as in Dupont's capture of Port Royal.

A blockade was established of the various southern ports from the Atlantic to the Gulf of Mexico ; despite this, much blockade-running was indulged in by the Confederates, partly in connection with the cotton-trade, a valuable export of the Southern States ; this was an export on which the Lancashire cotton industry was largely dependent. During the first year of the war the Confederates had the classic advantage of the aggressor, but as the war progressed, the Federal power, notably at sea, gradually increased. Steps were taken by the Federals to cut off the three westernmost of the Confederate States, by occupying the line of the Mississippi River ; but to ensure that the coastal blockade should be effective, it was essential to obtain possession of certain bases of operations on the coast ; one of these bases was Port Royal, in South Carolina.

In November, 1816, Flag-Officer S. F. Dupont conducted an attack on the harbour of Port Royal, where the only naval defence consisted of a small force of gunboats, commanded by Flag-Officer Josiah Tatnall, who had now joined the Confederate forces ; Tatnall prudently retired his small command up the harbour, of which the entrance on the south-west side was defended by Fort Walker, and on the north-east side by Fort Beauregard. Dupont, in the steam frigate *Wabash*, and accompanied by a force of steam frigates, sloops and gunboats, brought his ships up in a heavy gale and took them safely over the bar. On the morning of the 9th of November he led his squadron in to within eight hundred yards of Fort Walker, which was submitted to a fierce bombardment, the Confederates having no idea that defensive works on shore could receive such punishment from ships' guns. The squadron passed backwards and forwards, opposite the fort, submitting it to an intense fire, which was aided by an enfilade by Dupont's gunboats operating inshore. By one o'clock in the afternoon the Confederates were beginning to evacuate Fort Walker, and very soon afterwards Commander John Rodgers went ashore and hoisted the Stars and Stripes over the place. No serious attack was made on Fort Beauregard, which was seen later in the day to have been evacuated also.

A curious incident, which might have had unfortunate results, occurred in the same month. Two Confederate officials, Messrs. Mason and Slidell, were on their way to Europe, as Commissioners to the Governments of Great Britain and France, accompanied by two attachés. The four had taken passage in the S.S. *Trent*, a British mail steamer, proceeding from Havana to England. On the 8th of November, the ship was stopped in the Bahama Channel by the *San Jacinto*, Captain Charles Wilkes ; a boat was sent alongside and these four gentlemen were removed and taken to Boston on board the *San Jacinto*. Great indignation was aroused in Great

PLATE XXVII

DESPERATE ENCOUNTER BETWEEN THE ERICSSON BATTERY *MONITOR*
TWO GUNS AND THE *MERRIMAC* TWELVE GUNS, March 9th, 1862

Engraved by F. Newman

The momentous conflict between the *Merrimac* and *Monitor* (1862) which revolutionized the navies of the world. The *Merrimac* had previously sunk 3 Federal war vessels when the *Monitor* appeared. Neither ship suffered much damage in the subsequent duel, but the *Merrimac* had to sheer off. The *Merrimac* was eventually scuttled by the Confederates, while the *Monitor* foundered in a gale and took down 16 of her crew.

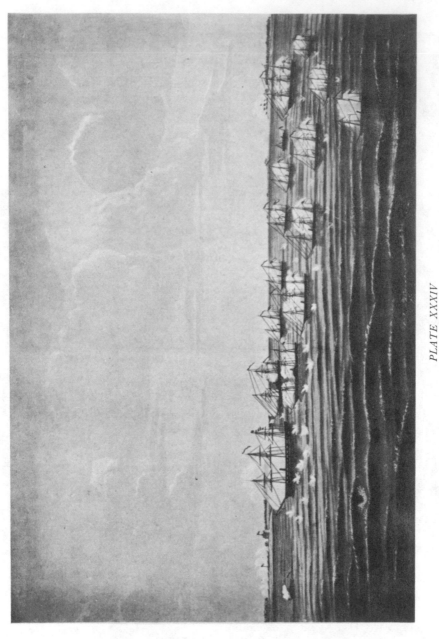

PLATE XXXIV

BATTLE OF PORT ROYAL, November 7th, 1861

By George Roberts, Yeoman, of the U.S.S. *Wabash*

The capture of Port Royal was one of the earliest naval episodes in the Civil War. The place was taken after a bombardment by a squadron commanded by Flag-Officer Dupont, in the flagship *Wabash*.

Britain, where public sympathy had always inclined more to the Southern than to the Northern States, and the case required the most careful handling, owing to the heat of American public opinion. Possibly the United States Government appreciated the humour of the situation; it had placed itself in the position of insisting on that very " right of search," against which its predecessors had protested so vigorously in 1812. For a time diplomatic notes passed between the two Governments ; then, with great breadth of vision, President Lincoln's Government conceded the point ; the Commissioners were transferred to a British warship and the incident was closed.[1]

In January, 1862, it was decided by the U.S. Government to capture Pamlico and Albemarle Sounds, together with Roanoke Island, which lies between them. Forts Hatteras and Clark, which commanded the principal entrance into the sounds of North Carolina, were taken ; but this was not sufficient to prevent the Confederates from conducting their coast-wise traffic in this neighbourhood. The task was entrusted to Flag-Officer Louis M. Goldsborough, aided by a military force under General Burnside. The naval ships and transports entered the sounds by way of Hatteras Inlet ; the former were placed under the command of Commander S. C. Rowan, who opened the attack on Roanoke Island on the 7th of February. At three o'clock the troops were embarked into light draught vessels and by 4.30 the first landing was made, some opposition being encountered, in which the Confederate gunboats rendered support ; ten thousand men were landed, and operations against the forts commenced on the 8th of February, the naval vessels co-operating with a bombardment. Soon afterwards the forts fell into the hands of the Federal forces, and the capture of Roanoke Island was completed. The enemy's gunboats were subsequently destroyed. Most of the sounds and inlets of South Carolina, Georgia and Florida had now fallen into the hands of the Federals, and the only important places remaining to the Confederates, through which they could obtain munitions of war or supplies from overseas, were Wilmington and Charleston, in the Carolinas.

An attempt to split the Confederacy in half had been decided on by the Federal Government and, in order to effect this, it was necessary to isolate the three western States of the South—Texas, Arkansas and the greater part of Louisiana—by occupying the line of the Mississippi River. A Western Flotilla of gunboats had been formed on the upper reaches of this river in 1861, and was placed by the Federal Government under the command of Flag-Officer Andrew Hull Foote. His depôt was at the town of Cairo, near the junction with the Ohio River.

During the first half of 1861 three wooden steamers had been bought, equipped as gunboats and manned for immediate service on the Missis-

[1] *The Naval History of the Civil War.* Admiral David D. Porter, U.S.N.

sippi, largely through the energy and skill of Mr. James B. Eads. These were the *Tyler* and *Lexington*, armed with eight-inch shell-guns, and the *Conestoga*, with thirty-two-pounder smooth-bores. In October seven ironclad gunboats, ordered by the Federal Government from Mr. Eads, were nearing completion, and the first one was launched at Carondelet under the name *St. Louis*, her name being afterwards altered to *de Kalb*.

Six vessels of a similar type were launched soon afterwards; these were named *Cincinnati*, *Cairo*, *Louisville*, *Carondelet*, *Pittsburgh* and *Mound City*, and other vessels were added to this force. In September, 1861, Flag-Officer Foote arrived in Cairo. By this time the rivers above Columbus, a little south of Cairo, had fallen into Federal hands, but the ironclad gunboats were not yet completed. The Western Flotilla was under the control of the War Department, and acted in co-operation with General Grant, who had his headquarters in Cairo.

In November Commander Henry Walke was sent down river, with the *Tyler* and *Lexington*, to convoy some troop-transports and to effect a reconnaissance. The troops were landed at Belmont, near Columbus, but the Confederate resistance was so strong that they and the gunboats had eventually to withdraw; the Confederates attacked and the Federal troops were obliged to re-embark, covered by the gunboats, whose fire scattered the enemy, who however was able to hold his positions.

An attack was made on Fort Henry, on the Tennessee River, in February, 1862. Four iron-clad gunboats, including the *Essex*, were employed on this enterprise, and the three wooden gunboats, Foote having his flag in the *Cincinnati*. The Tennessee River was much swollen by rain, which added to the difficulties experienced by the gunboats; they anchored for the night below Fort Henry, and were much relieved next morning to find a number of Confederate " torpedoes," floating down harmlessly, having been torn from their moorings by the force of the current; fortunately they did not break lose at night, and could be avoided.

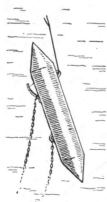

Confederate Torpedo.

On the 6th of February, the flotilla got under way again, and steamed up to within sight of the fort, which opened fire, and a vigorous exchange of shot followed. Eventually, after a brave defence of the Confederate garrison, General Tilghman lowered the Confederate flag, and the Navy occupied the fort, until it could be handed over to General Grant. Flag-Officer Foote received General Tilghman's surrender on board the *Cincinnati*.

During the following week an attack was made on Fort Donelson, on the Cumberland River. On the 12th of February the *Carondelet*, towed by the transport *Alps*, went up towards the fort, under Commander Walke;

the intention of this movement was to effect a diversion, while General Grant was getting his troops into position to invest the place. The *Carondelet*, having cast off the tow, proceeded alone to within sight of the fort, which was advantageously placed on a high bluff, at a bend in the river. There was no sign of life, so Walke loosed off his bow guns, partly to unmask the position of the enemy's guns, by inducing him to reply, and partly to apprise General Grant of his arrival. There was no response and, after firing a few more shells, Walke withdrew and anchored down stream.

Next day the *Carondelet* again advanced and bombarded the fort ; this time she received a spirited reply, which however did little damage ; the bombardment lasted for most of the day. In the evening Flag-Officer Foote arrived, with the *Pittsburgh*, *St. Louis*, *Louisville* and the wooden boats *Conestoga* and *Tyler* ; the decks of these ships were then protected, against plunging fire, by placing chains, bags of coal and other objects upon them, and in the afternoon of the 14th of February the ironclads advanced on the fort in line abreast. As the four ironclads approached, the fire from the fort became very intense ; boat-davits, anchors and even portions of the iron plating were torn away, and much other damage was caused, the casualties on board the ironclad gunboats being heavy ; these included Flag-Officer Foote, who was wounded.

The ironclads began to fall back on the wooden boats, which were nearly a mile to the rear ; in turning, the *Pittsburgh* struck the stern of the *Carondelet*, carrying away her starboard rudder. The pilots of the *St. Louis* and *Louisville* were killed or wounded, and the wheel-ropes of these two vessels were shot away : the two gunboats were obliged to retire, followed by the *Pittsburgh*. The *Carondelet* continued for some time to engage the enemy, but eventually she also was obliged to retire. Two days later Fort Donelson was taken by General Grant, and the gunboats proceeded back to Cairo for repairs.

Ironclad vessels had already been tried by the Federal Navy, in the gunboats of the Western Flotilla. The Confederates also experimented with this idea. One of the most remarkable actions of the war now took place—remarkable because it was the first fight between armoured vessels. Previously reliance for naval protection had been placed in most navies on the old wooden line-of-battleships. The introduction of armour now made these navies practically obsolete, since it appeared likely that naval battles of the future would be decided by ironclads and rams ; this action came, therefore, as a profound shock to most sections of naval thought. Great Britain had launched only two armoured ships, the *Warrior* and *Black Prince*, and France had launched one, the *Gloire* ; the departments of naval construction of both countries at once proceeded to reconstruct their fleets, by cutting down line-of-battleships and covering them with armour ; turret-guns also were introduced.

Early in 1861, Norfolk Navy Yard had been abandoned, for some reason, by the Federals, and, in order to render it useless to the Confederates, the yard had been set on fire. When the Confederates took possession of it, they found that a fine steam frigate, the *Merrimac*, had been burned at her moorings and sunk, together with a number of other ships ; a large number of guns had also been abandoned. The *Merrimac* was of three thousand five hundred tons and had forty guns in her original armament ; her engines and boilers were defective, and their long immersion did not improve them.

None the less it was decided to raise her. She was, therefore, raised and cut down in such a way that, when refitted, seventy feet at either end were just awash. The midship portion was a hundred and seventy feet long, and on this was built a structure of pitch pine, the sides of which came down to below the water-line and were inclined upwards at an angle of about forty-five degrees, this structure being covered with two thicknesses of iron plates. She had a kind of ram, fitted just below water at the fore end ; this was made of cast-iron, but proved to be of little use. Her " pilot-house " was also covered with iron plates, but her funnel was unprotected and she had no masts. The ship was rechristened *Virginia*, but is usually referred to to-day under her old name.

At each end the superstructure was rounded and accommodated two seven-inch " rifles," acting as pivot-guns at bow and stern. Ports were cut for these in the superstructure, as also for the remainder of the new armament, which consisted of two six-inch rifled guns and six nine-inch smooth-bores, making twelve guns in all. The Confederates had great difficulty in manning the ship, owing to the fact that there were few seamen available in the Southern States ; but a number of volunteers were eventually obtained from the army at Yorktown. Flag-Officer Franklin Buchanan was placed in command, and she started on what was expected to be her trial trip on the 8th of March, 1862.

The *Merrimac* showed that she was very unmanageable ; she could not make more than five knots speed and drew twenty-three feet of water ; but she steamed out from Norfolk, down the Elizabeth River, without mishap, being loudly cheered by the Confederate troops manning the batteries on the southern side of Hampton Roads ; she then set a course in the direction of Newport News.

Between Newport News and Fortress Monroe a number of Federal ships lay at anchor ; these were the frigates *Minnesota*, *Roanoke* and *St. Lawrence*, together with a few gunboats ; nearer Newport News lay the frigates *Cumberland* and *Congress*. The day was fine and the appearance of the *Merrimac* quite unexpected ; the ship's company of the Confederate ship did not, in fact, anticipate that this was the first occasion on which she would go into action.

As soon as the *Merrimac* had approached to within three-quarters of a mile, the *Cumberland* observed her and opened fire with her bow guns ; the *Congress* also opened, supported by the Federal shore batteries, on the north side of Hampton Roads.   The *Merrimac* took up a position across the *Cumberland's* bows and submitted her to an intense raking fire, and then struck her at right angles, near the fore chains on the starboard side ;   the ram broke off and was left sticking in the *Cumberland's* side. Broadsides were exchanged and Buchanan demanded the *Cumberland's* surrender ;   this was refused, and the *Cumberland* fought on.   Buchanan then rammed her a second time ;   with two big rents in her side, she could do little more, and was now filling rapidly.   Finally she sank, with colours flying, her crew gallantly fighting till the last.

Buchanan now steamed up the James River, where he had room to turn round and, coming back, turned his attention to the *Congress*, which had got under way and grounded in shallow water, where she was engaged by the deep-draught *Merrimac* at long range.   The *Congress* continued the fight for half an hour after the sinking of the *Cumberland*, suffering great losses, and finally she hoisted the white flag.   In this part of the action the *Merrimac* was aided by two small ships, the *Patrick Henry* and the *Jamestown*.   The gunboats *Raleigh*, *Beaufort* and *Teaser* were also present, and were ordered to take off the crew of the surrendered *Congress*, and to set her on fire.   The shore batteries were apparently unaware of what was going on, and continued to pour a hot fire into the Confederate ships.   Finally this humanitarian work had to be abandoned and the crew of the *Congress* left to their fate ;   the men escaped ashore by swimming or in boats.   Buchanan now ordered hot shot to be employed, and in a few minutes the *Congress* was in a blaze and eventually blew up.

Buchanan was wounded in the course of the action, also Lieutenant Minor, his flag-lieutenant, the total number of casualties on board the *Merrimac* being twenty-one.   The wounded were sent to Norfolk and Lieutenant Catesby Jones took temporary command of the ship.   She was leaking forward and her armour was strained at several points ; the muzzles of two of the guns had been shot off and her ram had gone. Night was now coming on, and the *Merrimac* withdrew to the entrance to the Elizabeth River, where she anchored.   The *Minnesota* had previously got under way and approached the *Merrimac*, but she grounded about a mile from Newport News ;   the *Merrimac* intended to deal with her on the following day.

Great dismay was caused in Federal circles, where it seemed as if the Confederates had at their disposal a vessel which was quite invincible, and the Confederates were proportionately jubilant ;   their jubilation was however short-lived.   During the rebuilding of the *Merrimac*, the Federals also had a new type of vessel under construction.   Both sides were feverishly working to complete these two ships and, by a coincidence, it happened that both were completed at about the same time ; both sides also were well aware of the main features of their respective vessels. The Federal ship was called the *Monitor*, and she was built from the designs of Captain John Ericsson.

The *Monitor* was an " ironclad steam battery," one hundred and seventy-two feet long, drawing eleven feet of water, and having a ship's company

The " Merrimac."

of fifty-eight, including her commanding officer, Lieutenant John L. Worden. Her sides had five inches of armour and only about a foot of them was visible above water. In the centre of the ship was a revolving turret, for the accommodation of two eleven-inch smooth-bore guns ; it was originally intended that these guns should be of fifteen-inch calibre, but eleven-inch Dahlgren guns had to be substituted, since the others could not be obtained in time. The turret was twenty feet in diameter and had eight inches of armour. In battle trim, the deck was absolutely unencumbered, except for the turret and a small armoured " pilot-house " right forward ; the absence of funnels, when cleared for action, was compensated for by powerful blowers, which maintained the necessary draught. She was described by the Confederates as resembling a " cheese-box on a shingle." [1]

The name *Monitor* is explained in a letter written by Captain Ericsson to the Assistant Secretary to the Navy, in which he opined that this ironclad vessel would prove to be a " severe monitor " to the leaders of the Confederacy. She was not intended to be a sea-going vessel, and her crew had a very exacting experience in bringing her down, in heavy weather, from New York, where she was built, to Chesapeake Bay. They left New York on the 6th of March and arrived on the night of the 8th, hearing the guns of the *Merrimac's* action off Cape Henry : the *Monitor* dropped anchor in Hampton Roads at nine o'clock the same night, close to the *Minnesota*.

At daybreak on the 9th of March the *Merrimac* and her attendant ships were seen near Sewall's Point, at the month of the Elizabeth River, and at about half-past seven they got under way, and made for the *Minnesota* ; the *Monitor* also got under way, and made for the *Merrimac*.

The duel between these two armoured ships now commenced ; but although they approached each other to within short range—from half a mile down to a few feet—their fire took very little effect. The shot dented the iron plates, but did no other apparent damage, though the *Merrimac's* funnel, which had been riddled in the previous action, was

---

[1] According to one account : " A tin can on a shingle."

now completely demolished. For two hours the cannonade continued; then the *Monitor* retired into shallow water, in order to replenish her ammunition from below, giving the *Merrimac* the opportunity of attacking the *Minnesota*, to which she did considerable damage, grounding in the attempt. She was then refloated and went into deeper water, with the *Monitor* in pursuit.

Catesby Jones now tried to ram his opponent, but the blow had no effect, since the *Merrimac* had lost her ram. Shortly after noon the *Merrimac* gave up firing on her adversary's turret, and concentrated on the pilot-house, breaking the top of it with a shell, and wounding Lieutenant Worden, who was temporarily blinded; Lieutenant S. Dana Greene took command. The *Merrimac* then gave up the battle, thinking that the *Monitor* was out of action; Greene, after assuring himself that his steering gear was unhampered, pursued her, firing all the time; but the Confederate ship retired, making for Norfolk.

The leak forward had now increased; the *Monitor's* fire had forced in the plates at one point and other damage had been done. The *Merrimac* needed a refit; but by the beginning of April she was again ready for action, and was placed under the command of Flag-Officer Josiah Tatnall. During the duel between the two adversaries, none was killed in either ship and there were very few wounded; the use of armour had justified itself.

Subsequent activities on the part of this vessel were brief; it was proposed that she should go up the Potomac River, to Washington, but she drew too much water to pass the shoals; similar difficulties obtained in trying to approach New York. She was not a sea-going ship, and was therefore largely confined to the waters around Hampton Roads.

On the 11th of April, she steamed down the Elizabeth River, with her attendant gunboats, expecting to meet a largely reinforced Federal fleet; but Hampton Roads were deserted of warships. Three merchant vessels, however, loaded with supplies for the Federal army, were at anchor there, and these the *Jamestown* succeeded in capturing. A few days afterwards, the *Merrimac* went down to the fort near the Rip-Raps, where she hoped to find the *Monitor* and to take her by boarding. Her engines then broke down, and she returned to Norfolk; but on the 8th of May she found the *Monitor*, with the ironclad *Galena* and other vessels, shelling the Confederate batteries at Sewall's Point. These ships retired, and again the *Merrimac* was disappointed.

Next day, while she lay at anchor off Sewall's Point, Norfolk was evacuated by the Confederates, and it was decided that the *Merrimac* must be destroyed, in order to keep her out of the hands of the Federals. The crew were therefore conveyed ashore and Catesby Jones set her alight; she was soon ablaze and subsequently blew up.

The *Merrimac's* crew then went to Richmond and, learning that the Federal fleet was now about to attack that place, they were moved down the James River, and took up a position in the batteries about seven miles below the city ; this was their last action with the *Monitor*. On the 15th of May, the *Monitor*, *Galena* and other ships arrived and came into action with the batteries ; but, making no impression on them, the enemy subsequently retired. Lieutenant John Taylor Wood, of the *Merrimac*, expressed the opinion that " The *Merrimac's* crew alone barred his way to Richmond." [1]

One of the points revealed by the remarkable action between the *Monitor* and the *Merrimac* was the fact that considerable inconvenience was caused by the small distance which separated the *Monitor's* turret from the pilot-house ; this meant that the turret-guns had not an all-round fire, and were unable to fire ahead, owing to the pilot-house being in the way ; the voice-pipe was cut by a shot during the action, thus rendering communication difficult. These drawbacks are said to have been afterwards overcome by a proposal which came from her First Assistant Engineer, who bore the scientific name of Isaac Newton ; he suggested that the pilot-house should be placed on top of the turret. This was done in subsequent vessels of the monitor class, but had already been considered by Ericsson, who was unable to arrange this in the case of the first *Monitor*, owing to the turret-roof having insufficient strength to bear the weight of the pilot-house, through the haste with which his ship had to be completed.

Owing to the success which attended the performance of the first *Monitor*, a number of sea-going ships of this class were built by Ericsson. In each case the pilot-house was placed on top of the turret, and in more than one the ship had two turrets on the centre-line. Among them were the *Weehawken, Passaic, Saugus, Montauk, Catskill, Nahant, Patapsco, Nantucket, Tecumseh, Monadnock, Mahopac, Canonicus* and *Dictator*. They at once attracted attention in Russia, whose Emperor ordered twelve to be built, according to the original plans ; Sweden and Norway, followed by Turkey, acted on similar lines. Rear-Admiral Dahlgren [2] is best known through the gun which bears his name. He was in charge of the Federal fleet, which blockaded Charleston in 1863, and here the prowess of the monitors was not remarkable ; but on the whole they proved themselves to be eminently successful. The term " monitor " became applied later to a smallish vessel of low freeboard, with a turret containing one or two heavy guns.

The gunboats of the Western Flotilla were soon ready for action again and, the enemy having now retired some fifty miles below Columbus,

---

[1] " Battles and Leaders of the Civil War." *Century Magazine*, March, 1885.
[2] The rank of Rear-Admiral was established during 1862.

PLATE XXXV

THE *ONONDAGA* ON JAMES RIVER IN THE CIVIL WAR

One of Ericsson's monitors.   In this case the ship has two turrets.   The
U.S.S. *Onondaga* remained in the U.S. Naval service for some years
following the Civil War.

"ADMIRAL FARRAGUT'S FLAGSHIP HARTFORD"

PLATE XXXVI

ADMIRAL FARRAGUT'S FLAGSHIP *HARTFORD*

The *Hartford* was Admiral Farragut's flagship in the operations during which he took New Orleans and subsequently carried his flag at the Battle of Mobile Bay.

they proceeded down river towards an island known as " Island Number Ten," where he was known to have taken up a strong position ; they were accompanied by some mortar-boats and troop-transports. Island Number Ten was near New Madrid, at a loop in the river ; New Madrid itself was occupied by the Federal troops, under General Pope, who intended to cross from New Madrid to the east bank of the river, and required the assistance of some gunboats in his attempt.

On the 15th of March, the flotilla arrived above Island Number Ten, and found a line of Confederate batteries on and below the bluff along the crescent-shaped east bank, and heavy batteries also on the island, so disposed as to command the river against an advance from the north. Two days later the flotilla engaged the batteries on the east bank. The *Benton*, bearing the flag of Flag-Officer Foote, was lashed between the *Cincinnati* and the *St. Louis*, and proceeded down the east bank, the *Carondelet*, *Pittsburgh* and *Mound City* being on the west. All the guns in the upper battery were silenced as a result of this attack. For over a fortnight the bombardment, in which the mortar-boats co-operated, continued at intervals, but without dislodging the Confederates from their positions.

Meantime the Navy co-operated with the Army in cutting a canal through the loop of the river, on its west bank, so as to short-circuit Number Ten, and through this canal the tugs and transports for General Pope's army reached New Madrid, which was immediately below it. It was quite clear that the bombardment by the gunboats was insufficient to dislodge the enemy, and means had to be found of getting one or two gunboats past Island Number Ten, in order to assist General Pope. Time was pressing, for the Confederates were known to have several gunboats in the lower reaches, and to have some powerful vessels, including the *Arkansas*, under construction ; if these ascended the river, great damage might be done to Pope's batteries, on the west bank below the city.

Commander Walke, of the *Carondelet*, volunteered to run the gauntlet, and it was decided that an attempt should be made to pass Island Number Ten. Hawsers and chain-cables were placed around the pilot-house and other more vulnerable portions of his ship, and the decks were covered with all sorts of material, as a protection against plunging shot ; also a coal-barge, loaded with coal and hay, was lashed to the port side, that being nearest to the batteries on the east bank.

At ten o'clock on the night of the 4th of April, the vessel started down stream. The moon had gone down, and a thunderstorm made the night more than usually dark, except for occasional flashes of lightning. The batteries on the east bank saw the vessel, and opened fire, but with little effect ; and as the *Carondelet* passed Island Number Ten, she was so close to it that she almost grazed the island, whose batteries were not able to depress their guns sufficiently to hit her, and nearly all their shot passed

U.S. Gunboat " Carondelet."

harmlessly over the vessel. She still had to pass a floating battery, but the fire from this also was ineffective, and the *Carondelet* arrived at New Madrid, almost unscathed, at about midnight.

On the 6th a reconnaissance was made down river by the *Carondelet*, whose ship's company captured and spiked the guns of a Confederate battery below the city. The enemy then prepared to evacuate his positions on Island Number Ten. The *Pittsburgh*, under the command of Lieut.-Commander Thompson, ran the gauntlet the same night, also in a thunderstorm, and Island number Ten surrendered to Flag-Officer Foote at about the same time, the remainder of the Confederates retiring before General Pope's advance, and being captured by his army subsequently.

The Confederate flotilla was known as the " River Defense " ; five gunboats of this force came into contact with the Federal flotilla a week later, but had to retire before it on Fort Pillow, above Memphis. The mortar-boats were most annoying to the enemy, who tried to capture them, but without success ; a force was landed by General Pope near Fort Pillow, and an attack on this place was projected, but was given up, his army being ordered elsewhere. Flag-Officer Foote was now obliged, owing to wounds and ill-health, to give up his command, dying in the year following. On the 9th of May, he was succeeded by Flag-Officer Davis.

Two battles followed, those of Fort Pillow and Memphis ; in both engagements hard blows were given and taken on either side. On the 10th of May, there was a slight fog, and a mortar-boat was towed down stream to bombard Fort Pillow, the *Cincinnati* accompanying her, when six Confederate " rams " were suddenly espied coming up river at full speed. The *Carondelet* and *Pittsburgh* at once got under way, and went to the support of the *Cincinnati*, followed by the rest of the flotilla. The ram *General Bragg* was ahead of the remaining Confederate vessels and attacked the *Cincinnati*, ramming her, and compelling her to retire out of action ; the *General Bragg* also drifted down stream, disabled ; the *General Price* and *General Sumter* also rammed the *Cincinnati*. The *Carondelet* engaged these three rams, and disabled all of them, while the *Pittsburgh* went to the aid of the *Mound City*, which had been rammed by the Confederate vessel *Van Dorn* ; she afterwards sank. The engagement had lasted a little over an hour, and the enemy retired, as a result ; long-range fire was then maintained on Fort Pillow, which was evacuated on the 4th of June.

The flotilla then proceeded down to Memphis, now accompanied by seven Federal rams, under Colonel Ellet, and anchored at " Island Number Forty-Five," a little above the city. On the 6th of June, the Confederate flotilla was seen to be lying off that place, and was at once attacked by the rams *Queen of the West* and *Monarch*, which sank one of the enemy and disabled another. The rams were followed by Flag-Officer Davis and the gunboats, who opened fire. The *Queen of the West* was now rammed by the *Beauregard* which, in attacking the *Monarch*, collided with the *General Price*, disabling her ; the *Monarch* then rammed and sank the *Beauregard*. The *General Lovell* was also sunk by the Federals, and the remainder of the Confederate flotilla was run ashore, only the *Van Dorn* escaping down river.

Memphis was taken, with the Confederate Navy Yard, containing the sister-ship of the *Arkansas*, which was on the stocks ; a large quantity of cotton was also captured, and the Mississippi was cleared down to the southern border of Tennessee. The splitting of the Confederacy had commenced.

CHAPTER VIII

THE CIVIL WAR (continued)

THE opening of the Lower Mississippi was entrusted to Flag-Officer David Glasgow Farragut. In November, 1861, it had been decided to capture New Orleans, but no attempt had been made previously to do more than blockade the mouth of the river, and the Confederates had in the meantime built powerful forts on the lower reaches of the Mississippi, nearly as far north as Memphis.

In 1862 a plan was formed whereby the Navy and Army were to take and hold New Orleans and, as soon as that was accomplished, to push up the river to Vicksburg, which was strongly fortified ; Flag-Officer Davis, with the Western Flotilla, which was then above Vicksburg, was to join hands with the Navy ships, thus clearing the Mississippi completely.

Farragut was a Southerner, and the South used their best endeavours to retain his services, but he remained loyal to the Union and, before his departure from Norfolk to New York, he is said to have observed to some Confederate officers : " Mind what I tell you : You fellows will catch the devil before you get through with this business." His parents had shown considerable kindness to the family of Captain David Porter, of the *Essex*, who adopted Farragut as his son, and took him to sea, where he was present at the famous action with the *Phœbe* and the *Cherub*. Both Farragut and Porter's son, David Dixon Porter, greatly distinguished

themselves during the Civil War, and Farragut was over sixty years of age when the operations on the Lower Mississippi commenced.

Confederate Ram " Manassas."   Advantage of the delay had been taken by the Confederates, not only in building forts, but also in constructing vessels for the defence of the Mississippi. The ram *Manassas* was already complete, and the ironclads *Louisiana* and *Arkansas* were building ; a number of tugs and converted merchant vessels were also used in this connection. Farragut's squadron consisted of the flagship *Hartford*, of twenty-five guns, and sixteen other ships and gunboats ; in addition he had a mortar-flotilla, under Commander David D. Porter, numbering six ships and several mortar-schooners ; the last-named had their masts well camouflaged with branches of trees secured to them. Farragut might also have had the services of the *Colorado*, a fifty-gun frigate, but it was found that she could not be lightened sufficiently to cross the bar at the mouth of the river.

PLATE XXXVII

THE SPLENDID NAVAL TRIUMPH ON THE MISSISSIPPI, April 24th, 1862

Currier and Ives Print

The ships are here seen forcing their way past the two forts at the entrance to the Mississippi. The *Hartford*, with Farragut's flag at the fore, is seen in the foreground.

PLATE XXXVIII

ADMIRAL PORTER'S FLEET RUNNING THE REBEL BLOCKADE
OF THE MISSISSIPPI AT VICKSBURG, April 16th, 1863

Currier and Ives Print

"At half-past ten p.m. the boats left their moorings and steamed down the river, the *Benton*, Admiral Porter, taking the lead. As they approached the point opposite the town, a terrible concentrated fire of the centre, upper and lower batteries, both water and bluff, was directed upon the channel, which here ran within one hundred yards of the shore. At the same moment

On the 18th of March, 1862, the mortar-flotilla crossed the bar, also the *Hartford* and *Brooklyn* ; Farragut had great difficulty in bringing the remainder of his squadron over, owing to their deep draught, but at last he succeeded. Two forts guarded the lower Mississippi : Fort Jackson on the right bank and Fort St. Philip on the left. The mortar-vessels were anchored under cover of the right bank, and on the 16th of April the ships were moved up to within three miles of the forts, that is to say, about a mile astern of the mortar-vessels.

Fire was opened on the 18th of April and continued all day, the Confederates replying. At sunset the latter ceased fire and Fort Jackson was seen to be in flames, but it continued firing next day. During the night the mortar-vessels renewed the bombardment, which continued night and day until the morning of the 24th. On the 20th, two steamers, the *Pinola* and *Itasca*, under Captain H. H. Bell, went up river to break the chain cable which extended across the river ; they succeeded in doing this near the left bank, despite a hot fire from Fort Jackson, and at two o'clock in the morning of the 24th of April, Farragut was ready to advance, past the forts ; chain cables had been hung over the ship's sides, as a protection to the engines, and other precautions were taken against the enemy's shot.

Farragut's force was divided into three divisions, of which the van consisted of eight ships, under Captain Bailey, in the gunboat *Cayuga*, and the rear of six ships under Captain Bell, in the *Sciota* ; Farragut himself had the centre division, with three ships, the *Hartford*, *Brooklyn* and *Richmond*. The squadron got under way about half-past two, making a considerable noise with their anchor-chains, and putting the Confederate troops on the alert ; the current was very strong and their progress against it was slow, so that Captain Bailey's ship, which was leading, did not come under fire till nearly three. The enemy's gunboats made some attempt at resistance, but were driven off. The mortar-flotilla meantime was detailed to keep up a bombardment of the forts, while the squadron passed them.

The escaping gunboats were pursued by the *Varuna*, Commander Charles S. Boggs, which outstripped the remainder of the first division, and found herself in the midst of the hostile vessels. As day broke, she was attacked by the *Governor Moore*, a vessel fitted as a ram, and was then rammed by the *Stonewall Jackson* ; she subsequently sank, her crew being rescued by the *Oneida*, Captain Lee. The two Confederate rams were then set on fire by their crews, who abandoned them. Captain Bailey's division had now passed the forts, which had maintained a heavy bombardment throughout.

Farragut's flagship, the *Hartford*, accompanied by the *Brooklyn* and *Richmond*, formed the centre as mentioned ; the *Richmond* passed the forts without much difficulty. Farragut engaged Fort St. Philip at close quarters and drove out its defenders, but a fire-raft, pushed by the Confederate tug *Mosner*, was seen coming down the river and, in trying to avoid it, the *Hartford* ran onto a shoal ; the fire-raft came alongside, and for a time the *Hartford* was in grave danger of being set on fire. The flames however were subdued, the flagship was refloated and passed on with little damage. The *Brooklyn* followed, and was attacked by the ram *Manassas*, which rammed her twice, but without causing her any injury, owing to the chain cables which had been hung over the *Brooklyn's* sides.

Captain Bell, in the *Sciota*, brought the third division past with little trouble, so demoralized had the garrisons of the forts become by this time. The *Itasca*, *Winona* and *Kennebec*, however, were slow steamers ; they became a target for the enemy's guns and were obliged to fall back on Commander Porter's mortar-flotilla. During this action the *Manassas* had rammed the *Hartford*, *Brooklyn* and *Mississippi*. Farragut ordered the last-named ship to run her down ; she tried to do so, but failed, and the *Manassas* then ran herself ashore and subsequently blew up. Lieutenant Dewey, afterwards a famous Admiral, was executive officer of the paddle-frigate *Mississippi* on this occasion.

Flag-Officer Farragut had now passed the forts of the Lower Mississippi and was proceeding up river towards New Orleans. In the meantime Porter, in the *Harriet Lane*, remained below the forts, in order to keep an eye on the Confederate ships *Louisiana*, *McRae* and *Defiance*, still in that neighbourhood. On the 25th of April Commander Porter sent a flag of truce to Fort Jackson, demanding the surrender of both forts. General Duncan, who was the Confederate officer in command, replied that he could not do this, until he heard from New Orleans ; whereupon Porter ordered a rapid fire on Fort Jackson, and on the 27th the Confederates announced their readiness to capitulate.

An awkward incident occurred during the discussions which followed, on board the *Harriet Lane*. The ironclad *Louisiana* was reported to be drifting down the river in flames ; fortunately she blew up before reaching the Federal vessels, and the proceedings continued undisturbed. Forts Jackson and St. Philip surrendered to Commander Porter's force, and were then occupied by the Federal troops, who had now arrived. When Farragut arrived before New Orleans, Captain Bailey and Lieutenant Perkins were sent ashore to demand its surrender, and the Louisiana State flag was hauled down over the City Hall and replaced by the Stars and Stripes at about the end of April, 1862.

The Upper and Lower Mississippi were now in the hands of the Federals ; the seizure of the centre portion was also a matter of some difficulty, owing to the resistance of the town of Vicksburg, which has been called by some the " Gibraltar of the Mississippi." The first attack on the place by Farragut's squadron was not successful ; he passed through, however, and effected a junction with Davis's Western Flotilla, above the town ; he was obliged to retire again towards New Orleans, engaging the Confederate ram *Arkansas* on the way. The famous *Monitor* now made a brief reappearance in history ; for she was unfortunately sunk in a gale off Cape Hatteras, foundering with the loss of two officers and twelve men at the end of 1862.

On the 29th of December, 1862, the paddle-steamer *Rhode Island* left Hampton Roads for Charleston, with the *Monitor* in tow. The weather was stormy with a westerly wind, and by the time the two vessels were off Cape Henry, waves were breaking all over the *Monitor*. By noon the next day the wind had backed to S.S.W. and had increased to gale force and, when night fell, the ships were off Cape Hatteras and were pitching and rolling in an alarming manner. At eight o'clock at night the *Monitor* was taking in water in such quantities that the small pumps could not cope with it, and the main pump had to be set going ; the coal was now so wet that steam-pressure had gone down considerably.

Half an hour later distress signals were made to the *Rhode Island* ; this ship then slowed down, and the *Monitor* rode more comfortably ; but the tow-lines had to be cast off, and they fouled a paddle-wheel of the *Rhode Island*. The *Monitor* now stopped her own engines, and used all her steam for the pumps. At ten-thirty the anchor was let go, in sixty fathoms, and as the cable tore out the packing in the hawse-hole, the water came in with redoubled force.

Eventually there was nothing for it but to abandon ship and endeavour to reach the *Rhode Island*, which was standing by, pitching and rolling to the enormous seas. A boat succeeded in making the difficult passage on two occasions, and shortly after starting on its third journey, the lights of the *Monitor* had disappeared. The *Rhode Island* cruised about all night without finding any sign of her, and then returned to Hampton Roads with the survivors of her crew.

At the beginning of the war there were seventy-two Captains in the United States Navy, and such an officer, when in command of a squadron, was recognized as a Commodore ; after 1857 he was given the title of Flag-Officer ; Captain was therefore the highest *permanent* rank. In 1862 the rank of Commodore was introduced [1] ; several Rear-Admirals were also appointed, and the rank of Lieutenant-Commander was instituted.

In October, 1862, Rear-Admiral David D. Porter was appointed to command the Mississippi Squadron in place of Rear-Admiral Davis, and in December another attempt was made to capture Vicksburg ; the squadron co-operated with the Army under General Sherman, and again

[1] This rank has been subsequently discontinued.

the attack was unsuccessful. The Mississippi, from Vicksburg down to Baton Rouge, was still in the hands of the Southerners. The port of Galveston, in Texas, was taken by the Federals in October and retaken by the Confederates in January, 1863 ; Farragut's attempt to recapture it was unsuccessful.

On the 14th of March, Rear-Admiral Farragut determined, in conjunction with General Banks, to advance past Port Hudson, on the Mississippi, and cut it off from supplies.   He started off with the *Hartford* and six other ships, and passed Port Hudson, losing the *Mississippi* on the way, and succeeded in getting up as far as the Red River, which he blockaded ; Baton Rouge and several other towns surrendered to the Federal forces. The only Confederate ram now in service on the lower Mississippi was the

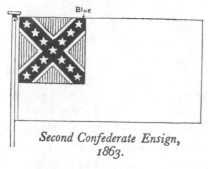

Second Confederate Ensign, 1863.

Arkansas, and she was destroyed by the Federal gunboat *Essex* on the 5th of April.

The Confederates had employed a red " battle flag " with their armies ; this flag was charged with a blue saltire, fimbriated with white and bearing thirteen white stars. On the 1st of May, 1863, the flag was used in the Confederate States Navy as a jack, replacing the jack of 1861, and a new ensign was employed, of plain white and having this design as a first quarter.

Vicksburg was now besieged by the Federal Army, and a third naval attack on the place was made on the night of the 15th of April, 1863. A few nights previously the rams *Switzerland* and *Lancaster* had run the gauntlet past Vicksburg, the *Lancaster* being sunk ; the *Switzerland* got through and joined Farragut's blockade of the Red River. On the 15th of April, the gunboats started down the Mississippi and, as they passed the batteries at Vicksburg, a lively interchange of gunfire took place ; they all got through and arrived at Carthage, below the town. Grand Gulf was captured, and Admiral Porter then joined Admiral Farragut at the Red River on the 3rd of May ; Porter went up the river, destroying several forts and capturing Alexandria.

The gunboat *Cincinnati* was sunk in a further attack on Vicksburg on the 27th of May, and the co-operation of the Navy with the Army, under General Grant, finally resulted in the capture of the town on the 4th of July ; Port Hudson also surrendered. The squadrons of the Upper and Lower Mississippi were now able to combine, the river was opened, and the Confederacy was split in two. Galveston was taken by Farragut shortly afterwards.

Charleston was still being employed by Confederate blockade runners and an attempt was made to capture this port early in 1863. In April

PLATE XXXIX

ADMIRAL FARRAGUT
The seated figure is Admiral Farragut, famous leader of the Federal
naval forces in the Civil War. After the War Farragut was made full
admiral, dying in 1870. Standing by him is Admiral Watson.

PLATE XL

KEARSARGE AND *ALABAMA*, 1864

From an original drawing by W. F. Mitchell

In the summer of 1864, the Confederate raider *Alabama* put into Cherbourg. Here she was surprised by the Federal ship *Kearsarge*, with which she fought an action. The *Alabama* was sunk. In the picture the yacht *Deerhound* is seen approaching to rescue survivors; the Confederate ensign has been hauled down.

Rear-Admiral Dupont, in the *New Ironsides*, and accompanied by a certain number of monitors, attacked the place. Fort Sumter was bombarded, but Dupont was forced to retire ; he was afterwards succeeded in command of the blockading squadron by Rear-Admiral Dahlgren, the inventor of the powerful gun which bore his name.

The monitors had more success two months later ; two of these vessels, the *Nahant* and *Weehawken*, were blockading the Wilmington River, in North Carolina, when they saw the Confederate ram *Atlanta* coming out. The *Weehawken* approached within three hundred yards and opened fire ; fifteen minutes later the *Atlanta* surrendered. Another attempt on Charleston was made in the same month, the military co-operating, under General Gillmore. One of the defending forts, Fort Wagner, was submitted to a continuous naval bombardment and to gallant assaults by the troops, but without success. Forts Wagner and Gregg were subsequently evacuated and Fort Sumter reduced to ruins ; operations against Charleston itself then ceased for the time being, but the port was definitely closed to blockade-runners by the end of 1863.

Another monitor was lost to the Federal Navy at the end of 1863, by the foundering of the *Weehawken* in a heavy sea, off Charleston. The " Davids " now made themselves felt. During the summer of 1863 a physician named Dr. St. Julien Ravenel [1] bought an old locomotive boiler, and conveyed it to his property about thirty miles inland from Charleston. Here he converted it into a cigar-shaped boat, fifty feet long and seven feet in diameter. It carried a steam-engine and, when launched, it was submerged, except for the funnel and a coaming round the hatch. A fourteen-foot hollow shaft projected forward, below the water-line, to which was attached a " spar torpedo."

Then the boat was taken to Charleston and launched and, on the night of the 5th of October, 1863, Lieutenant W. T. Glassell and three men of the Confederate States Navy took her down harbour, to where the Federal armoured ship *New Ironsides* was lying ; she ran at this ship at full speed and blew a large rent in her side, but without sinking her. The " David's " machinery was put out of action, and the crew swam for safety. Glassell and the fireman were captured ; the pilot and engineer swam back, succeeded in getting the boat going again, and returned safely to Charleston.

On the night of the 17th of February, 1864, the new wooden ship *Housatonic* was attacked by one of these vessels ; the *Housatonic* was sunk, and no trace was found of her aggressor. When divers were sent down subsequently, they found the " David " sticking in the hole which she had made in the ship's side, and on board her the corpses of the nine gallant men of her crew.

[1] *Reader's Digest.* December, 1941.

After the fall of Vicksburg, it was decided to send a naval and military expedition up the Red River, as far as Shreveport, in Louisiana. In February, 1864, Rear-Admiral Porter had about twenty vessels, ready for the attempt, at the junction of the Red River and the Mississippi, his flag being in the gunboat *Black Hawk*. The gunboats started on the 12th of March, followed by transports and, after encountering various difficulties and obstructions, arrived at Alexandria a few days later. From here they went up river, over the " Falls," in support of the troops. On the 11th of April, General Banks was defeated at Sabine Cross Roads and compelled to retire ; the gunboats conformed, fighting their way back, with the loss of one vessel, the *Eastport*. The river was now very low, and the " Falls " provided an effective obstruction to their further retirement.

It was then decided to construct a dam across the river, thus raising the level of the stream above it. The work was carried out in about eight days by the Navy and Army in co-operation ; finally an opening was made in its centre, wide enough for a vessel to pass, and between the 9th and 11th of May, the gunboats, which had been lightened of their guns and armour, passed through, and so down the rapids to safety. The gunboats then returned to their stations on the Mississippi River.

So far as the sea was concerned, the greatest damage to the Federal side during the war was caused by the Confederate commerce-destroyers. There were a great number of these, and they included the *Sumter, Georgia, Tallahassee, Chickamauga, Nashville* and *Retribution*. Some of the commerce-destroyers had been built or fitted out in Great Britain, and other help rendered to them ; at the close of the war, therefore, a claim was made by the United States Government against Great Britain for the amount of the damage caused by them. The ships in question were the *Alabama, Shenandoah, Florida, Sallie* and *Boston*.

Most damage was done by the *Alabama* and *Shenandoah*, and this was estimated at nearly four-fifths of the whole amount. An international tribunal was set up at Geneva in 1871, to consider the matter, and the " Alabama Claims " were fixed at a sum of a little over $15,000,000 ; they were amicably settled in the following year.

The *Alabama* was the ship which attracted most attention, possibly on account of her fight with the *Kearsarge*, which terminated her career. She was built by Lairds, of Birkenhead, and Captain Raphael Semmes was her commanding officer ; he had previously commanded the *Sumter*, which went into Gibraltar in June, 1861, and was there blockaded by the *Tuscarora, Ino* and the famous *Kearsarge* ; she was sold early in 1862. The *Alabama*, known at first as " 290," sailed from the Mersey on the 28th of July on a supposed trial trip, and put into a bay on the Welsh coast, where many of her crew joined her ; she then sailed round the north of Ireland and arrived in about a fortnight's time at the island of Terceira in the Azores. Here she was joined by a British ship, which brought out her guns and other war material. The Portuguese governor would not allow the work of fitting her out to be done in port, and some difficulty was experienced in carrying this out outside the three-mile limit. Eventually it was accomplished ; the *Bahama* arrived, bringing Captain Semmes and his officers, and the vessel became the Confederate States ship *Alabama*.

In the summer of 1862 she sailed from Terceira on her first voyage ; on a bright Sunday morning she left the island, in company with the *Bahama*. The officers, some of whom had been at Annapolis Naval Academy, were in full uniform, and the band played a Southern air ; the crew were mustered and numbered about one hundred and forty ; they were mostly experienced seamen, though throughout the voyage they showed themselves to be somewhat unruly. With steam and sail the *Alabama*, in favourable circumstances, was able to make fifteen knots having very fine lines ; she drew fifteen feet of water and was barquentine-rigged. The armament consisted of eight guns ; one rifled hundred-pound Blakeley gun, pivoted forward, and one eight-inch sixty-eight-pounder pivoted abaft the main mast ; there were also six thirty-two-pounder broadside pieces.

She took her first prize near the Azores on the 3rd of September—a whaling schooner ; she destroyed a number of whaling vessels in these latitudes, and then went northwards, towards the shipping lanes, where a number of grain ships fell victims. In one of the prizes the crew found a deserter from the commerce-destroyer *Sumter*, who was suitably dealt with, but proved to be a somewhat mutinous subject ; it was extremely difficult to maintain discipline on board, and fights used to break out, especially when the men had been amusing themselves ashore ; these drawbacks were not improved by the overcrowded state of the ship, and the need for providing accommodation for prisoners, when ships had been captured or destroyed.

Course was now set for Sandy Hook, and on the 16th of October, when off the Newfoundland Banks, the *Alabama* lost one of her yards in a gale, and decided to go down to a milder climate farther south. On the 18th of November she arrived at Martinique where she had a sympathetic reception from the French ; a few days later, she learned that the *San Jacinto* was outside, waiting for her. The crew wanted to fight, but the orders from the Confederate Government were to capture or destroy merchant shipping, and fighting a warship was regarded as no part of her duties. She succeeded in escaping from Martinique, and in getting to Blanquilla, where she coaled and put the mutinous deserter ashore. Puerto Rico was the next place to be visited ; thence she sailed through the Mona Passage, between Santo Domingo and Puerto Rico, and here she made a prize, the twentieth since the commencement of the voyage ; this prize she had to let go, under bond.

Arcas Keys, an island in the Bay of Campeche, was her next port of call, and thence she worked round the west coast of the Gulf of Mexico towards Galveston. From captured mails it was learned that General Banks was going to attack that place, and also to invade Texas ; Galveston was now in Confederate hands, and Captain Semmes, who had re-coaled and re-fitted at Arcas Keys, hoped to strike a blow for his side by attacking Banks's transports, while they were lying off the port. He calculated the time of Banks's arrival, and stood in for Galveston accordingly early in January, 1863.

Rather to his surprise, he found five warships in the port, one of which came out after the *Alabama*, which retired ; the warship approached to within hail, when the Confederate ship let her have the starboard broadside at fifty yards' range. She replied, but it was evident that her armament was weaker than that of her opponent and, after ten minutes' engagement, she was seen to be sinking and went down stern first. She proved to be the *Hatteras*, of four thirty-two-pounder guns ; all her ship's company were rescued and taken to Kingston, Jamaica, where they were paroled. This was the *Alabama's* first naval engagement.

From Jamaica she went to the coast of Santo Domingo, where she was nearly the victim of an accidental outbreak of fire, and then south, through the Mona Passage, and up again to a point south of the Azores Islands, capturing prizes all the time ; thence south again to the coast of Brazil. After some time spent in the South Atlantic, she headed across from the latitude of Rio de Janeiro, to the Cape of Good Hope, where she arrived in July ; on the way an amusing incident occurred : she tried to stop a British warship, H.M.S. *Diomede*, taking her for a Federal merchant vessel ; the *Diomede* took no notice of her warning gun, and the mistake was then discovered.

At Cape Town was the Federal ship *Vanderbilt*, whose captain announced his intention of running down the *Alabama* ; the latter however escaped thence at night, in a south-easterly gale, and stood east, hoisting her propeller and proceeding under sail. She passed by St. Paul Island, and then headed northwards for the Straits of Sunda, making no captures on this part of the voyage. The China seas were more productive of prizes, so much so that Federal trade in those parts was almost paralysed, and ships used to stay in port, for safety, leaving the carrying trade to neutrals. Here she met the Federal warship *Wyoming*, but managed to avoid action and arrived at Singapore on the 22nd of December.

From Singapore she sailed through the Straits of Malacca to the south of India and thence, through the Mozambique Channel, back to the Cape, making two captures on the way ; from the Cape she went over again to the coast of Brazil. Semmes anticipated that some day he would have to fight another action with a Federal warship, and one of the prizes captured off the coast of Brazil was converted into a target, on which good practice was made with the *Alabama's* guns.

She had now made over sixty captures and was badly in need of docking ; course was set for the neutral port of Cherbourg, with this intention. The ship arrived at Cherbourg on the 11th of June, 1864, and four days later, while she was awaiting permission to dock, the Federal ship *Kearsarge* entered the port.

The *Kearsarge* had been at Flushing, where she received a telegram telling of the arrival of the *Alabama*, and at once

U.S. Frigate " Kearsarge."

set out to capture or sink her. She was a barque-rigged steamer, commanded by Captain John A. Winslow ; she carried a larger crew than the Confederate ship ; also her guns, though less in number, were heavier. Semmes decided to engage her, as soon as the *Alabama* had coaled ship, and everything was got ready for action. The *Kearsarge* left Cherbourg and patrolled up and down the coast, about five miles off the breakwater.

On Sunday, the 19th of June, the *Alabama* came out of port and made for the Federal warship. The crew of the *Kearsarge* were assembling for church service when the *Alabama* appeared ; the drum beat to quarters, the ship was cleared for action, and headed out to sea. The French ironclad frigate *Couronne* escorted the Confederate vessel to the limit of territorial waters, and a small British steam yacht, the *Deerhound*, also came out.

About seven miles out at sea, the Federal ship turned and presented her starboard battery ; the *Alabama* did the same, the two being now on opposite courses. Broadsides were exchanged, and Captain Winslow then put his helm over, with the intention of passing under his adversary's stern, and raking her ; she avoided this manœuvre by putting her own helm over, with the result that the two ships circled round each other, still presenting their starboard broadsides, and being carried westwards by the tide.

The *Kearsarge* poured in her eleven-inch shells with deadly effect and only had three men wounded, during the engagement, whereas the *Alabama* suffered heavily in killed and wounded. Once a shot from the Federal ship carried away her spanker-gaff, with the ensign, but this was hoisted again at the mizen, and the fight went on. The *Alabama* now took on a heavy list to starboard, and it was clear that she was doomed. Her captain decided to set all sail as soon as the ship's bows headed again for the French coast ; but she was then in a sinking condition, and was obliged to surrender. She sank soon afterwards, stern first.

Captain Winslow did everything possible to rescue the survivors, in which the steam yacht *Deerhound* co-operated, and Captain Semmes and some of his men were saved by the *Deerhound's* boats, and escaped to England.

Thus ended the career of the best-known of the Confederate commerce-destroyers ; but there was another which, in spite of the immense damage which she caused, is rather less known. This was the *Sea King*, later known as the *Shenandoah* ; her activities took place largely in the Pacific Ocean. On the 8th of October, 1864, she cleared from London for Bombay, as an ordinary merchant ship ; but a few days later she was joined by another vessel, which put her guns and other equipment on board. She was now the commerce-destroyer *Shenandoah*, commanded by Commander James J. Waddell, of the Confederate States Navy. She cruised for some time in the Atlantic, then going to Australia ; she subsequently went to the Pacific and as far as the Bering Straits, where she destroyed a large number of whaling ships. Her activities continued until the Spring of 1865, when hostilities between the North and South had ceased.

Mobile Bay, in Alabama, was a port much used by the blockade-runners ; this was a large harbour, protected from the direction of the sea by two forts, Fort Morgan on the east side of the entrance and Fort Gaines on the west. Until these two forts could be reduced, Mobile Bay remained open to the Confederates. Farragut began to bombard the forts in February, 1864, but decided to wait until he received the help of some monitors, before attempting to enter the harbour. Inside this harbour were some Confederate vessels, including the formidable ram *Tennessee*, commanded by Flag-Officer Franklin Buchanan ; this ship arrived in Mobile Bay during the month of May.

By the 5th of August, four monitors had arrived, the *Tecumseh*, *Manhattan*, *Winnebago* and *Chickasaw*. Farragut had fourteen ships in his force, excluding the monitors. These ships were lashed together in pairs, and proceeded into the harbour in line ahead on the early morning of the 5th, the monitors being disposed abeam to starboard, that is on the side nearest Fort Morgan. The flagship *Hartford*, having the *Metacomet* lashed to her port side, took the second place, the *Brooklyn* (and *Octarara*) leading the line.

The fleet passed close to Fort Morgan and a fierce exchange of fire began and continued while it was slowly passing the fort ; just as it came abreast of it, the monitor *Tecumseh* struck a " torpedo " and sank immediately. The *Brooklyn*, anticipating that the fleet was running into what we should call a " mine-field," stopped and went astern. Farragut at once gave the order to his flag-captain : " Pass the *Brooklyn* and take the lead," followed shortly after by a hail to the *Brooklyn* of : " Damn the torpedoes! Follow me." The ships engaged the ram *Tennessee* and three Confederate gunboats, which were behind Fort Morgan, and then passed up the harbour and anchored.

During this part of the fight the three Confederate gunboats *Morgan*, *Gaines* and *Selma* were put out of action or forced to retire; no sooner was the fleet anchored than the *Tennessee* moved up harbour to attack it. The fleet got under way again and the ships closed round the *Tennessee*; the *Monongahela*, the *Lackawanna* and *Hartford* rammed her, without any apparent effect, but damaging their bows severely in the attempt, and the *Lackawanna* collided with the *Hartford*. Meanwhile the *Tennessee* was being submitted to an intense fire from the whole fleet, and soon afterwards she surren-dered; Flag-Officer Buchanan was badly wounded, but otherwise her casualties were light. Fort Gaines was bombarded on the 6th of August by the *Chickasaw*, and this was so effective that the fort

A Monitor.

surrendered two days later; with the aid of the military forces Fort Morgan was also taken later in the month.

The sounds of North Carolina were still being used by the blockade-runners; here the ram *Albemarle* had already disabled some of Captain Melancthon Smith's [1] gunboats. In October, 1864, Lieutenant W. B. Cushing, who had already been distinguished for gallantry, was given command of three steam torpedo-launches, armed with spar-torpedoes, and sent to Hampton Roads, to report to Rear-Admiral Porter, who was now in command of the North Atlantic Squadron. Two of these launches were lost on the way, through heavy weather; Cushing, in the third, succeeded in getting to Hampton Roads.

From here he proceeded by night towards Plymouth, in Albemarle Sound, where the *Albemarle* was lying; with great daring he came up to the ship, under an intense fire, and blew her up. The launch was sunk, while escaping, and Cushing swam ashore and, after great priva-tions, succeeded in getting back to safety. The sinking of the *Albemarle* opened the way for an attack on Plymouth, which was duly captured by Commander W. H. Macomb's flotilla early in November.

At the end of 1864 a large fleet had assembled in Hampton Roads, ready for an attack on Fort Fisher, which was on the Cape Fear River, leading up to Wilmington; this attack was to be made in co-operation with the military under General Butler. The first action taken was to send in a steamer, the *Louisiana*, full of powder, with the idea of blowing it up close to the fort. This perilous enterprise was undertaken by Commander Rhind, who succeeded in escaping with his men, after

[1] Formerly captain of the paddle-frigate *Mississippi*.

setting the fuzes ; the explosion took place, but without any appreciable results. This was on the night of the 23rd of December. On the 24th of December the fleet went in at daylight and engaged the fort ; on the next day the bombardment continued and the Army landed, but wa compelled to retire ; this attack was therefore unsuccessful.

In January, 1865, another attempt was made. The fleet went in in three columns ; the first was led by the *Brooklyn*, Captain Alden, the second by the *Minnesota*, Commodore Lanman, and the third by the *Santiago de Cuba*, Captain Glisson. There was also a reserve division under Lieutenant-Commander Upshur, making about fifty ships in all The *New Ironsides* and four monitors co-operated and opened fire within eight hundred yards of the fort ; the fleet anchored and did likewise, the bombardment continuing all that day. Next morning, the 15th of January the fleet again took up its positions and resumed the bombardment the troops, under General Terry, had been landed on the 13th, and these aided by a naval landing-party, succeeded in capturing the fort. The capture of Fort Fisher led to the surrender of Wilmington and, no doubt had an effect also on the defences of Charleston, which place was evacu ated by the Confederates on about the 18th of February.

Towards the end of this war an alteration was made in the design of the Confederate ensign. It was thought that the ensign of 1863 too closely resembled a flag of truce, and possibly that it bore some resem blance, at a distance, to the British white ensign which, in 1864, became the only ensign worn in the Royal Navy. On the 8th of March, 1863, therefore a broad vertical band of red was added to its outer edge. The decision of the Confederate Government was expressed in these terms : that the Union was " to have the ground red and a broad blue saltier thereon bordered with white and emblazoned with mullets, or five-pointed stars corresponding in number to that of the Confederate States ; the field to be white except the outer half from the union to be a red bar extending the width of the flag."

A joint naval and military attack under Rear-Admiral Thatcher and General Canby was made at the end of March on the city of Mobile, in Alabama, and the Stars and Stripes were hoisted over the City Hall in April. This concluded the activities of the U.S. Navy during the Civil War ; Richmond had been captured by the Federals and the surrende of General Lee at Appomattox Court House, in Virginia, brought the war to an end on the 9th of April, 1865.

Rear-Admiral Farragut was raised to the rank of full Admiral, which he held until his death, when he was succeeded by Admiral Porter, Rear Admiral Rowan becoming Vice-Admiral. These ranks existed in the U.S. Navy until 1875, when Rear-Admiral again became the highest rank, as it was in 1862.

PLATE XLI

U.S.S. *BROOKLYN* (ARMOURED CRUISER)

The *Brooklyn* was armed with eight 8-inch guns, in pairs, and twelve 5-inch; she had five torpedo tubes. She carried Commodore W. S. Schley's broad pendant in the operations off Cuba, being flagship of the Flying Squadron.

PLATE XLII

U.S.S. *OLYMPIA*

Protected cruiser, armed with four 8-inch guns and ten 5-inch ; six torpedo tubes.   The *Olympia* was Commodore Dewey's flagship at Manila, when he defeated the Spanish squadron under Admiral Montojo in May, 1898.

CHAPTER IX

WAR WITH SPAIN

THE United States Navy had not a powerful fleet at the commencement of the Civil War, and had to call in many of its ships on foreign stations, in order to maintain an adequate blockade and one which would satisfy neutral opinion ; after four years of war, the number of ships added to it was considerable. As soon as the war was over, the officers and men of the Confederate States Navy were placed on parole. The Confederate flags ceased to exist, and the Stars and Stripes became once more the flag of the whole country ; during the war Kansas, Nevada and West Virginia were added to the Union, and the number of the stars was increased in 1865 to thirty-six, one star being added subsequently whenever an additional State was admitted.

With the exception of the " Quasi-War " of 1798, France had always been friendly to the United States, who had not forgotten the help given by Lafayette, de Grasse and others during the War of Independence. Something closely resembling a threat to the Monroe Doctrine, however, occurred in 1863, when the United States were seriously embarrassed by the Civil War. In that year there were disorders in Mexico, and the Emperor Napoleon III supported with French bayonets a scheme to put the Austrian Archduke Maximilian on the throne of that country. The French troops were compelled to evacuate Mexico in 1867 ; the Emperor Maximilian was shot by the Mexicans, and the incident came to an end.

During the peace which followed the Civil War the United States gradually returned to normal. In the Navy, as in most navies, the period was one of transition, the wooden ships being replaced by steel and armoured, a change which was partly due to experience gained during the Civil War. In 1871 a difficulty arose in the Far East ; the inhabitants of Korea had been acting in a hostile manner towards the crews of American ships, and an attempt was made to conclude a treaty with Korea. With this intention the United States Minister to China went there with a small American squadron commanded by Rear-Admiral John Rodgers ; the flagship was the *Colorado*, and the other vessels were the *Alaska*, *Benecia*, *Monocacy* and *Palos*. The two last-named vessels were treacherously fired on by the Koreans ; whereupon a landing-party went ashore and, after severe fighting, captured the Koreans' main position. As a result friendly relations were established, a treaty was concluded with the United States in 1882, and in the year following with Great Britain also.

Again the United States played its part in Arctic exploration. In 1879 the steamer *Jeannette* set out for Polar Seas, the intention of the expedition being to explore the approaches to the North Pole by way of the Bering Strait. The ship was crushed in the ice and sank, and the explorers made their way over the pack towards the Siberian coast, but were all lost, some of the bodies being afterwards recovered. In 1881 Lieutenant Adolphus Washington Greely, of the U.S. Army, was selected to command an expedition, in order to make certain meteorological and other scientific investigations around the North Pole. The expedition went via Grinnell Land and reached what was at that time the farthest north, 83° 24′ North Latitude ; it got into difficulties, however, and had to be rescued, there being seven survivors. The relief expedition reached them in 1884, and consisted of the ships *Thetis*, *Bear* and *Alert* ; it was commanded by Commander W. S. Schley, U.S.N., who afterwards served as a Commodore in the Spanish War.

Trouble arose in Polynesia in 1889. The inhabitants of Samoa were engaging in tribal hostilities and the safety of other nationals was threatened. Warships of three Powers, Great Britain, the United States and the German Empire, were sent there, and the Germans showed themselves to be very difficult, coming into conflict especially with American interests. The harbour of Apia, in the principal island of the group, is a narrow anchorage, flanked by coral reefs and facing North ; here the international naval squadron was anchored. There were three American warships, the U.S.S. *Trenton*, *Vandalia* and *Nipsic*, under Rear-Admiral L. A. Kimberly in the *Trenton*. The Germans also had three ships, H.I.M.S. *Olga*, Captain von Ehrhardt, *Adler* and *Eber*. Great Britain was represented by H.M.S. *Calliope*, Captain Henry C. Kane, R.N. All these vessels were of moderate tonnage, being for the most part steam corvettes, of from twelve to fourteen knots speed.

On the 15th of March it came on to blow, and at midnight the wind went round to the north, thus putting the ships on a lee shore. H.M.S. *Calliope* raised steam in all boilers and steamed to her anchors, for by five in the morning the wind had increased to a hurricane. The ships began to drag their anchors ; H.I.M.S. *Eber* drifted onto a reef and sank ; H.I.M.S. *Olga* and the U.S.S. *Nipsic* collided and the *Nipsic* went ashore, as did H.I.M.S. *Adler* ; the *Olga's* anchors still held. H.M.S. *Calliope* had lowered her upper masts and lower yards, and as the U.S.S. *Vandalia* swung towards her, the lower fore yard fended her off. The seas were now " mountains high," and again the *Vandalia* collided with the *Calliope*, smashing her own quarter gallery and carrying away much of the *Calliope's* bowsprit gear.

During the forenoon of the 16th Captain Kane decided to make the attempt to get the *Calliope* to sea. The United States flagship *Trenton* was still lying to her anchors, though swept by the sea and with all fires extinguished, but in the narrow entrance to the harbour. With superb seamanship the *Calliope* was manœuvred past her, hardly making way against the immense seas, and at length succeeded in escaping from the harbour and into the open, the crew of the *Trenton* cheering her as she did so.

The weather improved, and three days later H.M.S. *Calliope* returned, much battered, to find that the other three vessels had all sunk or gone ashore ; she was the sole survivor of seven ships. Captain Kane wrote to Admiral Kimberly, who survived, condoling with him on the loss of his squadron and thanking him for his ship's greeting. The Admiral replied: " . . . in a time like this I can truly say with old Admiral Josiah Tatnall that ' blood *is* thicker than water ' ".[1] After the disaster at Apia the international difficulties there were smoothed out and, at the beginning of this century, Samoa came partly under the control of the United States, and partly under that of the German Empire.

At the end of the Civil War the U.S. Fleet was strong and numbered over six hundred ships, but in the years which followed it was allowed to become weak until, in 1882, it was thought well to reduce the Rear-Admirals' list to six ; the importance of sea-power seems to have been overlooked ; the mercantile marine also declined. In about 1890 the relative weakness of the United States Fleet was realized and a number of ships was built, which reflected the progress made at that date in armoured vessels ; with the result that, when war with Spain broke out, the U.S. Navy disposed of a number of up-to-date ships.

A difference of opinion with Great Britain arose in 1895. Venezuela was engaged in a frontier-dispute with that country over the boundary between British Guiana and Venezuelan Territory. President Cleveland saw in this dispute a possible threat to the Monroe Doctrine, perhaps through a fear that Great Britain might try to annex a portion of Venezuela. The question was referred to an Anglo-American commission and was settled without much difficulty.

Sentiments of an unfriendly character had existed between Spain and the United States at various dates, and the trouble came to a head when the disturbances in the island of Cuba, which was then Spanish, seemed to threaten the safety of American nationals there and the interests of the United States. In January, 1898, the U.S. battleship *Maine* was sent to Havana, and was blown up, three weeks later, while lying in the harbour, apparently by a mine ; this added to the delicacy of the

U.S.S. " Maine."

---

[1] *Sea Escapes and Adventures.* " Taffrail."

situation. Appropriate orders were sent to U.S. Navy ships in various parts of the world. One of these vessels, the U.S. battleship *Oregon*, was in the Navy Yard at Puget Sound, near the Canadian border in the Pacific Ocean. The Panama Canal was still non-existent and she received orders to proceed to San Francisco, for ammunition, and thence to the Atlantic Ocean, via the Straits of Magellan ; she made a remarkable voyage, arriving at Key West towards the end of May, having covered fourteen thousand seven hundred sea miles in fifty-six days.

At the end of March Captain W. T. Sampson, U.S.N., of the battleship *Iowa*, was promoted to Rear-Admiral and given the command of the North Atlantic Squadron, which included the battleships and armoured cruisers, Rear-Admiral Sicard being retired through ill-health, and on the 19th of April, the United States Government demanded that Spain should give up her authority in Cuba and should withdraw her forces. Spain was unready and her naval force was inferior to that of the United States, but she was evidently willing to fight, and a squadron of Spanish ships, under Admiral Cervera, was at the Cape Verde Islands, and expected to leave at any moment, possibly for Puerto Rico, east of Cuba. Pending a state of war, ships of the North Atlantic Squadron sailed from Key West ready to blockade the Island of Cuba. On the 24th of April war was declared and Cervera's squadron left the Cape Verde Islands for an unknown destination.

Meanwhile the Asiatic Squadron, which was under the command of Commodore George Dewey, U.S.N., was at Hong Kong. British neutrality compelled him to leave there for Mirs Bay twenty-four hours after the outbreak of war, and a couple of days later he sailed for the Philippine Islands. His force consisted of six ships, including the U.S.S. *Olympia*, his flagship, mounting four eight-inch and ten five-inch guns and the U.S.S. *Baltimore*, with four guns of eight-inch and six of six-inch calibre. These were protected cruisers, as were also the U.S.S. *Boston*, which mounted two eight-inch and six six-inch guns and the U.S.S. *Raleigh*, with one six-inch and ten five-inch guns. The other two ships were " unprotected " vessels, officially rated as gunboats, the U.S.S. *Concord* with six six-inch guns and the U.S.S. *Petrel* with four of the same calibre.[1] He also had in company the armed revenue vessel *Hugh McCulloch* and two store ships.

The island of Luzon is the northernmost large island in the Philippine Group ; on its south-western side are the town and bay of Manila. Just south of Manila is the naval base of Cavité, and here a Spanish squadron was anchored, under the command of Rear-Admiral Patricio Montojo, in the *Reina Cristina* ; this force consisted of seven ships, as here, and was therefore slightly superior to the American force in

[1] *The Relations of the United States and Spain.* Rear-Admiral F. E. Chadwick, U.S.N.

numbers, though not in armament, only three of the ships having guns larger than five-inch.[1]

	6·3-inch	5·9-inch	4·7-inch
Reina Cristina (flag)	6	—	—
Castilla (wood)	—	4	2
Isla de Cuba	—	—	4
Isla de Luzon	—	—	4
Don Juan de Austria	—	—	4
Don Antonio de Ulloa	—	—	4
Marques del Duero	I	—	2

Two other vessels, the *Velasco* and *General Lezo*, were under refit, and do not appear to have been manned when the action began. Some of the Spanish captains were ashore, and did not return on board their ships until the battle was in progress, though their ships' companies were on the alert and fought gallantly from the opening of the action until its close. Dewey slowed his squadron down, with the intention of arriving just at daylight on the 1st of May; he sent two ships forward to reconnoitre Subig Bay, to the north, but they found no trace of the Spanish ships, and reported that the lights on Corregidor Island and elsewhere had been extinguished; an American attack was clearly expected.

In perfect weather the American squadron steamed into Manila Bay from the south-west, a few shots being exchanged with the shore batteries near de la Restinga Point. No warships were lying off the city, which was reached about daybreak, and the squadron then turned to starboard and proceeded south towards Cavité, and here the Spanish squadron was found at anchor.

The action opened with a shot from Sangley Point, covering the arsenal at Cavité, and as soon as the American ships came into range, it became general. Commodore Dewey led his line to the westward and engaged, and during the action he turned alternately westwards and eastwards on five successive occasions. The Spaniards, who were also in a single line, remained where they were, except for an occasional sortie of an individual ship. The flagship *Reina Cristina*, supported by the *Don Juan*, tried to close the *Olympia*, but was compelled to run back, losing her captain and about a hundred and fifty men killed. Finally she blew up and sank; the wooden *Castilla* caught fire and went down, and Admiral Montojo's flag was transferred to the *Isla de Cuba*. At seven in the morning Commodore Dewey broke off the action, believing that his five-inch ammunition was becoming exhausted, but at a quarter-

[1] *The Relations of the United States and Spain.* Rear-Admiral F. E. Chadwick, U.S.N.

past eleven action was resumed ; the *Don Antonio de Ulloa* went down with colours flying, and at 12.30 firing ceased.[1]

As a result of these operations, the *Reina Cristina*, *Castilla* and *Don Antonio de Ulloa* were sunk and the following ships were burned : the *Isla de Cuba*, *Isla de Luzon*, *Don Juan de Austria* and the *Marques del Duero* ; also some minor vessels burned or taken. No lives were lost in the American squadron, and there were very few wounded ; the squadron anchored off Manila after 12.30. Requisite action was taken in order to destroy the shore batteries or to receive their surrender, but no attempt was made to bombard Manila itself.

Commodore Dewey's orders had been as follows : " War has commenced between the United States and Spain. Proceed at once to the Philippine Islands. Commence operations at once, particularly against the Spanish fleet. You must capture vessels or destroy. Use utmost endeavours." His task was completed, and great enthusiasm was aroused in the United States ; shortly afterwards he was promoted to Rear-Admiral ; but the United States found themselves with a large new colony on their hands, which was not yet conquered. It was necessary to send out an expeditionary force for this purpose, and Admiral Dewey's squadron remained at Manila.

At the same time Admiral Sampson decided to send part of his forces eastwards, in the hope of intercepting Cervera. He left for Key West on the 1st of May and on the 4th was under way for San Juan, Puerto Rico ; this is an island lying to the eastward of Haiti, and at that time belonged to Spain. He arrived off Puerto Rico a week later. The armoured cruiser *New York* was his flagship, and two battleships, the U.S.S. *Iowa* and *Indiana* were of his force, which included the monitors *Amphitrite* and *Terror* and some smaller ships.

The Admiral shifted his flag into the U.S.S. *Iowa* and approached San Juan before daylight, fully expecting to find Cervera's squadron in that port. There was a heavy swell, as the ships formed into line, and soon after five in the morning the American squadron opened fire on the forts and batteries ashore, taking them by surprise. Fire was returned from the shore, but there was no sign of the Spanish ships ; at 7.45, therefore, the action ceased and the American force withdrew, having suffered little damage and few casualties, and returned slowly Westwards.

A flying squadron had been formed and placed under the command of Commodore W.. S. Schley, U.S.N. This consisted of the battleships *Massachusetts* and *Texas* and the armoured cruiser *Brooklyn* ; the squadron was sent to Charleston, ready to reinforce the Cuban blockade or to defend Key West. Conflicting reports now began to come in, but these seemed to indicate that Cervera had taken a somewhat southerly course,

[1] *Autobiography of George Dewey, Admiral U.S.N.* 1913.

on leaving Cape Verde, and that he was at Martinique on the 11th of May and at Curaçao on the 14th; it appeared probable that he was bound for the south coast of Cuba. Sampson was ordered to return to Key West; Cervera arrived at Santiago de Cuba on the 19th of May and entered the harbour.

Commodore Schley's Flying Squadron was now reinforced by the addition of the U.S.S. *Iowa*, and he sailed on the 19th of May with the intention of blockading Cienfuegos, a port on the southern side of the island of Cuba, towards its western end. On the evening of the 20th Admiral Sampson received news of the presence of Cervera's squadron at Santiago; he therefore attempted to divert the Flying Squadron to Santiago, and proceeded to the Bahama Channel, in order to supervise the general blockade of Cuba; there was still doubt as to whether or not Cervera was actually at Santiago, and Schley continued his voyage to Cienfuegos. On arrival there, Commander McCalla took two ships inshore and met a group of Cuban insurgents, to whom he gave arms and ammunition, and from whom he ascertained definitely that the Spanish ships were not in Cienfuegos; whereupon the Flying Squadron immediately proceeded to Santiago, arriving off that port on the 26th of May.

The port of Santiago had a narrow and twisted entrance, thus making it impossible to see inside from the direction of the sea, so the exact strength of the Spanish squadron could not yet be determined. Owing to the impossibility of coaling, in the heavy seas, from the colliers, the Flying Squadron was in difficulties through shortage of coal, and it was difficult for this squadron to maintain a close blockade, but it had to hold on, pending the arrival of Admiral Sampson, who was now on his way there. The possibility of the Spanish squadron making a sortie was considered, but Admiral Cervera vetoed the suggestion. It proved to be his last opportunity of breaking out.

As the result of a reconnaissance made on the 29th of May, it was known that the new armoured cruiser *Cristóbal Colón* was in Santiago, also the armoured cruiser *Infanta Maria Teresa* and two torpedo craft, and two days later the American ships went in to within seven thousand yards' range, in an attempt to damage the *Cristóbal Colón*. Shots were exchanged with the Spaniards, and the volume of indirect fire, over the high land guarding the harbour, showed that the entire Spanish squadron was sheltering there.

On the 1st of June, Admiral Sampson arrived in the U.S.S. *New York*, and Commodore Schley went on board to report; his broad pendant was in the U.S.S. *Brooklyn* and he still had in his force the battleships *Iowa*, *Massachusetts* and *Texas*, also the protected cruiser *New Orleans* and some smaller ships. In Sampson's force was the battleship *Oregon*, which had now completed her voyage from the Pacific.

An expeditionary force under General Shafter was embarking at Tampa, in Florida, and consisted of about twenty thousand men ; the convoy was under the protection of a small naval force, of which the senior officer's ship was the battleship *Indiana*. A point had to be selected

U.S.S. " New York."

for the disembarkation of this force, and the friendly relations which had already been established with the Cuban insurgents, were now consolidated.

The flagship *New York* approached the harbour of Santiago on the morning of the 1st of June, and lowered a steam launch ; this was for the use of Assistant Naval Constructor Lieutenant R. P. Hobson, U.S.N., who wished to reconnoitre the entrance to the port, with a view to blocking the harbour by the sinking of the collier *Merrimac* on the following night. The launch was picked up again, and during the day preparations were made for this gallant attempt to block the port of Santiago de Cuba.

Ten explosive charges were fixed on the port side of the *Merrimac*, and anchors at bow and stern were slung, ready to be cut away ; a " catamaran " was carried aboard, for the rescue of the crew ; six men were selected from those who volunteered for the attempt, and were placed under the command of Lieutenant Hobson. The night was overcast, with clouds which partly obscured the moon ; the start was delayed, owing to various circumstances until between four and five in the morning, and after proceeding some distance, the *Merrimac* was recalled, owing to the approach of dawn. The attempt had to be postponed for twenty-four hours.

Next night the attempt was renewed. It was a clear moonlit night, and as the *Merrimac* approached the coast, she became a target for the shore batteries ; a shot cut the steering-gear and she drifted in. A picket boat had been detailed, under Ensign Powell, to pick up her crew, and she remained under a severe musketry fire, close to the shore, finally abandoning her post, when there was no further hope of picking up the survivors. Lieutenant Hobson had found it impossible to reach the point he was aiming for, and was obliged therefore to sink the *Merrimac* in comparatively deep water ; thus the channel was only partially blocked.

During the forenoon the Spanish tug *Colón* came out of the port, under a flag of truce, and came alongside the U.S.S. *New York*. Captain Bustamente, who was Admiral Cervera's Chief of Staff, went on board and delivered to Admiral Sampson a friendly letter from Admiral Cervera ; in it the Admiral stated that the *Merrimac's* crew were safe

PLATE XLIII

ADMIRAL DEWEY

In 1898 Commodore George Dewey was sent in command of a squadron to Manila, and here he defeated the Spaniards under Admiral Montojo. After the war he became Admiral of the Navy.

PLATE XLIV

REINA CRISTINA

The flagship of Admiral Patricio Montojo, in the fight with Commodore Dewey's force off Manila in May, 1898 ; she tried to close the U.S.S. *Olympia*, but failed, and finally blew up and sank. She is shown here fully rigged.

and expressed admiration for their gallant exploit. Cervera himself had effected their rescue, in his barge, finding the seven men in the water, clinging to their " catamaran," after the sinking of the *Merrimac*. Steps were afterwards taken for an exchange of prisoners.

Plans were now made for a more effective blockade of Santiago de Cuba. The ships were divided into two squadrons, one being under the direct command of Admiral Sampson and the other under Commodore Schley. The larger vessels formed a semicircle round the port, at about six miles distant, the smaller ships operating inshore.

It was now decided to capture Guantánamo, a port some miles to the eastward, and efforts were also made to cut some of the cables leading out from Santiago and elsewhere. Guantánamo was to be used as a coaling base ; it was practically undefended, and on the 7th of June, two small ships were sent there to capture the outer harbour, while Commander McCalla landed in order to get in touch with the Cuban insurgents, with the object of securing the land lying between Guantánamo and Santiago. General Shafter's command was in the nature of a reconnaissance in force, and intended to give encouragement to the insurgents, pending the arrival of the main army ; it was now on its way, and a few officers and men of the Marine-Corps had already been landed at Guantánamo, where they exchanged shots with the Spanish troops.

The naval blockade of the South coast of Cuba was now made effective ; Admiral Sampson organized the searchlights of his fleet in such a way as to prevent any vessel from emerging from Santiago unseen by night, and, after various experiments, a thoroughly efficient system was devised. A reconnaissance was made by Lieutenant Victor Blue, of the U.S.S. *Suwanee*, who landed at a point West of Santiago and, aided by a Cuban general, arrived at a point giving a view of the harbour, where he was able to establish the size and nature of the Spanish squadron. At about the same time news arrived to the effect that Admiral Camara had left Spanish ports, with a small squadron, and was bound for the Suez Canal and presumably for the Pacific ; this news also caused some anxiety to Admiral Dewey, in the Philippines. The U.S.S. *Oregon* and *Iowa*, and several smaller vessels, were ordered by the Navy Department to be held in readiness to proceed to the coast of Spain, if need arose ; but Admiral Sampson's protests prevailed, and they were retained on their station off Santiago.

On about the 20th of June the expeditionary force arrived, and on the 22nd a landing was made at Daiquiri, fifteen miles East of Santiago ; Lieut.-Colonel Theodore Roosevelt, afterwards President of the United States, served in this force. The blockading fleet co-operated, sending boats to assist in the landing, which was covered by its guns ; the disembarkation was completed in about four days. The rains, which were prevalent at this time of year, caused great discomfort to the troops, but on the 30th they were ready to advance along the coast to Santiago, which was already in acute distress, owing to lack of provisions.

Operations were now mainly of a military character, and the troops advanced westwards, suffering some loss in the taking of El Caney, on their right ; they then captured San Juan Hill and the advanced trenches of the Spaniards, covering Santiago from the east. The warships co-operated in firing on the enemy's positions, and the insurgent troops also gave some support. By the 3rd of July, the City was invested on the north and east, and General Shafter sent a message, under flag of truce, calling on its commander to surrender ; this request was refused, but in view of the large number of non-combatants involved, a general bombardment was postponed for two days.

General Blanco, the Governor of Santiago, had now assumed command of all the forces there, including Admiral Cervera's squadron ; and the admiral was ordered by him to make a sortie ; it was hoped by this means to save at least some of the ships, the only alternative being to destroy them at anchor, and so prevent them from falling into the enemy's hands. This action was approved by Madrid, and preparations were made to go to sea ; the men who had been sent ashore, to aid in the land defences, were re-embarked, and by the night of the 2nd of July the squadron was ready to proceed.

At about nine-thirty the following day the Spanish ships came out. The U.S. battleship *Massachusetts* had been sent eastwards, to Guantá-namo, but the other six big ships were waiting outside Santiago; still in an irregular arc of a circle. These were the battleships *Indiana, Iowa, Oregon* and *Texas*, and the armoured cruisers *New York* and *Brooklyn*. The first Spanish ship to emerge from the harbour-mouth was the *Infanta Maria Teresa*, which was Admiral Cervera's flagship ; after her came the *Vizcaya, Cristóbal Colón* and *Almirante Oquendo* ; these were all armoured cruisers. They were followed by the *Plutón* and *Furor*, which were destroyers, a type of vessel of which there were none available at that time in the U.S. Navy.

It was a fine morning, and the American fleet was at Sunday divisions, when " action stations " sounded. The *Teresa* fired a gun, as she emerged, and then turned westwards along the shore, followed by the rest of the squadron, apparently in the hope of reaching Cienfuegos. The American ships closed in and engaged, and the action developed into a chase, which lasted about four hours in all. The Spanish case was hopeless from the first ; at the outset they had some advantage of speed and were able to get ahead of the American battleships, which had not yet worked up to full power. This resulted in the two torpedo craft, which came out last, becoming a target for the concentrated fire of the big ships' guns ; the *Plutón* blew up and sank at about a quarter to eleven, and the *Furor* was run ashore at the same time.

Ten minutes earlier the flagship *Teresa* and the *Oquendo*, which had got some distance ahead, had been severely damaged, and had lowered their colours and gone ashore. In the smoke the *Vizcaya* and *Colón* had escaped farther Westwards, hotly pursued by the American ships. By half-past eleven the *Vizcaya* was in obvious distress, and almost immediately afterwards two great explosions occurred on board her ; she at once turned to starboard and ran ashore ;

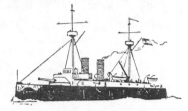

Cruiser "*Vizcaya*."

the U.S.S. *Iowa* was stopped, in order to attend to her ; the U.S.S. *Indiana* was ordered back to Santiago. The U.S.S. *Brooklyn, Oregon, Texas* and *New York* were meanwhile chasing the *Colón*, on which they gradually gained ; and by two o'clock the *Colón* had to haul down her colours and run ashore, seventy-five miles west of Santiago.

Admiral Cervera's squadron was no more. Had he tried to escape by night, he might have been more successful, but in his opinion the searchlights made navigation impossible. Cervera was one of the survivors of the action, and was received on board the American fleet with all the honours of war ; he was afterwards sent as a prisoner of war to the Naval Academy at Annapolis. During the action the Spaniards lost over three hundred killed ; the Americans lost one killed and one seriously wounded.

On the following day General Shafter made a further attempt to obtain the surrender of the city, again without success. At midnight on the 4th of July the fleet closed on the place, and were able to sink the unprotected cruiser *Reina Mercedes*, which had remained there ; the ships did not, however, enter the harbour, which was believed to be mined. Noncombatants were now leaving the city, and there was a lull in the operations. Reinforcements for General Shafter were now on their way, and the General endeavoured to arrange for a joint naval and military assault on the city, which was now completely invested.

Admiral Camara's squadron, which was in the neighbourhood of Suez, was still causing some anxiety, and it was desired to deal with Santiago as quickly as possible, in order to release ships for the East, if that should become necessary. On the 10th of July, the fleet commenced bombarding the city, and at about the same time General Miles arrived, bringing with him some reinforcements. The bombardment was resumed on the following day, and continued until the afternoon, when hostilities ceased, pending negotiations ; these were protracted and difficult, owing to

attempts to find a formula which would "save the face" of the Spaniards ;
but the Americans were determined that the city should surrender uncon-
ditionally.   Santiago de Cuba was finally surrendered on the 16th of
July, the Spanish forces marching out with the "honours of war."

During the month of July anxiety as to the safety of Dewey's force at
Manila, in view of a possible attack by Camara, was still exercising the
minds of the Navy Department, and orders were sent to Admiral Sampson
to reorganize his ships as follows : an Eastern Squadron was to be formed,
under Commodore Watson, which included the *Massachusetts* and *Oregon*,
and a Covering Squadron, including the other battleships and armoured
cruisers, with the exception of the *Texas*.   These forces were to proceed
east, as far as the Spanish coast, under the command of Admiral Sampson ; Commodore Watson's force was then to go on to Manila, while the
Covering Squadron returned to the United States, as soon as the safety
of the Eastern Squadron was secured as far as the Suez Canal.

Admiral Camara's force included one battleship, the *Pelayo*, carrying
two guns of 12·5-inch and two of eleven-inch calibre, and the armoured
cruiser *Carlos V*, armed with two eleven-inch guns ; these might have
proved a match for Dewey's protected cruisers at Manila ; as far as the
Suez Canal the Admiral had three destroyers in his force, which consisted
otherwise of vessels of doubtful value.   He left Cadiz on the 16th of June,
and arrived at Port Said a week later, passing thence through the Canal
to Suez.   Here he outstayed the twenty-four hours permitted by the
neutrality of the Egyptian Government and was asked to leave ; he went
into the Red Sea, and on the 8th of July was recalled to Spain, where
he arrived towards the end of July.   Camara's cruise was, therefore,
abortive, and the need for sending the American ships eastwards from
Cuba no longer existed.

It was now proposed to organize an expedition against the island of
Puerto Rico.   General Miles, with a strong force and accompanied by a
squadron which included the *Massachusetts*, went to the port of Guanica,
where he landed a part of his force on the 25th of July, afterwards landing
the remainder farther along the south coast, at Ponce ; the southern side
of the island was then occupied and the troops advanced on San Juan,
on the north side, which was the main objective.   By the 14th of August
the whole of Puerto Rico was in American hands ; Cuba had fallen, and
hostilities in this part of the world had come to an end.   The fleet returned
to New York on the 20th of August.

During July a force under General Wesley Merritt was sent to Manila ;
on the way Brigadier-General Anderson landed troops at the Spanish
island of Guam, and occupied it in the name of the United States.
Meantime Admiral Dewey had cut the cable from Manila, and his only
communication with the outside world was by ship to Hong Kong ;

wireless telegraphy was still non-existent. After his victory over the Spanish squadron at Manila on the 1st of May, he instituted a strict blockade.

The Filipino insurgents, under Aguinaldo, were now entrenched before the town of Manila, and the situation was rather similar to that existing in Santiago de Cuba ; provisions were running short ; anxiety, also, was felt lest the Spanish troops should get out of hand, thus endangering foreign nationals in the place. Men-of-war of Great Britain, Japan and Germany were sent to Manila, in order to protect national interests, The ships of the two Powers first mentioned preserved strict neutrality. but in dealing with the Germans, Admiral Dewey had to exercise the utmost tact, as indeed also in his dealings with Aguinaldo and his men.

When two countries are at war and a naval force of one blockades a port of the other, it is usual that no ship of a non-belligerent country should enter the port, or have any communication with the shore, without first obtaining the permission of the admiral commanding the blockading force. The Germans had the largest neutral squadron in Manila Bay, consisting of five ships, under the command of Vice-Admiral von Diedrichs. These ships came and went, much as they pleased, and troops were landed from a transport for exercises. Dewey protested and, after his protest had been upheld by Captain Edward Chichester, the senior British naval officer present, the German squadron became more amenable to International Law ; but a risk of foreign interference was thought always to exist.

The first troops of General Merritt's force arrived in Manila Bay on the 19th of July, and were landed under General Greene, at an open space just South of the town, the transports remaining at Cavité. The main body, under General Merritt, arrived on the 24th of July. No communication was held with the Filipino insurgents, under Aguinaldo, for reasons which appear later, and the American troops threw up their own entrenchments. On the 4th of August, Dewey's squadron was reinforced by the arrival of a monitor, the U.S.S. *Monterey*, armed with two twelve-inch and two ten-inch guns. Three days later the Governor-General was notified that it would be well to remove all non-combatants, since operations against Manila would begin within forty-eight hours ; advantage was taken of this concession, and no hostilities were indulged in on either side until the 13th of August, the delay being due to negotiations, which were now set on foot. The capitulation of Manila was a foregone conclusion ; but nearly a week's negotiations to that end were necessary between General Merritt and General Firmin Jaudenes, the Spanish Governor-General.

Had the naval and military forces bombarded Manila, great damage to life and property must have resulted, without the slightest benefit to the Spaniards, but the Spanish military code of honour stood in the path of a complete surrender, without resistance, and a way had to be found of getting over this difficulty ; consequently a " token " bombardment had to be arranged, to which the Spaniards could make a show of replying.

It was therefore arranged that on the 13th of August a joint naval and military attack should be made on a fort south of Manila and on the shore batteries and strong points. Admiral Dewey's squadron closed in at nine in the morning, and the U.S.S. *Olympia* began to fire on the fort. The

H.M.S. " Immortalité."

foreign warships had been asked by the Admiral on the 9th of August to shift their anchorages out into the bay, in order to be clear of the line of fire ; but there was still thought to be a risk of foreign interference and, as the American ships closed in, Captain Chichester, in H.M.S. *Immortalité*, followed by H.M.S. *Iphigenia*, steamed across, cleared for action, and anchored in such a position that he was between Dewey's squadron and the foreign warships. Dewey, in his autobiography, mentions this episode with appreciation, and compares it with the " Blood is thicker than Water " episode of 1859, as an example of " true international friendship."

At about noon a white flag was hoisted above the fort, in a position previously agreed upon between the opposing forces, and the surrender of Manila was an accomplished fact. Peace preliminaries had been under discussion for some time, and in these M. Cambon, the French Ambassador in Washington, had taken an active part. Hostilities were now generally suspended, the war having lasted a little more than three and a half months, and a Peace Treaty was drawn up through the good offices of the French Government. Admiral Dewey's services received due recognition ; he was given the unique position of " Admiral of the Navy," a rank which he held for life, and was presented with a sword of honour, voted by Congress.

For many years before the outbreak of war, the Philippine islanders had been endeavouring to shake off the Spanish yoke. In 1872 a revolt broke out, and another in 1896, when Aguinaldo led the insurgents ; the Filipinos tried to create a " Philippine Republic," and the intention of the United States to annex the islands came into conflict with this aspiration. This explains the care which was used by the American forces not to co-operate in any way with Aguinaldo or his followers. When peace was signed, and the Philippine Islands were duly ceded to the United States, unrest and guerilla warfare continued there for some time, but were finally brought to an end some years later, after the capture of Aguinaldo.

As a result of this war Spain gave up her sovereignty over Cuba, which eventually became an independent republic ; she ceded to the United States Puerto Rico, with the small islands depending on' it, and the island of Guam, in the Pacific Ocean. The Philippine Islands were also ceded to the United States, a large sum being paid in compensation. Spain retained her colonies in Africa, but her ancient empire in America and the Eastern Seas was now a thing of the past.

CHAPTER X

THE WORLD WARS

D URING the war with Spain the ensign and jack displayed forty-five stars, arranged in six alternate rows of eight and seven. In 1907 Oklahoma ceased to be a " Territory " and was admitted as a State; the stars were now increased to forty-six. In 1912 the same thing happened in the cases of Arizona and New Mexico, and the stars were increased to forty-eight; that is their number at the time of writing, the stars being arranged in six rows of eight each.

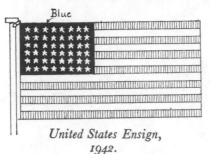

United States Ensign,
1942.

For fifteen years the peace of the Atlantic was little disturbed. The United States Navy was now strong, and the appearance on the Eastern side of the Atlantic of the *Dreadnought* in 1906 affected all the navies of the world ; some powerful " dreadnoughts " were added to the U.S. Navy. A threat to the tranquillity of the South Atlantic had occurred when the German Kaiser sent his famous telegram to President Kruger in 1896, but the British fitted out a flying squadron, and the steps taken by the British Admiralty during the South African War, three years later, averted the danger.

A threat to the Monroe Doctrine, however, became apparent in 1901. On account of a debt difficulty Germany made a naval demonstration against Venezuela, and tried to induce Great Britain and Italy to co-operate ; the American Fleet was mobilized. Fortunately President Theodore Roosevelt was able to persuade Germany to arbitrate, and war was prevented. Various other anxieties arose in Central America or the West Indies, but these were dealt with without much difficulty.

Arctic exploration still attracted the more venturesome spirits, and the North Pole, prize of arctic explorers, had not yet been won. From 1886 till 1902 an engineer officer, Commander Robert Edwin Peary, U.S.N., explored North Greenland, including Cape York and Whale Sound, and finally determined the insularity of Greenland. In 1905 he started out again, via Grant Land, in the specially constructed ship *Roosevelt*, and in 1909 he reached the North Pole.

In 1910 an American squadron visited Great Britain, and the ships' companies were entertained at a luncheon given by the Lord Mayor at

PLATE XLV

ANGLO-AMERICAN CO-OPERATION

A group taken at the end of the First World War.   Left to right : Admiral
Sir David Beatty, Rear-Admiral Hugh Rodman, U.S.N., H.M. King
George V, Vice-Admiral W. S. Sims, U.S.N., H.R.H. The Prince of Wales.

PLATE XLVI

U.S.S. *PENNSYLVANIA* (Battleship)

Completed June, 1916.   Armed with twelve 14-inch guns and twelve 5-inch.   Speed 21 knots.   The ship is seen with basket masts, coming through the Culebra Cut, in the Panama Canal.

the Guildhall. On this occasion Captain W. S. Sims, of the U.S.S. *Minnesota*, made a speech, in which he said : " If the time should ever come when the British Empire is menaced by a European coalition, Great Britain can rely upon the last ship, the last dollar, the last man and the last drop of blood of her kindred beyond the sea." The utterance not unnaturally came in for violent criticism, especially on the continent of Europe ; but when America entered the Great War, or as it is now called the First World War, it was remembered with great appreciation in Great Britain.

Trouble with Mexico again took place in April, 1914, when a boat's crew from the U.S.S. *Dolphin* was arrested on landing at Tampico and imprisoned. A force of American marines and bluejackets was immediately landed at Vera Cruz, and various buildings were seized. The city was then occupied, whereupon the Mexican President resigned. Peaceful relations with the United States were then resumed.

The First World War broke out in August, 1914, and in April, 1917, Rear-Admiral W. S. Sims arrived in England, in order to ascertain and report how the United States Navy could best co-operate. In April the German submarine menace to merchant shipping had reached an alarming stage, a fact of which the general public was ignorant, and during the same month the United States entered the war. Admiral Sims at once got in touch with Admiral Jellicoe, who was First Sea Lord, and the facts of the submarine situation were frankly explained. Sims took the view that available ships of the U.S. Navy should be used to " strengthen the weak spots in the Allied line," or, in other words, that they should reinforce the British Navy, instead of acting as an independent force : British destroyers and other anti-submarine craft were now insufficient in numbers adequately to deal with the situation alone.

Six U.S. destroyers crossed the Atlantic and arrived at Queenstown, in Southern Ireland, in May, 1917. Here they reported to Vice-Admiral Lewis Bayly, who was commanding the naval forces there, the liaison officer being Captain E. R. G. R. Evans. These ships consisted of the U.S.S. *Wadsworth, Conyngham, Porter, McDougal, Davis* and *Wainwright*, which received a great welcome from the local inhabitants. Commander Taussig, in the *Wadsworth*, led the flotilla. Admiral Sims recounts in his book [1] how, in the Boxer Rebellion in China in 1900, when British and American naval forces were among those which co-operated in an attempt to relieve the Legations, Taussig was wounded and found himself in the next bed to that occupied by another wounded officer, a certain Captain Jellicoe. A friendship sprang up between them and one of the first to extend a welcome was the British First Sea Lord.

Later, in May, a second destroyer flotilla arrived at Queenstown,

[1] *The Victory at Sea.* 1920. Rear-Admiral W. S. Sims, U.S.N.

and subsequently these two flotillas were supplemented by others. Admiral Sims became Commander of the U.S. Forces operating in European waters, which necessitated his presence in London ; but for a time he hoisted his flag at Queenstown, in the temporary absence of Admiral Bayly, who was on duty elsewhere. Commenting on the appointment of Admiral Sims, the flag-officer in command at Queenstown afterwards wrote : " I consider that the choice of Admiral Sims was a very fortunate one for the Allied cause in the war." [1]

British and American co-operation was marked by the greatest cordiality, though officers at first found a difficulty in understanding each other's slang. A story is told that on one occasion one of the American destroyers, when hunting for submarines, made a wireless signal reporting that she had sunk a U-boat, giving her position ; the message concluded with these words : " Where am I ? "

This puzzled the staff at Queenstown, since her position had been given. An American officer who was present came to the rescue by saying :

" Where is he ? Why, at the top of the class, I should think."

Portions of the ocean had been divided up into patrol areas, in each of which destroyers or other anti-submarine craft operated ; " mystery " or Q-ships were employed also ; but it became clear that these methods alone were insufficient to cope with the danger. The British Admiralty then decided to adopt, or to revive, a convoy system, of which Admiral Sims proved to be a warm supporter.

Convoys have been employed from very early times ; but grave doubts were felt, especially by the merchant captains concerned, as to whether or not a convoy propelled by steam would be capable of " keeping station," and of manœuvring at night with all lights out, without running a serious risk of collision. The convoys of past centuries had to be protected only against surface craft ; the invention of the submarine had altered the position ; convoys had to zigzag, which complicated the matter still further, especially since the zigzags had to be ordered by signal, a naval evolution to which the Merchant Navy was unaccustomed. The invention, during the war, of the depth-charge facilitated the task of the escorting ships, however, and during the month of May the first convoy made its passage and in perfect safety. The convoy system was thereupon seen to be an accomplished fact, and it subsequently defeated the submarine campaign.

The British merchant fleet was now being camouflaged, and many of the vessels used for escorting convoys were also so treated ; the American destroyers were among these ships. The following incidents may be quoted as examples of the action of American naval ships on convoy duty

[1] *Pull Together.* Admiral Sir Lewis Bayly, K.C.B., K.C.M.G., C.V.O.

In October, 1917, the U.S. Destroyer *Conyngham*, Commander Johnson, was escorting, with his destroyers, a large convoy off the East Coast, when he received a wireless message from the *J. L. Luckenbach*, a merchant ship which was about a hundred miles ahead of the convoy ; the message stated that she was being shelled by a submarine. German submarines made a practice at this time of using their guns on isolated merchant vessels, because by this means they were enabled to economise torpedoes, and could remain on the surface without danger to themselves. The U.S. Destroyer *Nicholson* was at once despatched to the *Luckenbach's* assistance, and came on the scene between two and three hours later. Meantime shells had set fire to a part of the cargo and had also damaged the machinery of the merchant ship. The *Nicholson* attacked the submarine, which at once submerged and disappeared ; the fire was got under, and eventually the *Luckenbach* joined the convoy.

The *Nicholson* also rejoined the convoy and resumed her station. Scarcely had she done so, when one of the escorting ships, the British armed merchant cruiser *Orama*, was torpedoed. Immediately afterwards a periscope appeared in the middle of the convoy. The U.S.S. *Conyngham* dashed to the spot and saw below water the shape of a submarine, on which a depth charge was dropped ; wreckage rose to the surface, but no more was seen, and it was presumed that the U-boat was sunk. The *Orama* subsequently sank, her survivors being rescued by the destroyers, and Commander Johnson was afterwards awarded the C.M.G. for his action.

During the summer of the same year the American yacht *Christobel*, while escorting a " straggler " from a convoy, saw a periscope and started for the spot, dropping a depth charge. Nothing more was seen until some hours later, when again a periscope appeared ; it was presumed that the submarine had been following the two ships. Again a depth charge was dropped and the explosion which it made was followed by a much more violent explosion ; masses of wreckage came up and quantities of oil. There was no further sign of the U-boat, but it was learned later that one of these craft, very badly damaged, had limped into Santander, in Northern Spain, where she was interned.

In November an American destroyer flotilla put out from Queenstown under Commander Berrien, in the U.S.S. *Nicholson*, in order to escort a west-bound convoy to its rendezvous in the Atlantic. Soon after the destroyers took up their positions on the flanks of the convoy, a periscope was seen to starboard of the U.S.S. *Fanning*. The *Fanning* at once turned and dropped a depth-charge near the periscope ; another depth-charge was dropped by the U.S.S. *Nicholson* ; there was no trace of wreckage or oil, and a few seconds of calm followed. Suddenly a U-boat came up stern first and lay on the water, showing no sign of damage outwardly, though serious damage had been done to her machinery, and she was quite helpless. The destroyers opened fire on her ; then the conning tower opened and the German commander appeared with his hands up, followed by his crew. Fire ceased and the submarine was taken to have surrendered. This did not prevent the Germans from following their usual plan of scuttling the ship and, as she sank, the U-boat's crew took

U.S. Destroyer.

to the water and, with one exception, was saved. The commanding officer of the U.S.S. *Fanning*, Lieut.-Commander Carpender, was afterwards awarded the D.S.O.

Queenstown remained the principal base for the American naval forces acting on convoy work, and when American Troops began to arrive in numbers in Europe during the summer of 1918, Brest and other French ports also became bases of prime importance. There was an immense and valuable trade passing through the Mediterranean Sea, and this became a target for the U-boats. In August, 1917, American naval vessels began to assemble at Gibraltar, in order to aid in convoying this trade ; the U.S.S. *Decatur*, and four other small destroyers from Manila, were joined there by the *Nashville*, the *Paducah* and other gun-boats, yachts, coastguard cutters—any craft, in fact, that could be spared from duties elsewhere. The force was commanded by Rear-Admiral H. B. Wilson, U.S.N., who took command at Brest in November, 1917, being succeeded by Rear-Admiral A. P. Niblack, U.S.N., at Gibraltar.

Towards the end of 1917 the writer found himself at Gibraltar, where he was detained for four or five weeks by the Flag Officer in Charge, in order to camouflage several Q-ships, boarding steamers and others ; some of these vessels came into dock ; many only moored for a few hours and had to be.dealt with piece-meal. One of these ships was the boarding steamer *Royal Scot*. Arrangements were made for a working pontoon to go alongside as soon as she came in ; as she was only in harbour for a few hours, it was decided that she should be painted by the ship's company, at sea or as circumstances would allow ; but the pattern had first to be marked out on her. The working party was divided, half working along her decks, and half on the pontoon, but this arrangement did not give the desired results.

The naval harbour of Gibraltar is of large extent, not greatly unlike that at Dover, and the shore was some distance away from the ship. The problem was how to choose a spot far enough away to get a good view of the ship, and near enough clearly to signal the necessary instructions by semaphore. A discussion with the commanding officer followed and, while this was proceeding, an American four-funnelled cruiser

PLATE XLVII

U.S.S. *OKLAHOMA* (Battleship)

Armed with ten 14-inch guns and twelve 5-inch. Completed May, 1916. Speed 21½ knots. The *Oklahoma* was badly damaged in the attack on Pearl Harbour. In foreground, a British battleship of the *Royal Sovereign* class.

PLATE XLVIII

U.S.S. *ARIZONA* (Battleship)

Completed in 1916. Armed with twelve 14-inch guns and twelve 5-inch. Speed 21 knots. The *Arizona* was damaged in the attack on Pearl Harbour and became a total loss.

of the *Birmingham* class, entered the harbour and secured to one of the buoys, in the ideal spot. The situation was explained to her by sema-phore and permission readily granted to go aboard her ; in a few seconds the writer and a signalman of the R.N.V.R. were pulling across to the American cruiser, whence the requisite instructions were semaphored over to the *Royal Scot* by the signalman.

A few years later the writer had a " one man show " at the Fine Arts Society's galleries in Bond Street. In hanging the pictures he was aided, among others, by a very smart young man, attired in a morning coat and striped trousers ; the young man edged over to him and whispered in his ear : " This is better, Sir, than ' Dazzling ' the *Royal Scot.*" It was the R.N.V.R. signalman.

The prompt action of the American cruiser on this occasion saved some hours, perhaps days, and was only one of the many ways in which the two navies showed a spirit of mutual co-operation, even over small matters. The same cordiality was visible everywhere. Each day at dusk a British naval officer and picket met an American naval officer and his picket near the Ragged Staff Steps and together they patrolled the town " on their lawful occasions " ; and the frequency with which American gunboats and yachts came into port, on their return from convoy duty, led to fraternization in each other's wardrooms.

So far as graver matters were concerned, the Gibraltar force did not lag behind its colleagues at Queenstown. It helped to escort more than ten thousand ships and had several successful engagements with the enemy. In May, 1918, the yacht *Venetia*, while escorting a convoy, depth-charged a submarine, and was later ordered to try and locate another submarine, which had just torpedoed the British ship *Surveyor* ; the submarine was found and depth-charged, and a few days later a badly damaged craft of this nature crawled into Cartagena, in Southern Spain, where she was duly interned. The yacht *Lydonia* too, in company with H.M.S. *Basilisk*, also sank a U-boat in the Western Mediterranean.

It became possible, owing to the convoy system, for the destroyers which acted as escort, to attack with gunfire or depth-charges any sub-marine which attacked the convoy, but only if it showed its periscope or otherwise gave evidence of its presence. Sometimes a U-boat thought that an attack would be too dangerous ; it allowed the convoy to pass unmolested, and waited for some other opportunity, or for some isolated ship. The problem now arose as to how to locate these unseen sub-marines, and destroy them before they were able to take the offensive.

Experiments were conducted in 1917 in connection with hydrophones or listening apparatus, by which the propellers of a submerged submarine could be heard and their direction estimated. Two or three craft, fitted with such apparatus and operating at some distance apart from each other, could get a " fix " on a propeller and so locate the submarine. The Allied navies worked on this problem and the U.S. Navy materially contributed to its solution ; the American submarine chasers proved to be eminently suitable for working the apparatus and, like the destroyers, were equipped with a number of depth-charges.

Shortly before the United States entered the war, several hundred wooden boats, 110 feet in length, had been built in American ports, to be used as patrol boats on that coast ; U-boats sometimes operated on the western side of the Atlantic, but not to any serious extent. A number of these wooden boats were sent over to European waters, where they acted as submarine chasers, and the British and French navies ordered a large number to be built of a slightly smaller type. Like the British motor-launches, or M.L.s, these submarine chasers were manned largely by amateur yachtsmen, but for the most part their crews were recruited from among the undergraduates of the great universities—Harvard, Yale and others ; the first boats to cross over went under their own power in January and February, 1918, in the face of severe weather, and arrived safely in Plymouth Harbour.

Squadrons of submarine chasers were based on Plymouth and at Queenstown, and craft of this type were sent subsequently to aid the " Otranto Barrage," this barrage being designed to stop the U-boats in Austrian ports from emerging out of the Adriatic Sea into the Mediterranean. The Otranto Barrage was maintained only by a few British destroyers, and this force of submarine chasers was based near Govino, in the island of Corfu.

Like the American destroyers, the submarine chasers also succeeded in accounting for several U-boats. One of these, the U 53, had sunk the U.S. Destroyer *Jacob Jones* by torpedo. It became known in August, 1918, that the U 53 was in the Atlantic 250 miles west of Brest, and the U.S. Navy naturally took a deep interest in her welfare ; two destroyers, the U.S.S. *Wilkes* and *Parker*, and twelve submarine chasers were sent out to hunt for her, and on the 2nd of September a conning tower was seen on the surface. This at once submerged and the U.S.S. *Parker* dashed to the spot and dropped a depth-charge ; three submarine chasers then came up, put their apparatus overside and began to listen. They came to the conclusion that the depth-charge had failed to hit the mark, and found that the U-boat was still going slowly ahead. They then obtained a definite " fix " on her position, and more depth-charges were dropped, after which there was a dead silence. Subsequently a battered U 53 limped back to Germany and never came out again, until the German submarines were surrendered at Harwich in November.

In September, nine submarine chasers were somewhere off Land's End, when they heard a submarine and got a " fix " on it ; some of the boats then dropped depth-charges, but with no apparent result. The U-boat was followed for two hours, when a good " fix " was obtained and a perfect shower of depth-charges was dropped. There was a dead silence for about twenty minutes, after which the revolutions of a pro- peller were faintly audible. For some hours there were sounds as if the U-boat's crew, of twenty-five men, was trying to effect repairs ; these became fainter and finally died away. More ships were summoned by wireless and a buoy marking the situation of the submarine was placed in position and lighted against the approach of darkness. For some hours longer the ships waited in silence, expecting the U-boat to blow her tanks, come to the surface and surrender. With dramatic suddenness the silence was broken by a revolver shot ; this was quickly followed by twenty- four other shots. The U-boat's crew had apparently committed suicide.

Later in September an enterprise was undertaken in the Adriatic Sea, in which the submarine chasers at Corfu co-operated. The intention was that a small force of Italian cruisers should bombard Durazzo, in Albania, followed by a force of British cruisers ; it was known that the Austrians had many submarines in the port, and the duty of the submarine chasers was to watch for and intercept any submarine

Submarine Chaser.

attack on the cruiser forces. Twelve of these boats were detailed for the operation, under Captain C. P. Nelson, U.S.N., and they proceeded to Brindisi, where the forces were assembled.

The submarine chasers left Brindisi by night and crossed over to Durazzo. Here they manœuvred about, without enticing any of the submarines to come out. A submarine chaser unit consisted of three boats ; two units, six boats, were detailed to screen the Italian cruisers, as soon as these arrived, three boats being stationed to the south of the bay and three to the north. Presently it was the turn of the British cruisers to continue the bombardment.

By this time the shore batteries were opening fire on the northern unit of chasers. Suddenly Chaser No. 129 turned to starboard and hastened after some object on the surface. No. 215, containing the commander of the unit, Commander Bastedo, also turned and at once became aware of a feather of foam just ahead of his port beam, making for the British cruisers ; a periscope became visible, and he opened fire on it and destroyed it. No. 128 had now joined in the chase. The submarine turned south and endeavoured to escape ; but Nos. 215 and 128 turned and followed it, dropping depth-charges. Steel plates and other debris rose in the air, and that submarine was out of action.

Meantime No. 129 was continuing to pursue her own prey, and made a signal to the effect that she had sighted a submarine ; this was followed by another signifying that her own engines were damaged ; this coincided with a great explosion of depth-charges. The commander of the unit closed this boat and enquired after the submarine.

" We sank her," said No. 129.

The British cruisers finished their bombardment of Durazzo unmolested and the whole force returned safely to Brindisi.

American submarines also played their part, and sometimes had narrow escapes, for any submarine was liable to be mistaken for an enemy. Seven of these submarines were based on Berehaven in Bantry Bay. On one occasion the American submarine AL 2 was manœuvring on the surface, when she saw a periscope. Preparations were made to fire a torpedo, when there was a terrific explosion ahead ; the AL 2 dived and tried to ram the enemy but failed. Sounds were heard for a time, but these died away, and it was concluded that the U-boat had fired a torpedo at the AL 2, which had circled and hit the U-boat herself ; but the solution of the mystery was never discovered.

U-boat activity on the western side of the Atlantic was not marked, but ships were occasionally torpedoed and mines were laid ; one of these sank the U.S. Cruiser *San Diego* off Fire Island, near Long Island. The U 151 sank a couple of schooners towards the end of May, 1918, off the New Jersey coast. American troops first crossed to Europe in June, 1917, and, when they began to come across in large numbers, the Germans took some of their U-boats off the shipping lanes, in the hope of sinking the troopships ; but they met with no success, as these ships were strongly escorted by the U.S. Navy.

It was during the Great War that the ability of aircraft to spot submarines was first realized. An American seaplane base was established at Killingholme, on the Humber, and American planes used also to operate from Felixstowe. Dirigible airships were also employed, especially on the flanks of a convoy, where they were almost as efficient as a destroyer. The principal naval problem during the last half of the war was the submarine danger, and to that the U.S. Navy directed its greatest efforts.

Attempts had been made to bottle up the German U-boats in their bases ; a valiant attempt had been made by the British Navy to block the ports of Zeebrugge and Ostende in April, 1918. The Dover Patrol and the barrage of nets and mines across the Straits of Dover were largely efficacious, but bad weather conditions there were continually rendering this work ineffective ; submarines were still able to slip through the Straits of Dover, and they could also pass northabout from Germany round the north of Scotland.

In 1918 it was decided to lay a mine-field right across the North Sea

PLATE XLIX

U.S.S. *NORTH CAROLINA* (Battleship)

One of the latest American battleships : she belongs to the *Indiana* class, one other of which, the *Washington*, is completed.   Armed with nine 16-inch guns and twenty 5-inch ; completed in August, 1941.   Speed over 27 knots.

PLATE L

U.S.S. *MINNEAPOLIS* (Heavy Cruiser)

There are seven ships in this class.   Commissioned in 1934.   Armament
nine 8-inch guns and eight 5-inch.   Carries four aircraft.   Speed 32·7 knots.

from the Orkney Islands to the coast of Norway ; a small minefield was first laid on the Norwegian coast, and it was decided to strengthen this and to continue it for the remaining 250 miles. This mine-field came to be known as the North Sea Barrage, or " Northern Barrage."

The British had laid mines in the Heligoland Bight and elsewhere, and these proved to be a serious obstruction to the egress of German U-boats, but here the Germans were able to sweep passages through the mine-fields from time to time, and they were extremely difficult to maintain. The laying of the North Sea barrage made its maintenance more easy, because it was more difficult for German mine-sweepers to operate in that area.

Much of the work of laying this mine-field was entrusted to the U.S. Navy. In 1917 a new type of mine had been evolved in the United States, which could be laid at any depth, and from which a copper wire extended upwards nearly to the surface, being held up by a small buoy ; any submarine striking this wire, and at any depth, would explode the mine. Thus a much smaller number of mines were needed than would otherwise be the case. One hundred thousand of these mines were manufactured and were loaded at Norfolk, Virginia, into ships for transport across the Atlantic ; all these ships but one arrived safely in Great Britain.

For this duty a mine-laying force was selected ; this consisted for the most part of converted coast-wise vessels ; they had three decks for the mines and lifts to bring them up to the upper deck, whence they could be dropped over the stern. They consisted of the U.S.S. *Housatonic, Roanoke, Guinnebaug, Shawmut, Aroostook, Canandaigua, Canonicus* and *Saranac* ; to these were added two old warships, the U.S.S. *San Francisco* and *Baltimore,* the former of which was the flagship of Captain R. P. Belknap, U.S.N., who had commanded the mine-laying squadron of the Atlantic Fleet.

Inverness and Invergordon were selected as the bases of this force in Great Britain, and here the mines were assembled and housed in vast store-houses ; here the personnel of the mine-layers received a warm welcome. The British officer in command of operations was Rear-Admiral L. Clinton-Baker, and the American officer was Rear-Admiral J. Strauss, U.S.N. About five thousand mines were laid each time the ships went out, which they did on thirteen occasions, but without serious mishap. The U.S.S. *Baltimore* also laid a mine-field in the north of the Irish Channel, which afterwards accounted for two German U-boats.

It was thought at one time that this mine-laying squadron might entice out the German High Seas Fleet, and it was usually well protected by British battle squadrons, sometimes aided by the American battleships, which had now joined the Grand Fleet. Screens of destroyers also accompanied these mine-layers ; once the latter got well out to sea, they formed into two columns and steamed over to the Norwegian coast. Here mine-laying began and continued for three or four hours, after which the exhausted crews returned again to their bases. Altogether, during the summer and autumn of 1918, seventy thousand mines were laid by the British and American forces in the North Sea Barrage, of which more than fifty-six thousand were laid by the U.S. Navy.

After the Battle of Jutland in 1916 the defeated High Seas Fleet retired to its bases ; it never emerged again, until it was surrendered in the Firth of Forth in November, 1918 ; the German bases, where the High Seas Fleet was sheltering, had to be watched and the greatest caution exercised. During this period a squadron of six American battleships, under Rear-Admiral Hugh Rodman, U.S.N., joined the Grand Fleet and became known as the 6th Battle Squadron, the 5th Battle Squadron, of the *Queen Elizabeth* class, being their " chummy ships."

These six battleships were all " dreadnoughts " and very different in design and armament to those vessels which had fought in the Spanish War. They consisted of the U.S.S. *New York*, Admiral Rodman's flagship, and the U.S.S. *Texas*, each mounting ten fourteen-inch guns, in double turrets, and a secondary armament of twenty-one five-inch guns ; they also had lighter guns, A.A., etc., and torpedo tubes ; they were completed in 1914. Two ships completed in 1912 were also of this squadron ; these were the U.S.S. *Arkansas* and *Wyoming*, each mounting twelve twelve-inch guns and a secondary armament similar to the two *New Yorks*. Two older ships made up the number : the *Florida* of 1911, with ten twelve-inch guns and sixteen of five-inch, and the *Delaware* of 1910, somewhat similarly armed.

In about 1910 the big ships of the U.S. Navy had been fitted with " basket " masts. The tripod mast had been introduced, or re-introduced, into the British Navy in about 1906. The theory of the tripod mast is that it is more rigid than an ordinary mast, and is better able to support the control station above it. The Americans made their masts of a network of steel, which was designed so as to allow shell-splinters to pass through ; this method was found, however, to be not sufficiently rigid, bearing in mind the delicate nature of the control instruments, and it was afterwards partly abandoned, tripod masts being introduced in about 1930 ; but during the Great War all American battleships had basket masts.

For long it had been the practice at sea to base all helm orders on the movement of the tiller ; so that if one wished to turn the ship's head to the left, or to port, the order to the Quartermaster was " Starboard," and vice versa ; this practice was abandoned some years after the Great

War. In the U.S. Navy the change had already taken place, and such orders as " Right Rudder " or " Left Rudder " indicated a desire to turn the ship in the direction named. A confusion over helm orders had already occurred at the Battle of Santiago, during the Spanish War,[1] and this may have affected the question. This matter only concerned the internal economy of the ship, and had no influence on the situation, where fleet movements were concerned. Here it was found to be convenient to bring the American methods into line with those obtaining in the

U.S.S. " Texas."

Royal Navy. Naturally the U.S. Navy had its own system of signalling and its own code of signal-flags ; in a remarkably small space of time the British signal-flags were adopted and the British signalling system ; the U.S. battleships were then able easily to take part in tactical exercises, as if they were a part of the Grand Fleet, which indeed they were for the time being. They also used range clocks, the outsides of turrets were marked out in degrees, and other details were adopted which were at that time ordinary practice in the Royal Navy.

There was a possibility that the German High Seas Fleet might try to interfere with the convoys which were bringing troops over to Europe from America. To guard against this possibility, a small squadron of battleships, under Rear-Admiral F. S. Rodgers, U.S.N., was based on Berehaven. This consisted of the new battleships *Nevada* and *Oklahoma*, which had been completed in 1916, and the *Utah*, a sister ship of the U.S.S. *Florida*. The U.S.S. *Oklahoma* and *Nevada* had ten fourteen-inch guns, six of them in triple turrets, and a secondary armament of twenty-one five-inch guns.

In September, 1918, there were reasons for thinking that the High Seas Fleet was coming out of harbour, and the Grand Fleet steamed out from Rosyth and elsewhere in readiness to meet it. The American battleships at Berehaven were also held in readiness, but the scare was found to be without any foundation. Two months later some of these ships took part in the reception of the German Fleet at its surrender at Rosyth.

Admiral Dewey lived till 1917, and with this exception, there was no flag-officer in the U.S. Navy since 1875[2] of higher rank than Rear-Admiral until 1915. In 1917, however, the Commanders-in-Chief of the Atlantic, Pacific and Asiatic Fleets were each given the rank of Admiral, and their respective seconds-in-command the rank of Vice-

[1] *Battleships in Action.* H. W. Wilson.
[2] *Naval Customs, Traditions and Usages.* Captain Leland Lovette, U.S.N.

Admiral. The Chief of Naval Operations also became an Admiral, and Admiral Sims was given this rank late in 1918.

After the Armistice it was decided to send back the American battle-ships, so that they should arrive home in time for Christmas. At about the same time President Wilson came over to Europe, in order to be present at the Peace Conference and its preliminaries ; it was arranged that he should have a naval reception in the Atlantic, on his way to Brest, and subsequently in Brest Harbour. Two divisions, each of four battleships, assembled at Portland, and went to sea under Admiral Sims, who hoisted his flag in the U.S.S. *Wyoming*. The writer was a guest in the U.S.S. *Texas*, of the starboard column, commanded by Rear-Admiral Rodman.

The force put to sea in two columns on a misty day in mid-December and proceeded westward through the night. At dawn on the following day, when about a hundred miles west of Ushant, the Presidential convoy hove in sight. The President had taken passage from America in the ex-German liner *George Washington*, which was preceded by the battleship *Pennsylvania*, bearing the flag of Admiral Mayo, the Commander-in-Chief of the Atlantic Fleet, and accompanied by a number of destroyers. Admirals' flags in the U.S. Navy are blue, and bear two to four stars according to the grade of the flag-officer concerned.

If a flag-officer commanding a squadron comes into company with another flag-officer of the same grade, whose flag is hoisted, the junior hauls down his flag and hoists a flag of exactly similar design, but of red. As the two forces approached each other, signals were exchanged by daylight searchlight, and Admiral Sims's flag was changed to red.

" My country, 'tis of thee " was often regarded in the United States as the national anthem, but the " Star-Spangled Banner " was usually so regarded in the U.S. Navy. The song was written by Francis Scott Key, during the siege of Fort McHenry by the British, under Vice-Admiral Sir George Cockrane in September, 1814 ; Key was detained on board the British fleet and, looking out on the morning after the bombardment, he saw the torn flag still floating over the fort, and immortalized the occasion in verse. The uncertainty over the nature of the national anthem sometimes caused international embarrassment, such as the occasion when " My country, 'tis of thee " was played on board Prince Henry of Prussia's flagship in China, in the presence of Admiral Dewey. Finally, in April, 1930, the " Star-Spangled Banner " was officially adopted.[1] It was played on this occasion, and was duly saluted by the writer.

Ships were manned, a salute was fired and, as the President passed through the lines, three cheers were given and the national anthem
----
[1] *Naval Customs, Traditions and Usages.* Captain Leland Lovette, U.S.N.

PLATE LI

U.S.S. *ANDERSON* (Destroyer)

Completed in July, 1939. Armed with five 5-inch guns and twelve 21-inch torpedo tubes. Speed 36·5 knots. U.S. destroyers are named after officers and men of distinguished service, in the Navy and Marine Corps, former Secretaries of the Navy, Members of Congress and Inventors.

PLATE LII

U.S.S. *KEARNY* (Destroyer)

This destroyer was commissioned in 1940. She is armed with five 5-inch guns and ten 21-inch torpedo tubes. Speed 36·5 knots. The *Kearny* was torpedoed in October, 1941, off Iceland, being the first American warship to be seriously damaged by the Axis forces, but was afterwards repaired.

played. The battleships then turned outwards and proceeded at full speed into Brest, where they anchored in two lines, and again rendered honours when the President landed a little later. Finally the eight ships weighed and proceeded across to the United States, while the guests returned to Plymouth in the flagship, U.S.S. *Wyoming*.

*   *   *   *   *

The Armistice of November, 1918, did not terminate American naval activities in European waters, and for a considerable time the U.S. Navy was obliged to co-operate in clewing up the loose ends, left by the war, in the Near East and elsewhere. In 1921 an International Conference assembled at Washington ; the Anglo-Japanese alliance was terminated and an agreement was reached, whereby parity in capital ships was secured between the British and the U.S. Fleets, Japan agreeing to three-fifths the strength of the other two navies ; a number of capital ships were scrapped while on the ways. Another Conference assembled in London in 1930 and imposed limitations upon certain other classes of ship.

In 1934 Japan gave notice of her intention to terminate the Washington Agreement, and since then has been pursuing her own policy with regard to capital ships and in some secrecy. At the outbreak of the present war both Britain and the United States had each fifteen capital ships completed, but the strength of the Japanese Fleet was a matter of some uncertainty, though there were believed to be ten battleships under the flag of Japan, thirty-five cruisers and nine or ten aircraft carriers.

After the Peace of 1919 polar exploration again attracted adventurous spirits in the United States. In 1926 Commander Richard Evelyn Byrd, U.S.N., was in charge of the naval unit of the McMillan Arctic Expedition and, on the 9th of May of that year he circled the North Pole in an airplane, making the first successful flight there, and returned to his base at Spitzbergen. In 1928–30 he led an expedition to the Antarctic, proposing to make a base on the Ross Barrier, south of New Zealand, and to explore from there south and east by airplane. On the 29th of November, 1929, Byrd made the first airplane flight to the South Pole ; he led a second Antarctic Expedition in 1933–35.

In 1937 an episode occurred which is slightly reminiscent of the " Blood is thicker than Water " episode, since it took place in the same latitudes, though in the presence of a different adversary. In that year hostilities commenced between China and Japan, and British and American naval ships were pursuing their usual lawful occasions on the Chinese coasts.

On the 12th of December Japanese troops on the Yangtse River commenced firing on a British gunboat, H.M.S. *Ladybird*, wounding her captain, Lieut.-Commander H. D. Barlow, R.N. ; another gunboat,

H.M.S. *Bee*, having on board Rear-Admiral R. V. Holt, the Chief of Staff to the Rear-Admiral commanding on the Yangtse, was also fired on. This incident caused a great stir in Great Britain; a still greater stir was produced in the United States by an incident, which took place on the same day and near the same place.

A United States gunboat, named the *Panay*, was moving up the Yangtse River from Nanking, in order to get away from that town, which was being attacked by the Japanese, when she was repeatedly bombed by Japanese aircraft; she had to be abandoned, in a sinking condition, losing three killed and fifteen wounded. The survivors succeeded in getting ashore, many of them being rescued by H.M.S. *Bee*. The U.S.S. *Panay* was machine-gunned also from a Japanese launch, and some of her survivors were fired on, while swimming ashore. Three Standard Oil Company Tankers were bombed from the air, and set on fire on the same day, and nearly a hundred deaths resulted. This barbarous and unprovoked attack produced the most painful impression in the United States.[1]

No warlike action was taken by the United States, but this incident no doubt had its influence on naval policy and, when the present war broke out in 1939, they were already speeding up their naval programme. A law was passed in 1819 by which American ships-of-war were to be named by the President, assisted by the Naval Secretary; this law is still in force. Ships of the line, which to-day mean battleships, are named after the States of the Union, and cruisers after the larger cities. Destroyers are named after famous seamen and other men of distinction, and submarines after fish and marine animals. Aircraft carriers take their names from famous ships of the past or from naval or military victories, and the nomenclature of other vessels is derived from the names of stars, rivers, Indian tribes, etc., according to the class of ship in question.

By December, 1941, when the United States entered the Second World War, their battleship-strength had been increased to seventeen, including two of the *Indiana* class, the *North Carolina* and *Washington*; this class is armed with nine guns of sixteen-inch calibre and twenty of five-inch, and one of them, the *Alabama*, was launched in February, 1942, nine months ahead of schedule. The next class, completed between 1921 and 1923, consists of the *Colorado, Maryland* and *West Virginia*, whose sixteen-inch guns number eight and the five-inch guns number

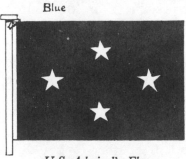

Blue

U.S. Admiral's Flag.

[1] *R.U.S.I. Journal,* 1938.

twelve. The *Tennessee* and *California*, completed between 1920 and 1921, have twelve fourteen-inch guns and the same secondary armament; and the *Idaho*, *Mississippi* and *New Mexico* are similarly armed. These last were built during the " Great War," as were the *Pennsylvania* and *Arizona*, also similarly armed. The *Nevada*, *Oklahoma*, *New York*, *Texas* and *Arkansas* have already been mentioned on an earlier page. The *Utah* had been converted into a target ship. The United States Navy had also thirty-seven cruisers of various types, one hundred and eighty destroyers, one hundred and nine submarines and seven aircraft carriers.

An important announcement was made in the middle of August, 1941, an announcement which probably could not have been made, had not the United States Navy, as the result of a century and a half of training and experience, attained to its present high pitch of strength and efficiency. It was announced that an agreement had been reached between the United States and Great Britain regarding the ultimate Peace Aims of the two countries. President Roosevelt had met the British Prime Minister, for discussion, somewhere in the Atlantic, and the resulting agreement became known as the Atlantic Charter. It is perhaps not too much to say that the Atlantic Charter depends upon the joint support of the naval and air forces of Great Britain and the United States.

Troops from the United States had already been sent to Iceland, and the supply-route between that island and America was maintained and protected. On the 4th of September, however, the U.S. Destroyer *Greear* was attacked by an Axis submarine off Iceland, and the following day an American vessel named the *Steel Seafarer* was sunk by a bomb in the Gulf of Suez. On the 11th of September, the S.S. *Montana* was sunk, and on the same day the United States announced that Axis vessels entering waters under U.S. protection would be fired on. Despite this warning, several other ships were torpedoed off Iceland, including the *Pink Star* and *Bold Venture*, and on the 17th of October the U.S. Destroyer *Kearny* was torpedoed in those waters, suffering eleven casualties.

On the 27th of October, President Roosevelt stated that " the shooting has begun," and three days later the U.S. Destroyer *Reuben James* was torpedoed and sunk in Icelandic waters, there being ninety-nine of her ship's company missing. The arming of merchant ships had already been considered by Congress and on the 7th of November a Bill providing for this passed the United States Senate.

During the first few days of December friendly discussions were still taking place in Washington, between the United States and Japan, with a view to the adjustment of certain differences between the two countries. Suddenly, on the 7th of December, American public opinion was electrified by the news that Japan had made a treacherous air attack on the U.S. Fleet in Pearl Harbour, Hawaii. There were six attacks in all, lasting from eight in the morning till nine in the evening.[1] Three battleships were sunk: the U.S.S. *Arizona*, *Oklahoma* and the old *Utah*; the *Arizona* was a total loss; the *Oklahoma* was capsized and sunk, but was afterwards declared capable of being righted and raised. Three destroyers were badly damaged: the U.S.S. *Shaw*, which blew up, and the U.S.S. *Cassin* and *Downes*, which were burned; a few smaller ships were also damaged, including the minelayer *Oglada*. Great damage was also caused ashore, and over two thousand seven hundred were killed in this onslaught, and about a quarter of that number wounded.

War was the immediate result between the United States and Japan, and the U.S. Destroyer *Ward* is credited with firing the first shot of this war at Pearl Harbour.[2] War also resulted with the other Axis Powers, and between Japan and Great Britain, who already had her hands full in Europe and Africa. Japan, having the initiative for the moment, at once began to spread southerly and fan-wise, with the object of securing naval and air bases, possibly prior to an attack on Australasia, always the goal of Japanese ambitions. She occupied Hong Kong, Singapore and Burma, the Dutch East Indies, Borneo and New Guinea and, despite General MacArthur's gallant defence, eventually secured the Philippine Islands. Admiral King was appointed Commander-in-Chief of the U.S. Naval Forces and in the spring of 1942 the Director of Naval Operations, Admiral Stark, came to London as Commander of these Forces in European Waters.

The Japanese began to land in the Philippines about the 9th of December, and also seized the American bases at Guam and Wake Island. In the attack on Wake Island, the American air forces sank a Japanese cruiser, and U.S. submarines were also active, sinking merchant ships in Tokio Bay and elsewhere, whilst their airplanes sank another enemy cruiser off the Philippines. On the 14th of January Axis submarines carried their activities into American waters, and sank or damaged a number of American merchant ships, especially tankers and, on the 23rd of January, one of these underwater craft shelled the Californian coast.

At about the same time two attacks were made on Japanese transports, landing supplies and men in the Philippines. A motor-launch, commanded by Lieutenant John D. Bulkeley, U.S.N., went at night into Binanga Bay under a hot fire, and there torpedoed a five-thousand-ton freighter; six nights later another motor-launch, commanded by Ensign George Cox, U.S.N., slipped into Subig Bay and sank another five-thousand-ton ship.

The Battle of the Macassar Strait resulted in serious loss to the Japanese. The Macassar Strait lies between the islands of Borneo and Celebes, and

---

[1] *Time.* The 22nd of December, 1941.
[2] *Life.* The 11th of May, 1942.

PLATE LIII

U.S. AIRCRAFT CARRIERS

Photograph taken from the deck of the U.S. Aircraft Carrier *Ranger*, showing aircraft lined up on the flight deck.   In the distance are seen the U.S.S. *Saratoga* and *Lexington*.   The U.S.S. *Lexington* was sunk, following the operations in the Coral Sea in May, 1942.   U.S. Aircraft Carriers are named after famous ships of the past and naval and military victories.

PLATE LIV

U.S.S. *NARWHAL* (Submarine)

This submarine was commissioned in 1930. She is 371 feet long and is one of the largest of this type of vessel in the world. Armament two 6-inch guns and six 21-inch torpedo tubes. Speed 17 knots surface, 8·5 knots submerged.

towards the end of January, 1942, the Japanese were bringing a large fleet of transports, escorted by naval vessels, south along it, presumably prior to an invasion of the Netherlands East Indies.   The transports carried a hundred thousand soldiers, to be landed at the southern end of Borneo and Celebes.   On the 23rd of January the convoy entered the northern end of the Strait ; here it was attacked by Dutch bombers, which sank one ship and damaged two.   For five days the voyage south continued and, during that time, United States and Dutch bombers and submarines, supported by cruisers and destroyers of Admiral Hart's force, sank eleven more ships and damaged another eleven.   The convoy put into Balikpanan, in Borneo, on the 25th of January, and the residue went on to Macassar and Banjermasin, farther South.

Six Japanese bases in the Gilbert and Marshall Islands were raided about a week later, the United States force being under the command of Vice-Admiral William F. Halsey, U.S.N.   At dawn bombers were sent out to attack hangars and aerodromes, the ships going up at night.   The Japanese bombers tried to attack the naval vessels, but were beaten back, one American cruiser having a narrow escape ; a Japanese pilot tried to crash-land on the deck of an American aircraft carrier, but was unsuccessful in his attempt.   Two Japanese submarines were seen and destroyed.

All next morning the fight continued, the ships bombarding the shore installations with high explosive shells.   As a result the Japanese lost sixteen ships, including an aircraft carrier, a light cruiser, a destroyer, two submarines and forty-one airplanes ; the American losses amounted only to eleven airplanes and one cruiser damaged.   Admiral Halsey also made a successful attack on Wake Island on the 24th of February, and on Marcus Island on the 4th of March.

Another example of naval co-operation between British and American forces, this time associated with the Royal Netherland Navy, took place in the Java Sea on the 27th of February ; the little squadron ran into a superior Japanese force, and was lost.   It was commanded by the Dutch Admiral Doorman, in the cruiser *de Ruyter*, accompanied by the cruiser *Java* and the destroyer *Kortenaer*.   The British ships consisted of the cruisers H.M.S. *Exeter* and H.M.A.S. *Perth*, and H.M. Destroyers *Encounter*, *Jupiter* and *Electra* ; the force was completed by the U.S. cruiser *Houston*.

At a quarter-past four in the afternoon of the 27th an enemy convoy was sighted, coming south, apparently for the invasion of Java, escorted by two ten-thousand-ton cruisers of the *Nati* class and a number of other cruisers ; the enemy also had thirteen destroyers ; the Japanese naval ships at once took up a position between the transports and the Allied force.

Action commenced, and in its earlier stages the enemy destroyers fired torpedoes and H.M.S. *Exeter* was hit in the boiler-room by an eight-inch shell, which greatly reduced her speed ; the *Kortenaer* was sunk by torpedo, and the *Exeter* was obliged to return to Sourabaya. The Japanese then laid a smoke screen, and the *Electra* was sunk, one of the enemy's big cruisers being seen to be on fire.

After dark Admiral Doorman engaged four enemy ships, and turned to sweep along the coast and intercept the invaders ; at this stage the *Jupiter* was sunk by torpedo. At midnight more Japanese cruisers were seen inshore ; they were engaged, but hit the *de Ruyter* with a shell. Immediately afterwards this ship and the *Java* were sunk by torpedoes, apparently from submarines. It was believed that, as a result of this action, one Japanese eight-inch cruiser and one of six-inch guns were sunk, and one destroyer ; also one eight-inch cruiser damaged and three destroyers left on fire and sinking.[1]

Early next day H.M.A.S. *Perth* reached Tanjong Priok, and the same evening endeavoured to pass south through the Straits of Sunda, in company with the U.S.S. *Houston*. Nothing more was heard and it was presumed that they ran into a superior force of the enemy at the north end of the Straits. The same night H.M.S. *Exeter* and *Encounter*, in company with the U.S.S. *Pope*, left Sourabaya. A wireless message was subsequently received from them to the effect that three enemy cruisers were seen approaching ; after that there was silence. H.M.S. *Exeter* was in the River Plate action with the *Admiral Graf Spee*, in which she had to retire from the fight in a damaged condition. The *Graf Spee* committed suicide. The *Exeter* presumably went down fighting.

War was carried into the heart of Japan on the 18th of April. A number of American bombers, on their way across to China, passed over Tokio, the capital city of Japan, and bombed it. They also bombed the naval port of Kobe, the port of Yokohama and the manufacturing city of Nagoya, causing great consternation among the Japanese. By the beginning of the month the U.S.S. *Kearny*, which had been torpedoed off Iceland, had been repaired and was back in service, and twenty-one Axis submarines had been sunk by the U.S. Navy.

The next event of importance in the Pacific Ocean was the Battle of the Coral Sea, which lies to the north-east of Queensland. In this action all the work was done by aircraft, since the ships were separated by many miles, and never came into action against each other.

In March, 1942, the Japanese were concentrating ships in Salamaua and Lae, in New Guinea, presumably prior to an attack on Port Moresby, in the south of the Island. On the 10th of March the U.S. Fleet made an attack on these ships, which resuted in twenty being sunk or damaged. The enemy then occupied points in the Solomon and Louisiade Islands,

[1] Rear-Admiral H. G. Thursfield. *The Navy*, April, 1942.

and on the 4th of May a portion of Admiral Nimitz's Pacific Fleet, under Rear-Admiral Frank J. Fletcher, found a number of enemy vessels near the port of Tulagi, in the Solomon Islands.

The enemy was taken completely by surprise, and lost most of his ships, twelve of them being sunk or damaged and six aircraft being accounted for, against a loss of three American aircraft. On the 7th of May the aircraft of Admiral Fletcher's force attacked the enemy's main body, which was sheltering in the Louisiade Islands. A Japanese heavy cruiser was sunk, and a new aircraft carrier, the *Ryukaku* ; twenty-five aircraft were shot down, against a loss of six American aircraft. On the same day the U.S. Destroyer *Sims* was bombed and sunk and an American tanker, the *Neosho*.

On the day following another Japanese aircraft carrier, the *Shokaku*, was badly damaged, and a Japanese air-attack resulted in the U.S. aircraft carrier *Lexington* being hit ; she subsequently sank. It was clear that these activities in the Coral Sea had resulted in a serious naval loss to the Japanese, from the communiqué which they issued immediately afterwards, partly for home consumption. This stated that they had sunk a *California* class battleship, an aircraft carrier of the *Saratoga* class and one of the *Yorktown* class, two heavy cruisers of the *Portland* class, and a British destroyer ; the Japanese also claimed to have damaged a British battleship of the *Warspite* class, an American battleship of the *North Carolina* class, one heavy Australian cruiser of the *Canberra* class, two light cruisers of the *Louisville* class and a tanker. This communiqué was apparently issued also in the hope of extracting information as to the whereabouts of the ships in question ; the only Allied ships lost were the *Lexington*, *Sims* and *Neosho*.

On the other hand, the losses suffered by the Japanese amounted to fifteen warships sunk, including one aircraft carrier, three heavy cruisers, one light cruiser, and two destroyers ; some transports also were sunk and considerable damage done to other vessels. This was followed by a Japanese attempt on the 7th of June to attack Midway Island, which was still in American hands. Admiral Nimitz, the Commander-in-chief of the Pacific Fleet, had made dispositions which rendered this attack completely unsuccessful, and it was beaten off with considerable loss to the enemy ; the Japanese lost two heavy cruisers sunk and three destroyers, thirteen other vessels, including three battleships, being damaged. Four aircraft carriers also were sunk ; thus the Japanese had lost half their strength in this class of ship. On the 15th of June the Japanese made an attack on Dutch Harbour, in the Aleutian Islands, and in this attack they are believed to have lost three cruisers, three destroyers, one gunboat and a transport vessel.

The fog of war still hangs about the Midway and Aleutian Islands, but it is evident that, although the United States has only been in the Second World War for a few months, the revenge for Pearl Harbour has already commenced. Japanese losses in aircraft carriers, cruisers and destroyers are considerably greater than those of the United States, which have lost only one of the first named, one of the second and thirteen of the third, against five, ten and sixteen of the Japanese Fleet.

The Stars and Stripes were adopted on the 14th of June, one hundred and sixty-three years ago.[1] On the 14th of June this year, at President Roosevelt's suggestion, the twenty-nine United Nations celebrated the occasion as United Nations' Day. The presence of American warships, in collaboration with the Royal Navy, in the Mediterranean, is a further proof of the unity of the nations, and the agreement recently signed by Great Britain, the United States and the Soviet Union of Russia makes the Atlantic Charter an even more powerful instrument.

It appears now as if a real Association of Free Peoples has been formed, and one by which peace can be maintained against aggressive nations, as experience has again proved to be necessary—by force.

After the close of the Napoleonic War, there followed a peace of a hundred years at sea which, owing to Great Britain's naval pre-eminence, is often referred to as the *Pax Britannica*. It may well be that, as a result of Anglo-American solidarity forged in the present conflict, the new peace will be known as the *Pax Atlantica*—possibly the *Pax Oceanica*.

Communications become daily quicker and more reliable, and the American Continents are now no less liable to attack than is an European country. The Freedom of the Seas may require securing from both sides of the Atlantic Ocean.

The U.S. Navy is likely to play a large part here, as it has done during the present war. Time has been necessary to bring a full realization of the truth ; but the history of that Navy shows that an appreciation of the importance of sea-power, both for the preservation of peace and for the defeat of an aggressive enemy, has gradually been borne in upon the peoples of the United States, as it was in the case of the elder branch of the English-speaking peoples.

[1] Chapter II.

Eendracht maakt macht.

PLATE LV

ATLANTIC CONVOY

Towards the end of 1941, it became known that ships of the U.S. Navy were co-operating in the defence of Atlantic convoys. This official photograph shows a convoy under way, and, in the foreground, an American bluejacket on watch, on the deck of a warship. The warship's guns at the ready are seen above.

PLATE LVI

ATTACK ON WAKE ISLAND

In February, 1942, a force under Vice-Admiral W. F. Halsey, U.S.N., attacked Wake Island, then in the occupation of the Japanese. The photograph shows the guns of a U.S. warship bombarding the place, and anti-aircraft crews standing by, ready to ward off an air attack.

INDEX

Names of ships set in italics.   U.S. and British warships, privateers, etc., set in small capitals, the British being followed by letters H.M.S. or H.M.A.S.   British and U.S. merchant ships and ships of other nations distinguished by "G.B., U.S., French," etc. * signifies text illustration.   C.S.N. signifies Confederate States Navy.